THE LAW
AND
YOUR HORSE

Edward H. Greene

Published by
Melvin Powers
WILSHIRE BOOK COMPANY
12015 Sherman Road
No. Hollywood, California 91605
Telephone: (213) 875-1711 / (818) 983-1105

Printed by

HAL LEIGHTON PRINTING COMPANY
P.O. Box 3952
North Hollywood, California 91605
Telephone: (213) 983-1105

Printed in the United States of America
ISBN 0-87980-202-2

CONTENTS

PREFACE

SCIENTISTS ESTIMATE A SPAN OF 60 MILLION YEARS FROM *Eohippus,* the "dawn horse," to the horse as we know it today. Yet from all indications the greatest advancement of the pleasure horse began in the mid 20th century. From a low ebb of 3.5 million in 1940 the horse population of the U.S. reached 7.5 million in 1969, with a prediction by the United States Department of Agriculture that there would be 10 million horses in America by 1975. It is hard to believe that 82 million Americans will ride a horse one or more times in 1975, but this, too, has been forecast by the Department of Agriculture. Yet we know the horse industry today is a business of more than $7 billion. Over 200,000 horses are involved in 4-H Club projects alone.

Such an economic impact of the horse industry requires knowledge not only of breeding, raising, training and showing horses but some knowledge of the owner's rights, liabilities and responsibilities under the law governing him and his horse. When an owner knows his rights as well as his liabilities, he will be able to enjoy the horse more.

For the above reason, and from the author's observations, there is a need for a legal guide to the everyday activities of the horse owner—not only to point out his rights but to warn him of his liabilities. In my attendance at many horse shows and horse auction sales and in my

7

visits to horse farms, I have seen careless and uninformed transactions consummated with the chance of misunderstandings and disagreements left to lady luck. As a lawyer I know how expensive, how time consuming and how nerve racking a law suit can be for the parties involved.

It is the purpose of *The Law and Your Horse* to fill a long-needed gap. Yet this book is not intended to be a substitute for legal advice from an attorney when one is confronted by a transaction or controversy which may lead to Court.

A book of this kind by necessity must contain many cases and opinions of the courts to illustrate the principle of the particular law under consideration. The facts of each case give a better understanding of the reasons behind the opinion of the court. In law it is not sufficient to merely state a general legal proposition that a certain mule is vicious and could "kick molasses out of a ginger cake" and therefore the person kicked should recover. In truth, the facts may place an altogether different light upon the situation leading up to the kicking. The actual facts may be that the person kicked was tormenting the mule or that he knew of the mule's tendency to kick and should therefore not have passed within reach of the mule's heels. If presented with such facts the court could rule that the person kicked was guilty of contributory negligence and should not recover. On the other hand if the person was not tormenting the mule or if he had no prior knowledge of the mule's disposition to kick, then the court could find that the person kicked was entitled to recover.

During the preparation of this manuscript I have obtained much encouragement from feeding, currying, and riding my gentle, wise, and faithful appaloosa mare, Amber. And finally I extend to David G. Todd, a senior at the College of Law, West Virginia University, my appreciation for his help in the research of the material on statutory regulations; to my wife, Marie, for her willingness to help and to put off other work that badly needed to be done around the house in order that I might meet the publishing date. It goes without saying that my partners, Chad W. Ketchum, David M. Baker, and Lawrence L. Pauley, have contributed much to make this book possible.

I dedicate this book to the many wonderful horse owners and friends whose reward is the pleasure they enjoy from their horses.

EDWARD H. GREENE

INTRODUCTION

THE DATE MAN FIRST DOMESTICATED THE HORSE IS LOST in the mists of history; but soon after man acquired the horse as a useful item of property that he discovered he could use to obtain the necessities of life, he realized that in order to protect his new property rights he would be required to enact rules and regulations. Laws were soon formulated to protect man's interest in his horse and other animals.

Early jurisprudence separated animals into two classes, wild or *ferae naturae,* and domestic or *domitae naturae.* Animals *ferae naturae* were wild by nature and disposition and belonged to the state unless acquired and made tame. Animals *domitae naturae* were those animals which were tame and gentle as a result of long continuous contact with humans and made subservient to the use of man. Except for the wild mustang in a few of our western states, horses are a domestic animal having intrinsic value, just as other personal property possessed by man. Wild animals under common law had no intrinsic value and were not subject to the laws of larceny, whereas domestic animals were subject to them. Historically, punishment for theft of a horse ran the gambit of punishment. Considered to be a minor crime in eastern states, in the western territories the offender was treated more harshly: even to hanging to the nearest cottonwood. Damages

11

seemed to come under the penalty of the Mosiac Code, which provided that: "If the theft be certainly found in his hand, alive, whether it be ox or ass or sheep, he shall restore double." Modern statutory provisions in all the states make it a crime to steal domestic animals and the punishment ranges from a misdemeanor calling for a jail sentence to a felony calling for a term of years in a state penitentiary.

Because horses are classified as personal property, ownership, sale and transactions are controlled by the law governing personal property. In all states horses are taxed as personal property. Most of the law governing business transactions involving horses has developed through court decisions. Whereas, the control over horses is generally statutory.

It is interesting to note that the present-day rule of liability for injury done by animals can be traced back to Exodus 21, wherein it is stated:

28 "When an ox gores a man or a woman to death, the ox shall be stoned, and its flesh shall not be eaten; but the owner of the ox shall be clear. 29 But if the ox has been accustomed to gore in the past, and its owner has been warned but has not kept it in, and it kills a man or a woman, the ox shall be stoned, and its owner also shall be put to death.

30 "If a ransom is laid on him, then he shall give for the redemption of his life whatever is laid upon him. 31 If it gores a man's son or daughter, he shall be dealt with according to this same rule. 32 If the ox gores a slave, male or female, the owner shall give to their master thirty shekels of silver, and the ox shall be stoned.

33 "When a man leaves a pit open, or when a man digs a pit and does not cover it, and an ox or an ass falls into it, 34 the owner of the pit shall make it good; he shall give money to its owner, and the dead beast shall be his.

35 "When one man's ox hurts another's, so that it dies, then they shall sell the live ox and divide the price of it; and the dead beast also they shall divide. 36 Or if it is known

that the ox has been accustomed to gore in the past, and its owner has not kept it in, he shall pay ox for ox, and the dead beast shall be his."

As you will see in Chapter 3, the present-day rules governing the liability of the owner or keeper of a vicious animal causing death or injury to others does not call for the death penalty against the owner or keeper, nor does it require the animal to be forfeited. It provides only for the recovery of damages against the owner or keeper.

Common law protected domestic animals from theft but it did not protect the animals from cruel abuse by man. The common law seemed to consider the animal as having no inherent right to protection from the pain and torture inflicted by man. Some courts in the United States held that malicious and willful mistreatment of an animal belonging to another was malice toward the owner and subject to prosecution under the common law crime of malicious mischief, but the great majority of the early cases did not follow this theory. However, through the efforts of the humane societies and the changing attitudes of the public, statutory laws were passed to protect animals from ill treatment and cruelty, making it a crime to willfully or wantonly abuse, neglect or mistreat them. Under the cruelty statutes the term "animal" embraces "every living brute creature."

The typical example of how the courts have changed their attitudes toward the treatment of animals is found in an opinion by the Supreme Court of Maryland in 1914 where the Court said:

The change of sentiment respecting animals and the light in which they are regarded at the present day are admirably shown in provisions of the law punishing cruelties inflicted upon them, and their sweeping character is indicated in the provisions that the word animal as employed in our statutes upon this subject includes every living brute creature.

The legislative purpose for enacting laws against cruelty to animals is the protection of the animal. Statutes in all the states make it a misdemeanor to willfully and/or maliciously torture or mistreat neglected or abandoned animals. If a person is found guilty, he may receive a fine, or a jail sentence, or both. Since cruelty to animals is prohibited only by statute, the statutes of each state must be examined to determine the specific acts constituting cruelty. However, the statutes of the various states are similar. The following is a typical statute against cruelty to animals:

> If any person shall cruelly, unnecessarily or needlessly beat, torture, torment, mutilate, kill, or overload, overdrive, or wilfully deprive of necessary sustenance, any horse or other domestic animal, whether such horse or other animal be his own or that of another person, or shall impound or confine any such animal in any place and fail to supply the same with a sufficient quantity of good, wholesome food and water, or shall carry in or upon any vehicle, or otherwise, any such animal in a cruel or inhuman manner, or knowingly feed a cow on food that produces impure or unwholesome milk, or shall abandon to die any maimed, sick, infirm or diseased animal, or shall be engaged in or employed at cockfighting, dogfighting, bearbaiting, pitting one animal to fight against another of the same or different kind, or any similar cruelty to animals, or shall receive money for the admission of any person, or shall knowingly purchase an admission, to any place kept for such purpose, or shall use, train or possess a dog or other animal for the purpose of seizing, detaining, or maltreating any other domestic animal, he shall be guilty of a misdemeanor, and, upon conviction, shall be fined not less than five nor more than one hundred dollars, and, in the discretion of the court or justice, may be imprisoned in the county jail not exceeding six months.

In addition to authority of public officials to enforce the laws against cruelty to animals, many states recognize humane societies whose main purpose is to protect animals. In some states humane societies are given governmental authority to enforce the cruelty law and to take charge of abandoned or mistreated animals.

Another regulation governed by legislative enactment is the control of diseased animals. This phase of the control over horses and other animals is becoming more important due to the increase in the transportation of horses across state lines either for sale, show or breeding. It is therefore important to the owner and keeper of horses to consult state statutes before transporting animals into another state. It is always advisable to have a health certificate issued by a licensed veterinarian before transporting horses from one state to another, since Congress passed the Animal Industry Act of 1884 prohibiting the transportation from one state to another of animals suffering from contagious diseases (USCA Title 21).

States have the power to control diseased animals to prevent the spread of contagious or infectious diseases even to the point of establishing quarantines. The power to require a health certificate for all animals entering the state has been upheld under the police power of the state.

The following is an example of the statute controlling the importation of animals into a state:

It shall be unlawful for any person or his agents or employees knowingly to drive, cause to be driven, bring or cause to be brought into this State any domestic animal infected with any communicable disease. Every domestic animal being brought into the State for any purpose, by any means of transportation, shall be subject to the restrictions imposed by section twenty-one of this article, unless such animal is accompanied by a certificate of good health issued by the state veterinarian or other accredited authority of the state from which such animal originates, or the certificate of a veterinary inspector of the bureau of animal industry of the United States department of agriculture, setting forth that such animal is free from all communicable diseases and does not originate from a district of quarantine or infection, and showing inspection to have been made within a period of thirty days prior to the arrival of such animal: Provided, however, that in the case of bovine animals the duration of such period of test shall be sixty days or such other period as shall conform to the regulations of the United States department of agriculture. Such certificate shall be made in triplicate, the original to be retained by the owner or person in charge of such animal, and by him attached to the bill of lading accompanying shipment of the animal, the duplicate to be forwarded to the commissioner, and the triplicate to be retained by the veterinarian making the inspection.

One important regulation every horse owner must take into consideration when he is about to purchase a horse and keep it on the property where he lives is the matter of zoning.

For the horse owner who desires to keep his horse in his back yard, on plots of land within corporate limits of a municipality or within an urban area, it is important for him to consult the zoning ordinance to see if there are any restrictions against the keeping of horses. Zoning is of comparative recent origin. Most zoning regulations are local ordinances covering a municipality, a county or certain zoning districts; therefore, the horse owner must consult his local governmental authority for zoning laws. Since there is a rapid and basic change in zoning ordinances and many cities and counties are rewriting and making changes in them, a prospective horse owner should check with local zoning authorities before purchasing a horse to be kept at home. Local circumstances and problems of each area make it impossible to set forth zoning restrictions which would be helpful other than to say that such restrictions are found in the zoning ordinances under *Agricultural Uses.*

In Chapter 11 the legislative acts controlling the ownership and liability of horses are set forth. Upon reading the laws of the different states it is apparent that in the general purpose and meaning they are all similar. Yet each must be examined in detail to determine when and under what circumstances each statute applies.

For those horse owners not trained in the law, the definition of certain terms will be helpful.

Tort cases are actions filed in court resulting from one party wronging another. They are limited in this work to personal injury caused by horses, damages to property or animals and the stealing and mistreatment of horses. The injured party who files the suit is called the *Plaintiff*. The party who is sued is called the *Defendant*. The amount of money the injured party sues for is called *Damages*.

Contracts are agreements between two or more persons. They can be oral or written. Both are recognized by our courts and one is just as binding as the other. The difficulty with an oral contract is proving just what the parties agreed to and their understanding at the time they made it. When one of the parties violates the contract, it is called a *Breach of the Contract*. An example of a written contract often used in the horse business is the *Bill of Sale*. This has been defined as a written statement certifying that the ownership of something (the horse) has been transferred by sale. A *Bill of Sale* should include the description of the horse to be sold, the consideration paid, or in case payments are otherwise than for cash, the method of payments, and the conditions of delivery and warranties, if any.

The courts have been called upon from time to time to define terms used by the horse industry. Some of the most frequently used terms defined by the courts are as follows: A "cutting horse" is a horse trained to separate cattle from a herd. A "span of horses" are two animals that may be connected together or united for the purpose of making a team. A "Lady's and amateur's horse" is one that can be ridden by a lady without fear of being hurt. A "green broke horse" is a horse that has had very little training and the prospective purchaser is on notice that the horse is not broke and can and may cause injury if not handled properly and carefully. "Vicious domestic animals" are such animals as are likely to injure other animals or persons. "Strays" are animals wandering at large whose owners are unknown to the person who takes them up, an animal that has strayed away and lost itself, or a wandering beast that no one seeks, follows or claims. When a boundary line has been established and an animal is permitted to go upon said land without the permission of the land owner, the animal is a "trespassing animal."

And finally "horsemanship" was defined by an early federal case of *United States v. Buffalo Park* as "the act or art of riding or training or otherwise managing horses."

1

OWNERSHIP AND SALE

BECAUSE HORSES ARE VALUABLE PERSONAL PROPERTY, ownership is acquired in the same manner as other personal property—by possession. *Actual transfer* of possession occurs when the owner agrees to give up all rights and possession to the horse. *Implied transfer* is where the owner agrees to keep actual possession of the horse for a certain length of time, or until the new owner requests the actual possession.

The sale and transfer of horses is controlled by the same laws that govern the sale of personal property. A *sale* has been defined as the transfer of ownership for valuable consideration. It is a contract founded on a valuable consideration by which the property is transferred from the seller to the buyer. A *contract of sale* takes place when the owner of a horse signifies his willingness to sell and another person signifies his willingness to buy the horse for a specified price. The courts often speak of the "meeting of the minds" in dealing with contracts of sale. To have a binding contract there must be a meeting of the minds on all important elements involved in the contract. The agreement must include the particular horse, the price, and the time and place of delivery. In

21

a recent decision the court said, "an acceptance, to be effectual, must be identical with the offer in all material points and unconditional; prior to unconditional acceptance of the offer the offer may be withdrawn."

Thus, when an owner of a horse states in a letter to another that he will sell a certain horse at a certain price, and asks the purchaser to wire or write stating if he desires to purchase the horse, and the purchaser sends a letter stating that he agrees to purchase the horse at the price stated, a binding contract now exists. When an offer is made, for the acceptance to be binding it must be identical with the offer and it must be unconditional. The seller is at liberty to withdraw his offer to sell at any time prior to the buyer's accepting his offer.

The contract of sale may be in writing, it may be oral, or it may be an implied contract from the actions and conduct of the parties. A contract exists when the parties agree on the sale, the price, and the particular animal. Large numbers of horses and other animals are sold under an oral agreement.

When the buyer asks the seller what price he will take for a horse, to which the seller replies that he will take a certain sum, and the buyer says he will give it, the courts have said under such circumstances "it is difficult to conceive how, by acts or words, they could have given a better definition or more appropriate illustration of a contract of an immediate sale."

In either a written or oral contract to sell, the sale is consummated upon the payment of the consideration and the delivery of the animal. In *Chapman v. Campbell*, 13 Gratt. 109, the Virginia Supreme Court defined a consummated contract of sale of personal property as where there is a "contract for an immediate sale of a chattel and nothing remains to be done by the vendor, as between him and vendee, the vendor immediately acquires a property in the price and the vendee a property in the goods and then all the consequences resulting from the vesting of the property follows."

The delivery may be direct to the purchaser or to an agent designated by the purchaser. The seller may retain possession of the horse for a limited time even though title and ownership passes to the buyer. An example of this is when a professional handler owns a horse and he sells it to a person who then permits the handler to keep the horse for purposes of training or showing the horse. This is called symbolical or constructive delivery. Title passes, but actual possession remains with the seller under the terms and conditions agreed upon by the parties.

The sale of a purebred horse can be consummated and ownership can pass to the new owner without transferring or assigning the certificate of registration of breed club. The requirements of the breed club for the registration of horses do not affect the title to a horse as between the seller and the purchaser. The transfer of the certificate of registration is therefore not necessary to consummate the sale of a registered horse. But in order to register the offspring, there must be a compliance with the rules and requirements of the breed club.

Warranty in the Sale of Horses—General

In the sale of personal property, a *warranty* is an expressed or implied state of the existence of a fact or a condition of the property which the seller guarantees as true. It is an agreement to be responsible for damages arising from false statements or assurance of a fact. For example, if the owner of a horse warrants that the horse is a purebred horse and registered with the breed club and the purchaser buys the horse relying upon these facts and later it is determined that the horse is not purebred and is not registered with the breed club, the purchaser has the right to rescind the contract of sale and may sue for damages incurred. Warranties may be either expressed or implied.

Expressed Warranty

An expressed warranty can be either in writing or an oral statement. No particular form is required to constitute an expressed warranty. Any statement of condition, quality or fact about the animal during negotiations leading up to the sale which the purchaser relies upon in making up his mind to buy the animal is an expressed warranty.

A good example is the case of *McNeir v. Greer-Hale Chinchilla Ranch*, 194 Va. 623, 74 S.E. (2) 165. McNeir purchased five pairs of chinchillas from Greer-Hale Chinchilla Ranch for $6250. McNeir claimed that it was represented to him that each pair was composed of young, normal animals of breeding age and that they were normal reproducing-type chinchillas and not barren or impotent. He further alleged that he had relied upon those statements, but that the animals did not meet or measure up to the representations and warranty in that they were not young and normal, but were impotent or near-impotent, and did not produce a normal number of young. Greer admitted that McNeir told him he knew nothing about the business of breeding chinchillas, that he wanted Greer to select his stock, and that McNeir was buying the animals for breeding stock. Upon learning that the animals did not measure up to the seller's representations and warranty, McNeir offered to return them but this offer was declined.

The Court held:

The representations and statements that defendant (McNeir) claimed were made by plaintiff (Greer) concerning the breeding qualities of the several pairs of chinchillas constituted a warranty of quality if, when the seller made them, he intended that they would be relied upon, and if they were in fact relied upon by defendant (McNeir) as an inducement to purchase.

The form in which representations of the vendor are made, and the words in which they are expressed, are, comparatively, unimportant. The true question is always the effect and intentions of the statements made by the vendor, and this (except when writings are to be construed) is a question for a jury.

It is important that the statements of the seller are expressed as facts distinguished from mere opinions or belief. The expression of an opinion with no intention of giving a guarantee or warranty is not binding. "I think this colt will make a champion" is no warranty. It is merely an opinion or belief. But if the seller states: "This colt is free of disease and is a healthy colt," it is a warranty. Should the colt die of a disease it had at the time of the sale, the seller is liable for breach of the sale contract. The buyer may recover the amount paid for the horse and reasonable expenses. But if the owner of a horse states orally or in writing that he warrants his horse to be sound in every way, free from disease and is a purebred horse eligible to be registered with the breed club, this is a guarantee to the buyer that if the horse is not as the seller has warranted, the seller will be liable for breach of the sales contract and the buyer may rescind the contract, and recover the amount paid for the horse plus reasonable expenses.

Written warranties generally are not difficult to understand and leave very little for implications. The difficulty arises when there is an implied warranty.

Implied Warranty

An implied warranty is an understanding as to the conditions of the property to be sold that is assumed without being openly or directly expressed. It may be inferred from the circumstances of the sale.

It can be said that generally there is no implied warranty of competency or fitness in the sale of a horse where there is no fraud or misrepresentation. The maxim of *"Caveat Emptor,"* let the buyer beware, generally applies. For example, a young colt is purchased at a horsetrader's barn and nothing is said and the purchaser has had an opportunity to see and examine the colt; he purchases it at his own risk. The same rule applies when purchasing "show stock." If the buyer of the show stock examines the animals before entering into the contract of sale, for the purpose of satisfying himself as to their quality, he is estopped from claiming that there was any implied warranty as to the quality of the horse for show purposes.

The above general rule of law has many exceptions. There are numerous situations where the rule of implied warranty applies. In the states where the new Commercial Code is in effect there is an implied warranty of fitness for a particular purpose for sale of all goods including animals. It provides that if the seller knows the particular purpose for which the goods are required, and the buyer relies on the seller's skill and judgment, there is, unless excluded, an implied warranty that the goods shall be fit for such purpose. For example, the purchase of a stud horse for breeding purposes would be a particular purpose, while the purchase of a horse for pleasure riding would not be a particular purpose. The key is the term "fitness for a particular purpose."

In the states where the Commercial Code is not yet the law, the courts are holding that there is an implied warranty for fitness for a particular purpose.

An early case: where one sells another a jack to be used for the purpose of breeding mules, there is an implied warranty that the jack is reasonably suited to the use intended.

In the case of *Balch v. Newberry*, 253 P. (2) 153, (1953) Okl., the evidence disclosed that the defendant seller was engaged in breeding and raising pedigreed dogs and had sold the plaintiff buyer a "stud" dog. In fact, he had sold the plaintiff other highly bred dogs. It was established that the seller knew that the dog was bought to be used exclusively for breeding purposes and the plaintiff relied upon the seller's judgment that the dog was of high breeding and fit for such purposes. Upon discovering the dog to be sterile, the buyer brought an action against the seller seeking to rescind the contract of sale. The court held that where a buyer trusts the judgment of the seller, who is engaged in the business of raising and selling stock to be used for breeding purposes, there is an implied warranty of its fitness. The buyer may rescind the contract for breach of implied warranty and recover what he paid under the contract and expenses necessarily incidental to the caring for the dog.

Where a horse is in the seller's possession, there is always an implied warranty that he owns the horse.

The law of the place where the sale was made and executed, although the parties may have resided elsewhere, governs as to whether warranties are to be implied or not.

In Missouri a Court considered a case where the owner was sued for damages for false and fraudulent representation in the sale of a horse. The facts as disclosed by the Court in *Nagel vs Christy*, 330 S W (2) 754 are as follows:

"Plaintiff and her husband, Earl C. Nagels, live in Topeka, Kansas. She has engaged in showing horses for fifteen years. Tom Davis trained plaintiff's horses.

R. B. Christy, defendant, owns . . . [a] . . . farm near Scott City, Kansas, where saddle horses are bred, trained, shown and dealt in. . . . Miss Irene Zane, who had been in defendant's employ for twenty years, is defendant's manager and secretary in charge of the farm, and had authority to advertise and sell defendant's horses. J. B. Utz was defendant's head trainer.

Sug Utz, J. B.'s brother, owns the Blue Ridge Stables near Raytown, Missouri, where he trains and deals in show horses. He testified that people sent him horses to sell; that on some transactions he received all over a stated amount the owner wanted for the horse, and on other transactions he received a commission on the sale price.

Northern Breeze was foaled June 1, 1951, and was purchased by defendant and delivered to Sunny Slope Farm in February, 1954. She was considered a top show prospect and was trained as a five-gaited show horse. She is a half sister to Southern Breeze, winner of a three-gaited championship.

Witness B. F. Vsetecka worked as a groom at defendant's Sunny Slope Farm. He testified that about August, 1954, Northern Breeze was continually in heat and would become unruly after making several rounds around the track; that they would feed the mare as much as two tubes (about 1 to 1½ inches in diameter and 4 to 5 inches long) of saltpeter a week; that Miss Zane also had them place a copper boiler in the mare's manger for her to eat from and nail copper pennies in her grain box to help control the heat cycles. If the mare was quiet she would not get the two tubes of saltpeter. This feeding of Northern Breeze continued until she left Sunny Slope Farm.

Defendant, Miss Zane and J. B. Utz decided that Northern Breeze and several other horses were ready for sale, and Miss Zane prepared an advertisement of their sale for the April, 1956, issue of "Short Snorts," a magazine circulating among people interested in horses. This advertisement, so far as material, stated that Northern Breeze was a "five year old five-gaited show mare * * * out of Mary E. Books who is also the dam of Southern Breeze"; that Northern Breeze was "completely trained," "ready to show," of "very fine disposition," "can rack and trot with great speed and action," and "is always in form and no mistakes."

The first week in April, 1956, Miss Zane purchased three horses from Sug Utz for defendant. Sug mentioned that he had a prospective buyer for a lady's or amateur's mare. Miss Zane told him about Northern Breeze; and that Northern Breeze was a lady's and amateur's horse, ready for showing and in sound condition. Miss Zane talked to defendant, and thereafter informed Sug Utz they would send Northern Breeze to him; he should keep and show her to prospective customers, and they would have to have $1500 net to them.

The purpose was for Sug to offer the mare for sale. The horses purchased from Sug Utz were delivered to Sunny Slope April 6, 1956, and the truck took Northern Breeze to Sug's stables on its return trip. Sug's customer wanted a lady's and amateur's mare for his thirteen year old daughter and, after looking at Northern Breeze, did not purchase the mare.

Plaintiff was interested in a five-gaited horse, and, reading the advertisement of Northern Breeze, was interested in the mare. Tom Davis met Sug Utz and Sug told him to come over and look at the five-gaited mare he had. Plaintiff and Davis went to see the mare the latter part of April. On this trip plaintiff rode Northern Breeze and liked her but in a short time, when plaintiff started to canter the mare, she acted very nervous. Plaintiff questioned Sug about the mare and asked whether she was a "hot mare," one that became nervous, unmanageable, and lunged. He said she was not a hot mare, and directed their attention to the mare's front fetlocks, which were quite raw and sore, indicating this might have caused her actions. These sores are comparable to blisters on a person's heel. Sug agreed to treat the fetlock condition and plaintiff was to return in a couple of days.

Plaintiff returned to Sug's a second time and again rode Northern Breeze, experiencing the same difficulty as on the first occasion. The fetlock condition was still present. Plaintiff was undecided about Northern Breeze but wanted a five-gaited horse to show at Oklahoma City and Tulsa, and Sug told her to enter the mare and if there was anything wrong with the mare that he did not know about, he would make it all right. Sug asked plaintiff $3500 for Northern Breeze.

On each trip Sug Utz represented Northern Breeze to be a lady's and amateur's horse, sound, and ready for showing. A lady's and amateur's horse is one that a lady can ride and show without fear of being hurt.

Plaintiff discussed the mare with her trainer, Mr. Davis. She made a third trip to Sug Utz's on April 25, 1956. Having seen the advertisement in "Short Snorts," and knowing Mr. Christy and Mr. Utz, and that Mr. Christy had owned Southern Breeze, and relying upon the representations of Sug Utz regarding Northern Breeze, plaintiff made an offer of $1250 and her horses Glorious Melody and Mr. Peepers for Northern Breeze. Sug excused himself, made a telephone call, and, when he returned, informed plaintiff he had sold Glorious Melody and would accept her offer. Plaintiff paid

Sug Utz the $1250, and he later remitted $1250 to defendant. The horses were exchanged about two days after the sale. Plaintiff forwarded Glorious Melody and Mr. Peepers to Sug Utz, with their registration papers, and Northern Breeze was delivered to plaintiff. Sug sold Glorious Melody as she came off the truck for $250, and Mr. Peepers about three months later for $600, which amounts were retained by him.

On account of the unmanageable behavior of Northern Breeze at the Oklahoma City horse show, the mare was returned to Topeka and examined by Dr. John S. Haley, a veterinarian, on May 31, 1956. He testified Northern Breeze was diseased with cystic ovaries; that she had suffered from nymphomania for a year or more; and that a common symptom of this disease is for the mare to become unmanageable after being warmed up.

There was testimony that Northern Breeze was worthless in her diseased condition.

The rules of the American Saddle Horse Breeders' Association require the registration papers of horses therein registered to be endorsed by the owner to the purchaser. Miss Zane, upon inquiry of Sug's wife, was informed to whom Sug had sold Northern Breeze and under date of May 16, 1956, R. B. Christy, defendant, endorsed the official registration certificate for Northern Breeze directly to Mrs. E. C. Nagels, plaintiff.

Plaintiff timely informed Miss Zane and, after repeated efforts, defendant of the condition of Northern Breeze, offering to lose her two horses involved in the trade if her $1250 be returned. Plaintiff's offer was rejected.

While not usually liable for physical activities of a broker or factor resulting in damage to third persons, a principal is liable for material misrepresentations of his property by his broker or factor, acting within the scope of the authority conferred, inducing a third person to enter into transactions therefor.

The facts establish the relationship of principal and factor between defendant and Sug Utz for the offering of Northern Breeze for sale, making defendant liable for his factor's misrepresentations. Miss Zane, defendant's general manager, made the representations to Sug Utz about Northern Breeze that he repeated to plaintiff. There was testimony that these statements were material misrepresentations; that plaintiff believed said statements, and was deceived and induced to purchase said mare in reliance upon their truthfulness. Defendant received from his factor his authorized price for the sale of the mare, which plaintiff paid and which he retains under the erroneous belief that Sug Utz acted as a dealer.

The Supreme Court held that where horse owner delivered his horse to a horse dealer, for the purpose of having dealer offer it for sale, with owner to receive $1500 net, relationship of principal and factor existed between horse owner and dealer, for the offering of owner's horse for sale, and therefore, owner was liable to buyer for dealer's misrepresentations as to the condition of the horse.

A prospective purchaser may not rely upon an advertisement that a horse is "safe for women and children" and ignore the usual traits of a saddle horse to be playful and too shy at times. So held a Louisiana court in the case of *Braswell v. Central Mutual Insurance Company*, 223 So.2d 204.

This is a damage suit brought for injuries sustained when plaintiff Mrs. Braswell fell from a horse owned by one of the defendants. There was judgment for the defendants in the trial court, from which the plaintiffs appeal.

The Lawtons owned an American saddle horse named Sonny, thirteen years old and five-gaited. Desiring to sell the horse, they placed a classified advertisement in the local newspaper as follows:

"BIG Bay American Saddle horse, safe for women and children. Highly trained."

On Sunday, May 1, 1966, Mrs. Braswell met Mrs. Lawton at Murrell's Stables to ride the horse, with a view toward purchasing him.

Neither Mrs. Braswell nor Mrs. Lawton were accomplished horsewomen, although each had had some prior experience with horses. Doctor and Mrs. Braswell owned two horses, but they were not gaited saddle horses.

Mrs. Braswell contends that she relied on the representation that Sonny was a gentle horse, suitable for women and children; that while she was riding the horse, he shied for no apparent reason and bolted out from under her. Mrs.

Braswell suffered serious back injuries as a result of the fall.

The evidence does not establish any vicious propensity or dangerous habit in the horse in question. The record contains the testimony of previous owners of the horse and of several persons, including children, who had ridden the horse. The witnesses uniformly testified that the horse was of a gentle nature and had never been known to be unruly or to exhibit any dangerous tendency.

On the day of the accident, Mrs. Braswell rode the horse down the road and was pleased "with the way he had gone into his gaits." Mrs. Braswell had then taken the horse into the riding ring; she testified that while going at a "brisk walk" the horse suddenly shied, bolted forward and to the left, throwing Mrs. Braswell off to the right. Mrs. Braswell described the horse's actions as jumping out from under her. She had been riding the horse about fifteen or twenty minutes when the accident happened.

A fourteen year old witness, Nancy Tyler, testified that Mrs. Braswell was riding Sonny at a trot when, at a distance of ten or twelve feet from the crossties, Sonny "just sort of stepped sideways," and Mrs. Braswell fell off backwards. This witness testified that the horse did not change his gait and did not rear or buck.

Numerous witnesses testified to the nature of the horse. It had been owned by the owner of the stable, and was rented to those who wanted to ride, except for periods when the horse was owned by other persons. Even when the horse was owned by those other than the operator of the stable, he was boarded at the stable. Except for the two incidents involving Mrs. Lawton's own falls, there was no evidence of any previous difficulty of any nature with Sonny.

In *Tally v. Travelers Insurance Company,* La. App., 197 So.2d 92 (1967), it was stated:

"The law with respect to personal injuries caused by domestic animals is well settled. For one to recover for such injuries, they must satisfy the burden of proving (1) the existence of dangerous propensity of the animal inflicting the damage, and (2) knowledge of such propensity on the part of the owner of the animal. These dual requirements for liability have been uniformly accepted by our courts."

The evidence in this case negatives the existence of any dangerous or vicious propensity in Sonny.

The added element of the classified advertisement, which

attracted Mrs. Braswell's attention to Sonny initially, is conceived by the plaintiffs to make this case, in some way, different from other "horse cases." Mrs. Lawton's advertisement said the animal was "safe for women and children." However, there is no evidence that Mrs. Lawton did not believe the horse to be "safe for women and children," or at least as safe for women and children as any other gaited saddle horse. A "safe" horse is still a thing of motion with a mind of its own, intended to be directed and controlled by a rider elevated several feet above the surface of the earth, who must maintain his equilibrium with a minimum amount of mechanical assistance. If the word "safe" is to be understood with scientific precision, with no latitude and no shades of meaning, then it would be reasonable to say that no horse is "safe for women and children," and that Mrs. Braswell, having had some experience with such animals, should have known it.

Words, however, must be taken in their ordinary and usual meaning. The evidence discloses that Sonny was about as safe as might be expected of any thirteen year old gaited saddle horse, that he did not possess any dangerous propensity, and that the numerous persons who testified at the trial knew him, without exception, as a gentle animal. The record is not convincing that Mrs. Lawton should have reasonably anticipated that Sonny would do anything unexpected which might result in injury to Mrs. Braswell. The injury to Mrs. Braswell was not Mrs. Lawton's fault.

2

AUCTION SALES

AUCTION SALES HAVE BECOME POPULAR IN THE HORSE AND cattle business. An auction is defined as a public sale of property to the highest bidder. Competitive bidding is an important element of an auction sale. Auction sales originated with the Romans, which sales were known as "auctio." Auction sales may be made by oral bid or by submitting one in writing.

The person who conducts the sale for another is called an "auctioneer" and he is generally deemed the agent of the seller.

Generally, there are four kinds of auction sales where registered horses are sold: The Production Sale, The Near-Dispersal Sale, The Estate Dispersal Sale, and The Consignment Sale.

The Production Sale is a sale by the breeder of horses he bred himself. Sometimes a breeder will permit a few horses from a friendly breeder to be sold in the Production Sale, but a true Production Sale is one where the breeder sells only his offspring.

The Near-Dispersal is just what the term indicates. The breeder is not selling all his horses. He is keeping some for his own use.

The Estate Dispersal Sale is a sale by the executor or

34

administrator of an estate after the death of the owner, and is generally for the purpose of settling an estate.

The Consignment Sale is a wide open market sale where any owner of horses may consign his horses to the sale. The sale is generally under the management of an auction company or a horse dealer. The owners of the horses pay a commission to this auction company on the amount for which the horse is sold.

Club Consignment Sale is one that is managed and controlled by a horse club. For example, a Quarter Horse Club may have a Consignment Sale and encourage all the members to consign horses to the sale. Generally, such sales have a committee to inspect the horses and decide if the Club will accept them.

States and municipalities may, and often do, regulate auction sales and auctioneers. In those states and cities which regulate auction sales, the auctioneer is required to have a license. In those states and cities which have no statutory regulations, anyone may be an auctioneer and carry on the business of auction sales.

It is a general rule that the auctioneer has no authority to warrant the goods he offers for sale, and without expressed authority from the seller he cannot bind the seller. However, where the auctioneer makes a warranty in the presence of the seller and the seller makes no objections, the warranties are binding on the seller.

Terms in advertising matter or catalogs distributed before an auction sale may set forth the terms and conditions of the sale. Most auction sales of horses use advertising notices and catalogs. Catalogs of horse sales usually contain the following terms and conditions:

Terms and Conditions of Importance to Bidders

Bidding:

The highest bidder shall be the buyer. In event of dispute, the auctioneer will recognize the person from whom he accepted the last bid and open the bidding to those involved.

Responsibility:

The seller is the responsible party for all representations and warranties. The sponsors, sales managers and auctioneers are acting as agents only and are not responsible in any way, but will endeavor to protect the interest of both buyer and seller. Anyone associated with this sale is not responsible for any accident at the place of sale. *In case typographical or other errors are discovered, the auctioneer or sales manager will announce them and a memorandum will be kept of such corrections, which takes precedence over printed matter in the catalog. Buyers are therefore cautioned to pay attention to the sales manager's announcements.*

Soundness:

As a service to buyers and consignors, all animals will be examined by the official veterinarian and his findings as to soundness will be announced by the auctioneer at the time the animal is put up for sale. All animals are sold according to the findings of the official veterinarian. Status of pregnancy of mares to be sold, from veterinarians' examinations within ten days prior to sale, will be announced at time of sale. The guarantee of soundness of any animal is made on the part of and is the responsibility of the consignor and does not extend beyond 24 hours after the start of the session at which the animal is sold or when the animal is fully paid for and delivered, whichever is sooner.

Risk:

All horses are at buyer's risk as soon as struck off. Horses may remain at the barns a reasonable length of time at buyer's risk until convenient to move them, providing buyer arranges for care.

Mail Bids:

See Bid Page, back of catalog.

Terms:

Cash. Checks to be made payable to National Quarter Horse Sales, who in turn, will pay the consignors. Parties unknown to the sponsors should bring late Bank references. No horse to be removed from place of sale until these terms are complied with.

Registrations and Transfers:

All horses registered in the American Quarter Horse Association. Transfer fee to be paid by the purchaser.

Regulations:

Any animal listed in the sale catalog can be withdrawn only upon being released by the Sales Manager or Sale Committee.

The owner of the horses to be sold at auction has the right to prescribe the manner, conditions and the terms of sale. These terms may be either stated in the catalog or they may be announced at the sale. Generally the terms are binding on the purchaser even if he is not present at the time of announcement and did not hear or understand them.

In addition to the terms and conditions set forth either in the advertising, catalog, or orally at the auction, the rule of law that a seller of horses impliedly warrants he has good title to the property also applies. Of course the seller may state that he does not own the horses and thereby negate the implied warranty. Other than the implied warranty of title on the part of the seller the maxim of *caveat emptor* applies at auction sales. Purchaser of horses at an auction buys at his own risk unless the seller expresses certain warranties to the horses to be sold.

Generally, in the absence of expressed authority from the seller, the auctioneer has no power to make any warranties concerning the horses to be sold so as to bind the seller. The relationship between the seller and the auctioneer is one of agency. There is no implied or apparent authority to warrant what he sells. However, the seller may ratify the auctioneer's statements and thereby bind himself. Some states have passed statutes giving the auctioneer authority to make certain warranties except where the seller specifically restricts the auctioneer.

The business of an auctioneer is a private business and his authority is obtained from his agreement with the owner of the property he is selling. The extent of the auctioneer's right to warrant or represent facts concerning the property to be sold is limited by the agreement he has with the seller. There are exceptions to this general rule. An important one is the failure of the auctioneer to disclose the name of the seller. In such a case the auctioneer is considered the vendor and is responsible to the buyer for title or for a breach of any warranty made during the sale.

A case in point is *Pasley v. Ropp,* 334 S.W. (2) 1254 (Missouri) where Pasley, an operator of a public auction barn at Osceola, Missouri, followed the practice of having the seller bring the livestock to the sale barn where they were placed in pens and given numbers for identification purposes. A slip was made out by Pasley's employee showing the number of cattle, the seller, and the pen number. The seller was given one copy when the cattle checked in. When the cattle was paid for the sales barn employee marked one copy "paid" and the buyer had to have that copy to get his cattle. Most cattle was sold through the auction but it was not uncommon for a buyer to buy stock from the seller while they were still in the pens and before the auction sale began. In such event the owner of the auction barn receives a commission on the sale just as though the cattle had gone through the sale ring.

On the Thursday morning in question, one Bridges brought 8 head of cattle which were placed in pens in the sales barn. There Mr. Mooney acting on behalf of Ropp saw the cattle and Bridges, and undertook to buy them from Bridges. He and Bridges agreed to their sale at 17½ cents per pound. The sales barn did not have scales so they and Ropp loaded up the cattle and took them into Osceola and weighed them, and returned them to the sale barn pens. The agreed purchase price was $1213.62.

They reported the sale to Pasley's bookkeeper, and upon Bridges' request the bookkeeper issued a check to Bridges for the reported sales amount less the customary commission and handling charge. Bridges took the check to a local bank and after being identified by telephone by the bookkeeper as the one to whom the check was issued, cashed it and disappeared.

The ring sales that day were over about 7:00 P.M. and Ropp, as was customary, went to Pasley's office, settled up for his day's activities, including giving to Pasley a check for the purchase price for cattle in question. Ropp then placed the cattle in his truck and took them to the stockyards in Kansas City, placed them in pens there with directions they were to be held until the following Monday and then were to be sold. On Monday Ropp returned to Kansas City where he was informed the cattle were stolen and had not ever belonged to Bridges. Later their true owners came and took them.

Ropp immediately stopped payment on his check to Pasley and contends he owed Pasley nothing as Pasley should bear the loss resulting from the sale of the stolen cattle. Pasley had never met Bridges and had no knowledge of the sale arranged by Bridges and Mooney until some time after it had been made. Nor did he or his employees know the cattle had been stolen. He contended the loss in question should be borne by Ropp.

Pasley sued Ropp for the amount of the check. The court held that Ropp was under a duty to pay Pasley the sale price. The court said:

> Ropp knew who the pretended owner was and made his purchase by negotiating with him directly. Pasley did not have anything to do with the agreement they reached. But even if we would say he did, the situation at most would be that of an auctioneer who had fully disclosed his principal to the buyer and who, as such agent, had done nothing to make himself personally responsible for the failure of the principal to have been the owner of the cattle.

> Ropp did avail himself of some of Pasley's sale barn services. He knew when he reported the sale he and the pretended owner of the cattle had arranged that the pretended owner could and might get his portion of the sales price immediately and that before the sales barn closed that day appellant would be expected to pay the sales price to Pasley. Under the circumstances he had a duty to pay Pasley and he is not relieved therefrom perforce of any of the applicable principles of the law of agency or contracts.

> It is true that broadly stated an auctioneer, in selling property for another, is the agent of the seller, and his rights and liabilities, in the absence of an applicable statute changing them, are governed by the general principles of the law of agency.

> It is a settled principle of the law of agency, as of contracts, that where the agent has disclosed his principal, the principal is considered to be the vendor himself, and, as such, responsible to the vendee for title. The agent, in the absence of other facts that may make him liable, is not responsible for the principal's failure to have good title.

> In 2 Williston On Sales (Rev Ed) Section 296, page 202, it is expressed: "When a contract has been completed the auctioneer is personally liable upon it, unless prior to its formation he disclosed the principal for whom he was act-

ing . . . if the principal is disclosed, he is the only person
who has a contractual relation with a bidder." These results
are in accordance with the general principles of law governing undisclosed principles.

In 7 CJS Auctions and Auctioneers §13, p. 1270, the rule
is stated, "An auctioneer is personally responsible as vendor,
unless at the time of the sale he discloses the name of his
principal, since his general employment as auctioneer is not
per se notice that he acts as agent."

In 5 Am Jur, Auctions, Section 57, page 488, the rule is
expressed: "Accordingly, an auctioneer selling for a known
principal is not responsible to the buyer for the title, in the
absence of his own affirmative agreement, for an auctioneer
does not impliedly warrant the title of his vendor."

Several cases are of particular interest. In *Corn Land
Farms Co: v. Barcus* 105 Neb 869, 182 N.W. 487, 489, 23
AlR 119, plaintiff sued the clerk of the auction for the
purchase price paid for a span of stolen mules sold at public
auction which plaintiff innocently earlier attempted to pri-
vately purchase from the purported owner who had stolen
them. The court in denying recovery quoted with approval
from *Mercer v. Leihy,* 139 Mich 447, 102 N.W. 972, "Where
an auctioneer discloses the fact of agency and his principal,
the law presumes that he does not contract upon his own
behalf but for the principal." In the instant case, while the
auctioneer did not announce for whom the property was
being sold, it was immaterial as the plaintiff's agent knew,
as a matter of fact, as heretofore stated, who was the pre-
tended owner, and, as far as any declaration of the ownership was concerned, it was unnecessary as to him.

In *Fox v. Wilson,* 36 Tenn App 324, 255 S.W. 2d 416,
the sale barn operator sued the seller and the buyers of
a cow which died in the barn after being returned by
the buyers as sick and after the buyers had stopped payment on their check. The Tennessee court ruled that the
sales barn operator was entitled to look to either or both
the buyers and the seller for his money.

In *Schell v. Stephens,* 50 Mo 375, defendants were auctioneers in Kansas City who sold a span of horses and a
wagon which were bid in by plaintiff. The property turned

out to be stolen and was reclaimed. Suit was brought on warranty of title by the auctioneers. There the court stated at page 370: "The mere fact that defendants were acting as auctioneers is not of itself notice that they were not selling their own goods, and they must be deemed to have been vendors, and responsible as such for title, unless they disclosed at the time the name of the principal."

This general rule that an auctioneer is liable for warranties where he fails to disclose his principal is inapplicable where the auctioneer orally discloses his principal to the persons attending the auction sale.

Of course the auctioneer may pledge his own responsibility either by expressed or implied implications. In such cases he is liable to the purchaser for any defect in the title to the animals sold.

In the case where the auctioneer publicly announced a warranty that the horse being auctioned had good wind, worked well, without stating that he was selling the horse for some other person, the court held the auctioneer liable and ordered judgment for the purchaser.

Advertisement as it Affects an Auction Sale

The prime purpose of advertisement of an auction sale is to give notice of the sale to prospective purchasers, and very often give the public the terms and conditions of the sale. There is a conflict of authority as to whether the representations contained in the advertisements, catalogs or brochures are binding as an expressed warranty. Some courts hold such advertisements are for the purpose of interesting the public to attend the sale. But if the statements in the advertisements and catalogs are adopted at the sale then they become warranties. Most catalogs contain the terms and conditions of the sale and the principal. Otherwise the auctioneer may state on the day of the sale that the terms and conditions in the catalog govern the sale. On the other hand the terms and conditions set forth in the catalog may be modified at the sale. When such modifications are announced before the sale starts, the changes of course supersede the terms and conditions stated in the catalog.

The Bids

The sale of a horse at an auction, like every other sales contract, must result from a meeting of the minds of both the seller and the buyer. When the auctioneer puts the horse up for sale he is inviting those present to make offers by bidding. The sale contract becomes final and the sale complete only after the bid is accepted. Generally this is denoted by the fall of the hammer. The buyer has a right to withdraw his bid any time before the fall of the hammer. By the same token the seller has the right to withdraw his horse at any time before the fall of the hammer. If, however, it is announced that the sale is "without reserve" the seller can not withdraw after a bid has been made. The seller does have the right to withdraw before there is a bid in a sale "without reserve." After the bid has been accepted there is a binding contract on both the seller and the buyer.

There seems to be no particular mode of making bids at an auction. The old rules say that a bidder may wink, blink or nod. Bids may be by spoken word, or some auction sales make provisions for prospective buyers to bid by mail. Any method that conveys to the auctioneer the intent of the bidder is acceptable.

The most used method of accepting a bid at auction is by the fall of the hammer. Many terms are used such as, "knocked down," "knocked off," "struck off," or such statements as, "going, going, gone," and "once, twice and three times and gone," or any method that is understood by the bidders that the auctioneer has accepted the final bid and the sale is consummated. The modes of bidding and accepting bids differ in different localities.

The auctioneer has to use a large degree of discretion in conducting a sale. He may reject a bid whenever he feels that the bid is not in good faith, or the bidder does not have the capacity to bid intelligently—such as a man too drunk to know what he is doing, or a person under 21 years of age. The auctioneer must use his best judgment under the circumstances to protect the seller.

Very often two persons may claim to have bid the highest bid. In such cases the auctioneer has the right to exercise his discretion in determining who made the highest bid first; he may go back to the last highest bid he acknowledged and start the bid again, or, he may use any method he may determine in the exercise of his best judgment.

Most courts hold that the owner of property who is holding the sale may not bid unless it is expressly announced that he reserves such privilege. He may not make secret bids for the purpose of raising the price. "By-bidding" or "puffing" is a fraud on legitimate bidders and if such occurs and the bidder can prove such facts it is grounds to rescind the contract.

At most auction sales delivery of horses is made upon payment. In the event a check is accepted in sales of registered horses the certificate of title is not transferred until the check clears the bank.

3

THE LEGAL OBLIGATION OF OWNER AND BAILOR OF HORSES

General

SINCE HORSES ARE PERSONAL PROPERTY AND THERE IS A delivery of the horse in both the training and boarding stable arrangements, the law of bailment applies. Bailment is defined as the placing of personal property in the care, custody and safe-keeping of another for certain purposes agreed upon by the parties, upon the understanding that the animal will be redelivered to the owner after the purposes have been fulfilled. An example would be the case of an owner of a horse delivering his horse to a trainer for the purpose of training, showing or racing the animal, or to a boarding stable for the purpose of boarding him. In order to constitute a bailment, there must be a transfer of possession of the animal, the title to remain with the owner, with the understanding that the animal will be redelivered as agreed upon. There is also a term used in dealing with cattle, horses, sheep and the like when the owner desires to deliver the animals to another for pasturing and feeding. The law of "agistment" also applies in the broad general terms.

The owner of the personal property is called the "bailor." The one who receives the property for a specific purpose is called the "bailee." To understand the court decisions, one must keep in mind that the owner of the horse would be the "bailor." The trainer or the owner of the boarding stable would be the "bailee."

Bailment Is Distinguished from Sale as Follows

A sale has been defined as being a transfer of the absolute or general property in a thing for a price in money and the difference between a sale and a bailment lies, to a great extent, in the fact that in a bailment no such absolute or general property in the thing passes, but only a special property passes to the bailee. It is, furthermore essential in the case of a bailment that the identical article which is the subject of the understanding shall be returned to the bailor, when the object for which it was entrusted to the bailee shall have been completed.

Liability of Owner to Bailee

In general the owner of an animal (and this includes liverymen, ranchers, riding stable owners and all persons who furnish horses to the public for hire) owes a duty to furnish a horse reasonably fit and suitable for the purpose for which it is let. The owner is not an insurer of the suitability of the horse he furnishes, but he owes the duty to furnish a horse suitable for the purpose contemplated in the hiring. He is under a duty to use ordinary care and diligence in furnishing a horse reasonably safe for the rider. The following case is in point for the proposition that an owner of a horse for hire is answerable for injuries to the rider who hired the horse if the horse is vicious and dangerous, and the owner knows or should

have known it (*Gober v. Nolan,* 81 Ga.App. 16, 57 S.E.2d #1
700 [1950]) :

Ruby Gober brought suit against W. H. Nolan for personal injuries she received when she was thrown from a horse she had rented from Nolan. The action was based on negligence: (a) That Nolan knew the horse for which he charged and accepted money from Gober to ride upon was a wild, dangerous and vicious horse which would likely run rapidly and recklessly and violently and suddenly turn and throw her, as it did on this occasion, (b) that Nolan knew the said horse was not gentle and safe as requested, (c) that Nolan failed to properly tighten and fasten the saddle on said horse, thus allowing it to sway from side to side as the horse ran rapidly and recklessly and turned off the road, and (d) that Nolan failed to give her any warning whatsoever that the horse was wild, reckless and vicious.

The evidence adducted by Ruby Gober is as follows: On the afternoon of April 26, 1947, 26-year-old Miss Gober, who was with two young men and two young women, rented horses from a riding academy operated by Nolan. She specified that she wanted a gentle horse. After being seated on the horse she asked the attendant if the horse was one that would stop when she said "whoa," and he assured her that it was a gentle horse. The group left the stable on horseback, but about twenty minutes later the horse she was riding suddenly bolted and started running without apparent cause. She tried to stop the horse by pulling on the reins and calling "whoa" but this had no effect on him. The saddle girth was loose, and the saddle started slipping and swaying. The horse turned to the right into some woods and Miss Gober was thrown from the horse and knocked unconscious when she hit the ground. She received injuries to her back and wore a brace constantly for about five months. (The horse also threw the attendant on way back to the barn.)

The Court held that knowledge on the part of Nolan as to the wild and dangerous character of the horse hired is not a necessary ingredient to sustain an action for injuries to the person to whom the horse was hired; it was only necessary to show a lack of ordinary care or negligence in furnishing an animal not suitable for the intended use. The fact that the horse ran and threw Miss Gober and later threw an attendant is evidence only of the character of the horse at the time, and unless there was evidence of prior acts of a similar nature or some evidence showing that Nolan knew of the character of the horse in this respect, or that he could have known of the same by the exercise of ordinary care, her case with respect to these grounds of negligence would fail.

A person who lets a horse for hire is not an insurer of the horse's fitness, but is under an obligation to furnish an animal which is reasonably safe for the purpose known to be intended as the Court held in the case of Koser vs. Hornback, 75 Idaho 24, 265 P (2) 988. The facts are as follows:

The morning of July 10, 1949, Koser with four companions arrived at the ranch intending to proceed from there by horseback on a fishing trip. Hornback and another, referred to as his "wrangler," were on hand to receive Koser and his party. The horses previously arranged for were saddled and ready. The horse ridden by Koser was assigned to him by Hornback. Hornback and his wrangler loaded the fishing equipment, brought by the guests, upon their respective horses. Koser and one Simpkins were in the rear as the guests started down the trail. After going a short distance, Koser discovered he had forgotten a metal tackle box containing tackle belonging to himself and Simpkins. He rode to the barn, where Hornback put the tackle box in a gunny sack, tied a string around it, and handed it to Koser, and this conversation occurred:

"What is the matter, is the horse skiddish or something?"
Koser asked.

Hornback said, "No, there is nothing the matter, just
sometimes it scares him a little bit to start out with." He
then said, "Just turn right down the trail—start down the
trail and hang it on the saddle horn."

Koser proceeded back along the trail and having gone
about one hundred yards, he hung the sack containing
the tackle box on the saddle horn, and the sack containing
the box either fell or rolled against the horse's neck.
Whereupon the horse jumped, dislodging Koser from the
saddle and he fell to the ground. His right foot being
caught in the stirrup, he was dragged for some distance
over rough, stumpy ground and kicked by the horse.

Koser was born and reared to the age of fifteen on a
farm where there were cattle and horses. Since that time
and in recent years he has owned one horse and has
many hunting and fishing trips by horse. The Court ruled:

> Whether the bailor had knowledge, or probable cause for
> knowledge, of the dangerous propensities of the animal hired,
> has been held to be the proper test in actions for injuries
> to third parties, due to the exercise of such propensities, but
> not in actions for injuries to the bailee, the test in the latter
> case of actions being whether there was a failure to exercise
> due care to furnish a suitable animal.
>
> One who lets a horse for hire, although not an insurer of
> the horse's fitness, is under an obligation, sometimes spoken
> of as an implied warranty, to furnish an animal which is
> reasonably safe for the purpose known to be intended, and
> for a failure to use due care to discover dangerous propen-
> sities in such animals, or to disclose them to the hirer, he may
> be held liable for personal injuries or death resulting from
> such neglect.
>
> It has been held that such an action may be brought
> either in contract for breach of an implied warranty of fit-
> ness, or in tort for negligence in furnishing an unsafe animal.
> However, the form of action is of no real consequence,
> because the courts all agree that the bailor is not an insurer,

and that a mere breach of the implied warranty is not alone sufficient ground for recovery. In addition thereto, the plaintiff must prove that the keeper had some knowledge, or the facts are such as to charge him with knowledge, of the unsuitability of the animal; or negligence in failing to take reasonable precautions to determine its suitability; or in failing to warn the prospective rider of the facts. So, whether the action be ex contractu or ex delicto, the required proof is the same. Dam v Lake Aliso Riding School 6 Cal 2d 395, 57 P2d 1315.

In the foregoing case, 57 P2d at page 1317, the Supreme Court of California, in a quote from Conn v Hunsberger, 224 Pa 154, 73 A 324, 25 LRA NS 372, held it to be the duty of a liveryman to inform himself of the habits and disposition of horses he keeps for hire. He must exercise reasonable care to ascertain such facts, and if he fails to exercise such care he may be held liable even though he did not actually know the horse was unsuitable for the service intended. In discussing the nature of the proof required to show a breach of this duty of due care on the part of the bailor, the California court said:

"We agree with appellants that it is not always necessary for the bailee to prove actual acts of misbehavior on the part of the horse prior to the accident. But in some way the bailee must prove such facts as will justify a jury in finding that at the time and place in question the horse was unsafe and unsuitable for the purpose for which it was hired. [Dam v Lake Aliso Riding School, 6 Cal2d 395, 57 P2d 1315, at page 1318.]

We agree that one act of sudden jumping or other misbehavior on the part of a horse would not ordinarily be sufficient to determine the character of the horse, depending of course upon the circumstances and the procuring cause. But, assuming the propensity of the horse to so act is established, proof that the liveryman had kept the horse over any considerable period of time, would justify the jury in concluding that he knew or should have known its characteristics. On the other hand, if the keeper had not kept the horse a sufficient time to become acquainted with it, he might be held negligent in hiring it to a bailee without warning him of his lack of knowledge of the horse.

Owner must keep in mind not only the purpose of the

use but the ability of the rider to control the horse if that is ascertainable.

In Bulkin vs. Camp Nockamixon 79 Atl. (2) 234 a ten #3 year old boy was placed on a horse contrary to specific instructions by the mother not to let the boy ride horses at the summer camp. The boy was inexperienced in handling and riding horses. He was left on the horse unattended.

The horse started running and kicking up his heels and the boy was thrown and injured. The court upheld a jury verdict of $7000 saying that the case presented a question for the jury as to whether the employee was guilty of negligence so as to render the summer camp liable for the injuries sustained by the boy.

The owner must exercise reasonable care in permitting persons to ride his horses. A youth with no experience with horses required a gentle horse and constant supervision if he is to ride a horse. The owner in furnishing a horse must have in mind all the existing and foreseeable circumstances.

On the other hand when the owner of a horse farm agrees to instruct a fourteen-year-old girl in horseback riding, to provide an instructor to ride with her, and to furnish a safe and dependable horse, he is not an insurer against every accidental injury which she might receive. (Smith vs. Pabst, 288 N.W. 780.)

If a gentle horse suddenly and unexpectedly inflicts injury on a person who rented it, the owner is not liable.

A man and wife both hired riding horses. The wife became alarmed at an approaching car and the husband reached for her reins, his horse shied to the right, he dropped one of his reins, dismounted, and while reaching under the horse's head he was struck when his horse reared. The evidence of the stable owner established that the horse was purchased some fifteen years earlier, that the horse had been hired out for riding for eight years.

The owner had never received a single complaint and it had been gentle, well trained and safe horse. The court held that the rider failed to prove negligence on the part of the owner and that one act of viciousness was not sufficient to hold the owner liable.

Liability was denied in the case where the rider sustained injuries when her horse ran away and fell. There was no evidence that the horse had ever run away or fallen before. The only negligent act relied upon by the rider was the horse's persistent habit of moving his head up and down and sideways when ridden. The court held there was no casual connection between the tossing of the horse's head and his running or falling.

In Clifton vs. Holliday 88 NE (2) 304 an experienced rider was unable to control the horse he had rented when the horse turned back toward the stable and ran through an unbarred stable door. The rider struck a beam in the stable. The evidence disclosed that it was a normal characteristic of horses to return to their stalls if permitted to do so. The Supreme Court of Ohio held that the facts did not constitute evidence of any known trait or propensity of the horse which would subject the rider to greater risk than ordinarily attaches to horseback riding.

A person who keeps horses for hire to the public must inform himself of the character, disposition, habits and traits of the horses he rents. He cannot overlook the bad habits or peculiarities of his horses, which may under varying circumstances cause injury to riders. The law places a duty upon a livery stable keeper to exercise reasonable care in determining if the horses he lets are unsuitable or dangerous for persons to ride. Or putting it another way: if it is known or in the exercise of reasonable care it should be known that the horses the owner lets are unsuitable or dangerous, he is liable for injuries resulting from vicious habits or propensities of the horses.

The operator of a riding stable breached his implied

warranty to furnish a suitable horse in Evans vs. Upmier, 235 Iowa 35, 16 N.W. (2) 6 when he furnished Evans, who had little riding experience, a horse which was unbroken to ride, high spirited, and had a tendency to run and rear up. The academy did not usually assign it to beginners but they claimed that the horse was gentle and could be ridden by anyone. Evans claimed the horse was hard to control and it wanted to gallop in spite of his efforts to restrain him. Evans fell when the horse bumped into another horse.

The Texas Court found the stable owner liable in Shanklin vs. Rogers, 213 SW (2) 730, for furnishing a blind or a partially blind horse to a fifteen-year-old girl. There was sufficient evidence to find that the horse was blind or partially blind in one eye and that the owner knew or in the exercise of ordinary care should have known of the horse's condition. The horse ran into the side of an automobile. One witness testified that the horse was "one-eyed"; the animal did not bat its left eye when he put his hand up in front of it. The owner had had the horse for three or four months and testified that it was not totally blind.

There is a duty to warn a person who hires a horse of vicious propensities of the horse if the owner is to avoid liability. A riding academy was held liable (in Hodge vs. Montclair Riding Club, 32 A (2) 840) for an injury sustained by a rider as a result of a horse's rearing up on its hind legs. The academy had failed to inform the rider of this habit.

The liveryman was not liable for failing to inform the rider that a horse was a jumper even though the horse injured the rider when it leaped in crossing an almost level trail. (Dam vs. Lake Aliso Riding School (1935) 57 P (2) 1315.) Here the owner purchased a horse and was told that the horse was an excellent saddle horse with some ability as a jumper. It had been used to jump hurdle. There was no evidence that the owner knew that the horse would suddenly leap when not facing a hurdle.

The owner or hirer of a horse is relieved from liability for personal injuries resulting from the unsuitability of a horse if the rider or bailee either assumes the risk of such a horse, or is guilty cf contributory negligence. There is a certain ordinary risk incident to horseback riding, and this ordinary risk all persons assume.

In Clifton vs. Holliday, 88 NE (2) 304, the Ohio Court held that the rider failed to prove the owner knew of any trait, condition or propensity of the horse which would subject the rider to greater risk than ordinarily attaches to horseback riding.

Liability of Owner to Public

The authorities generally agree that all domestic animals, whether horses, mules, cattle, dogs, cats or others, are not presumed to be dangerous to persons, and before recovery of damages may be had against the owner the injured party must prove that the particular animal was of a dangerous, or vicious, nature and that this dangerous propensity was either known, or should have been known, to the owner. The negligence that imposes liability upon the owner is the keeping of a dangerous animal with knowledge of its dangerous tendency, or in the failure to restrain it from injuring persons.

A good case that discusses the law applicable to an owner of a horse that injures a person is Mango vs. Bennett, 119 SE (2) 522, a North Carolina case.

The plaintiff, Ernest Mungo, brought an action for damages for personal injuries suffered by him when kicked by a stallion belonging to the defendant, Carl E. Bennett. The plaintiff charged the defendant with negligence (1) in keeping a horse known to have a vicious nature, (2) in failing to warn respondent of its vicious nature, and (3) in failing to keep the horse under control. Facts are as follows:

On the day of the injury in response to a call from Bennett, Mungo went to Bennett's backyard to see him. There he found him currying his horse. When he approached, Bennett was holding the bridle with one hand and currying with the other. Mungo did not know anything about the horse and had never seen it before. While Mungo was talking to Bennett, standing about five feet from the right front shoulder of the horse, it suddenly whirled around and kicked Mungo, as Bennett belatedly hollered to Mungo, "Look out, Jay." Immediately following the kicking, the horse jumped his lot fence and ran away. Bennett went to Mungo and thought him to be dead. A few days after the accident, and while Mungo was in the hospital, Bennett visited Mungo and told him, as Mungo testified, "that he was sorry that the accident happened, and that he was sorry that he failed to warn me about the horse being dangerous."

There was no showing that the horse had previously kicked anybody.

The Court said:

"From the foregoing evidence, it is reasonable to draw the conclusions that the horse was dangerous or vicious, as those terms are used in the applicable law, and that Bennett was aware of it. Furthermore, it is reasonable to draw the conclusion that Bennett was negligent in calling Mungo to the place of danger without any warning."

And, a vicious disposition ". . . is a propensity or tendency of an animal to do any act that might endanger the safety of the persons and property of others in a given situation. Although an animal is actuated solely by mischievousness or playfulness, rather than maliciousness or ferociousness, yet, if it has a tendency to do a dangerous or harmful act, it has a vicious propensity within the

meaning of the rule holding the owner or keeper liable
for injuries resulting from vicious propensities of which
he has knowledge."

Bennett claimed Mungo was contributory negligent in
standing close to the horse. But the Court found that
Mungo did not go to the horse's heels, but that he was
standing facing the horse and while in that position the
horse suddenly whirled around, without warning and
kicked him. The Court then discussed the law of contributory negligence:

Under our decisions the affirmative defense of contributory
negligence rarely becomes a question of law for the Court.
The authorities relied upon by Bennett are three cases from
other jurisdictions, all of which the Trial Judge held were
not persuasive in this case, and we agree.

In one of the cases, Heath v. Fruzia, 50 al. App. 2d 598,
123 P. 2d 560, the Court held as the Trial Judge here, that
the question of contributory negligence of the plaintiff was
for the determination of the jury. In the other cases relied
upon by Bennett, Miller v. Atlantic Refining Co., 210 Pa.
628, 60 A. 306, and Tolin v. Terrell, 133 Ky. 210, 117 S. W.
290, 291, the Court stated in each case that the plaintiff was
guilty of contributory negligence in that he had deliberately
walked directly behind the heels of the animal, and was
there at the time of getting kicked.

The Tolin case uses the strongest language of the cited
cases, and shows in the statement of facts that the person
injured by being kicked by the mule was working it at the
time of getting kicked. The action was not against the owner
of the mule, but against the owner of a horse which had
reached about three feet over a fence, shoulder high, and bit
the mule on the rump, causing the mule to kick. This vicious
act by the horse was the basis of the action. The Court held
that the plaintiff failed "to show that the negligence of defendant was the approximate cause of plaintiff's injuries,"
and in course of the opinion said: "In spite of the fact that
there was testimony to show that this mule was of so gentle
a disposition the children could play at his heels, it is a
matter of common knowledge and common experience that
there is no telling when or under what circumstances a mule

will or will not kick. The only way to escape danger from the feet of a mule is not to go within the radius of his heels."

We doubt that this is a correct statement of common knowledge experience. It is our observation and experience that a horse or mule, if properly trained, does not kick. We do know as a matter of common knowledge that it is impossible to work such an animal without going "within the radius of his heels," and being exposed many times daily to the danger of being kicked. For example, in harnessing the animal the crupper and breeching must be fitted under the animal's tail, and this requires not only standing at the animal's heels but annoying it as well by handling its tail. Again, every time the animal is hitched or unhitched it is necessary to take hold of each trace and fasten it to the singletree at the animal's heels. And when the hitching is to a plow, and many other farm implements, the singletree is very near the ground and requires the worker to take a completely helpless position as he stoops over and places his head near the animal's heels and hitches or unhitches the trace chains. Similarly, the hitching of a team to a wagon, or other vehicle, requires the worker to squeeze between the singletree and heels of the animal to hitch the inside traces.

Such exposures to being kicked in working an animal are many and often. And, yet, in this State boys on the farm . . . in past years before machinery replaced horses and mules, worked those animals with the entire confidence of their parents.

When this writer was a boy on the farm the older . . . farm workers had a common expression to give their view of the difference between the well trained animal and one that would kick, and the impossibility of working the latter, by saying that "A kicking horse or mule will kick molasses out of a ginger cake."

Of course, just as in the cited case, it is probable that most any horse or mule may be made to kick, just as most dogs can be made to bite, and most people, for that matter, made to fight.

Furthermore, the doctrine of those cases if applied here, is illogical as heretofore pointed out, the authorities generally agree that there is no presumption that a domestic animal is dangerous to man. It must be proven. Also, knowledge must be proven. Now, the Court, in each of the two cases relied upon by appellant, without repudiating those generally accepted principles, when it reached the affirmative defense of contributory negligence took judicial notice of the fact that the animal was dangerous, and charged the plaintiff with knowledge thereof, as a matter of law: the identical facts that a plaintiff is required to prove to make out his case.

A study of the Miller case shows that is exactly what the Court did. In that case the person who was kicked (and who died as a result thereof) passed near the rear of the horse, which was standing on a sidewalk. The Court found that there was no permanent or unreasonable obstruction of the sidewalk in the temporary stoppage of the horse at that point." And, further found, "There was no testimony to show that the horse was vicious, or that it had been known to kick before." Then, after having exonerated the defendant of all charges of negligence, the Court, in considering the defense of contributory negligence, said: "But, even if there was any question as to this, we are unable to regard the action of William Miller in walking deliberately past the heels of the horse, and within reach of them, without giving any warning or speaking to the horse, as being anything other than negligence which contributed to the happening of the accident. . . ."

In addition to the authorities hereinbefore cited, there is a note in 26 A.L.R. 871 discussing the duty of a master to warn his servant of the viciousness of a horse or mule used in the master's work, which, though not controlling, is helpful in understanding the trend of the decisions of the Courts on the subject here. Of course, a master would not be required to warn his servant of matters that are of common knowledge. However, an examination of the review of the cases covered in this note will show that all of the courts hold that the law imposes upon the master the duty of warning a servant of the known dangerous propensities of horses and mules, which are not actually known to the servant; and this is true even though the servant be experienced in handling such animals. In the case reported therewith, Boatman v. Miles, 27 Wyo. 481, 199 P. 933,935, holding a master liable for injuries to a servant in being bitten by a stallion furnished the servant in his work, expressed a sounder view of common knowledge and experience. Quoting briefly therefrom: "It is not likely that the temper of the animal changed overnight. The jury had a right to consider common experience. The stability of characteristics, inborn or acquired, is well known, and manifested alike in the vegetable and animal world. The traits exhibited by us in childhood are often still noticed when we reach the age of maturity. A balky horse is apt to be always balky. A gentle kitten is apt to manifest that gentleness in early life. Changes in nature are generally slow; sudden, radical changes the exception. For this reason evidence of viciousness by an animal subsequent to an accident, acting, as it does, according to its natural instincts, is admitted." Again in refusing to hold as a matter of law that the danger was apparent, said, "Courts will not declare that mules are judicially known as vicious; neither can we do so as to stallions. . . . The Jury, taken from all walks of life, were probably better to pass judgment upon that than the court, and the question was properly left to them." 199 P. 938, 26 A.L.R. 866, 871.

But we do not have to reject as authorities the Tolin and Miller cases to sustain the verdict in the case at bar, for the reason that there are important distinctions between the cases. Instead we have reviewed the Tolin and Miller cases in the light of other authorities for the purposes of clearly showing that, at least, they should not be extended further by applying them as controlling or persuasive in this case.

There are three important distinctions between those cases and the case now before us.

First, in the case at hand Mungo has proven negligence of Bennett which was the proximate cause of his injuries.

Again, on the defense of contributory negligence, Mungo testified that he did not go to the horse's heels, but that he was "standing facing the horse, more to the right side of the horse, facing it," and while in that position, the horse suddenly whirled around, without warning, and kicked him.

And finally, in this case it is an admitted act that Bennett called Mungo to the scene of his injuries, without giving him any warning, although appellant knew the horse to be dangerous, and would kick.

"From a review of all the decisions of the California appellate courts, it may be announced as the law relating to the liability of the owners of horses that if the owner knowingly keeps a mean or vicious beast, he is liable for injuries to another who has been invited to the premises where the animal is kept. . . ." O'Brien et al v. Gateway Stables et al., 104 Cal. App. 2d 317, 231 P. 2d 524, 526."

Obligations of Bailee or One Who Receives the Horse for a Specific Purpose

Generally speaking where a horse is loaned without compensation to a person (the bailee), that person is bound to exercise extraordinary diligence and care. Where the horse is hired or rented the bailee is bound to exercise ordinary care and diligence in the use and care of the horse. Of course a special contract providing the kind and degree of care to be exercised in caring for the horse will alter the general rule.

The care required by a bailee and, in this case, a trainer, is found in Schlamonitz vs. Pinehurst, 351 F. (2) 509 (1965). Mrs. Schlamonitz sought recovery of the value of two race horses that were destroyed when the barn in which the horses were stalled caught fire. Mrs. Schlamonitz employed a horse trainer to train, exercise and transfer them from racetrack to racetrack when they raced during the season. During the winter months she stabled the horses in the Pinehurst Stables. On the night of January 3 or 4, 1963, Mrs. Schlamonitz brought action against the professional horse trainer and the owner of the land upon which the stable was constructed, Pinehurst, Inc.

The evidence disclosed that the horses were stabled in a modern horse barn, constructed of concrete blocks. However the barn was not equipped with automatic fire alarm system or chemical fire extinguishers, although the stable did have three fire barrels and buckets. Mrs. Schlamonitz alleged three specific grounds of negligence: (1) that no groom was asleep in the barn the night of the fire; (2) that there were no chemical extinguishers in the barn; and (3) that it was not equipped with an automatic fire alarm system. (The origin of the fire was never determined.)

The Court examined the specific claims of fault alleged against the professional trainer as follows:

"We need not speculate whether a sleeping groom in a barn room might have avoided the loss. The fact is that no one in the business had thought that a sleeping groom in a barn such as this was a reasonable precaution against fire or other hazards. Their presence at night during the winter season was not because of any recognition of their usefulness. There was testimony that a conscientious groom, relieved of duty at 4:30 P.M., who had in his charge a horse who drank more water than most horses, might return in the late afternoon to replenish the water bucket. They were not required to do that, and the most conscientious of them did no more. A requirement of twenty-four hour groom service would have greatly increased plaintiff's maintenance costs. Bearing in mind the fact that the duty Edmunds (horse trainer) owed was one of ordinary, not extraordinary, care, we cannot affirm a finding of negligence because of his failure to take the possibly expensive and most extraordinary precaution of requiring the presence of a groom throughout the night."

"We cannot read the testimony as a whole as providing a reasonable basis for a finding that a prudent horseman would have provided his barn with an automatic fire alarm system. Of course, had an effective alarm system been in place, there would have been assurance of earlier warning of the fire, but that fact cannot support a finding of negligence."

"Finally, the plaintiff (Mrs. Schlamonitz) contends that the defendants should have placed chemical fire extinguishers in the barn, rather than the three fire barrels and buckets. Such extinguishers were not unknown in horse barns. They were available in Edmund's Barn No. 5, only a few feet away, but there was no attempt to use them in Barn No. 4, for the obvious reason that the people on the scene could not get to the fire. The fire was in the center of the barn and had burned through the middle of the roof when first discovered. The barn was 188 feet long, and was so filled with dense smoke that no one could enter it. Had chemical extinguishers been inside the barn they could not have been reached, and, if reached, their contents could not have been sprayed upon the fire. Moreover, by the time the would-be rescuers reached the barn and got the doors open, the horses were dead or dying. The most efficient fire fighting apparatus could not have revived them. There is no basis for a finding that the absence of chemical fire extinguishers in Barn No. 4 was a proximate cause of the destruction of the plaintiff's horses."

The Court then stated the legal principles relevant in such cases.

"When there is a bailment for the mutual advantage of bailor and bailee, the bailee is required to exercise ordinary care for the preservation and protection of the goods. He is not an insurer. He is required to exercise that degree of care which a person of reasonable prudence would use with respect to his own goods. The fact that Edmunds (the trainer) stabled his own horses and pony in Barn No. 4, rather than in Barn No. 5 is not conclusive, for imprudent men may take imprudent care of their own property, but the fact may be relevant and, in some instances, persuasive."

The same legal principle applies to an agister. In Nichols vs. Union Stock Yards & Transit Co., 193 Ill. App. 14 the Court stated: "It is conceded that the defendant was a bailee or agister of the cattle at the time they were destroyed by the fire, and that it was bound to exercise ordinary care for the preservation of the cattle."

Failure to return a horse in as good condition as when it was received for it creates a liability on the bailee greater than that imposed by the general law of bailment. The following case (Grady vs. Schweinler, 113 N.W. 1031) is a good example of a case in which the parties enter into a special contract that makes the bailee obligated to use more than ordinary care.

Grady, the plaintiff, brought an action for damages against Schweinler, the defendant, for the value of a stallion delivered by him to the defendant on a contract of bailment.

The stallion was delivered to the defendant for serving his mares for the agreed sum of $5 a foal. The complaint alleges plaintiff's ownership of the stallion, the value thereof, his delivery to the defendant under an express contract that defendant would return him to the plaintiff, or in case he were unable to return him defendant would pay plaintiff the value of said stallion, and that plaintiff demanded his return to him or payment of the value thereof, which was refused by the defendant. Judgment is demanded for the sum of $400.00.

The answer admits that said stallion was delivered to the defendant for the purposes alleged in the complaint, but denies that he agreed to pay for said stallion in case of his inability to return him upon demand. The answer further alleges that the stallion was sick when delivered to defendant. Plaintiff testified: "He said: 'I will take the horse and return him in as good or better shape than I get him, and, if I don't, I will pay for him. I am good for him.' I agreed to let him have the horse to breed his mares at $5 a colt, provided he returned the horse as he got him, and, if he didn't, he should pay for him. Mr. Schweinler said he would take him on those terms, and, if he didn't return him as good as he got him, he would pay for him." A witness for plaintiff testified: Mr. Schweinler said he would fetch the horse back in as good condition as he took him, or, if anything happened, he would pay for him."

The Court said:

> Parties are permitted to make their own contracts in reference to their mutual rights and liabilities under bailments of property as well as in reference to other subjects, but, of course, are not permitted to contract in contravention of positive law or public policy, and perhaps may not in all

cases relieve themselves from the results of their own negligence. In this case the language was positive and unequivocal that the bailee was to pay for the horse if he was unable to return him for any reason. If anything happened to the horse, making a return impossible, payment was to be made. Without any special contract, the law would impose on the defendant the duty to use ordinary care, and, in case of the death of the animal without defendant's fault, he would not be responsible. In this case, as we have shown, the contract went further, and enlarged the obligation of the bailee in respect to those devolving on him where no special contract exists. The principle contended for, therefore, has no application. The fact that the horse died while in defendant's possession without his fault is not a defense in view of the existing contract shown by the evidence and presumed to be true for the purpose of this appeal. The plaintiff having alleged and proved the contract, a breach thereof, demand, and a refusal to comply therewith, stated a cause of action in the complaint, and the same was established by the evidence without any showing of negligence.

Cameron vs. Bissonette, 152 V. 87 decided by the Supreme Court of Vermont illustrates the degree of care required of a gratuitous bailee. W. J. Cameron and wife, the plaintiffs, instituted action against Emile Bissonette and wife, defendants, to recover the value of a mare that belonged to the plaintiffs and that was found dead in a brook while in the possession of the defendants.

"On October 3, 1928, the plaintiffs purchased from the defendants a farm on which the latter then resided and certain livestock, including the mare in question; that the defendants were to have time (how long did not appear) in which to move off the farm, and were to have the mare, without charge, to use in moving; that there was a barn on the farm in which she could have been kept, but that she was left in the pasture the day and night of October 18th, when it was cold and rainy, and the following morning was found dead in a brook in said pasture; that the normal depth of the water in this brook is about two feet, and that its depth at the time the mare was found therein was from four to five feet.

The plaintiffs contend that the defendants were gratuitous bailees of the mare, since the bailment was for their sole benefit. This is not questioned by the defendants, so we treat that as an established fact," said the Court.

The Court further said that "The plaintiffs contend that as such bailees the defendants were bound to exercise a high or extraordinary degree of care and diligence in caring for the mare. This is true. Schouler in his 1905 edition on Bailments, at page 28, in speaking of this class of bailees, says: 'The bailee is bound to exercise what is called great, or more than ordinary diligence, and to respond for every loss which is caused by even slight negligence on his part.' To the same effect are Elliott on Bailments (2d Ed.) par 40, and Story on Bailments (9th Ed.) par. 237. In the absence of a special contract, however, such bailees are not insurers of the subject of the bailment and are only liable for such loss or damage as results from their negligence."

A case in 1893 of Wilder vs. Stanley 26 A. 189 sets forth the law of concurrent negligence of the bailee and a third party. A colt belonging to the plaintiff, Wilder, escaped from its pasture through a break in the division fence. The defendant, Stanley, had the duty to maintain the fence. A neighbor, Tracey, attempted to drive the colt back to the pasture. Tracey negligently drove the colt into a barbed wire fence causing injuries from which it died. The Court said:

"The escape being through the negligence of the defendant, that negligence accompanied the colts while roaming, by reason of it, away from the plaintiff's pasture. Inasmuch as Tracey was not the servant of the plaintiff, if he voluntarily negligently started up or drove the colt at the time it was injured, Tracey's negligence would be concurrent with that of the defendant in causing the death of the colt. In such a case, both or either of the wrong-doers are liable for the injury and damage caused by their concurrent negligence."

When negligence is established, liability attaches for all the injurious consequences that flow therefrom until diverted by the intervention of some efficient cause that makes the injury its own, or until the force set in motion by an negligent act has so far spent itself as to be too small for the law's notice.

4

TRESPASSING HORSES: LIABILITY OF THE OWNER FOR DAMAGES

IN THE DAYS WHEN AMERICA WAS RURAL AND AGRICULTURE was the most important factor in the economy, domestic animals were permitted to pasture without limitations. This was termed "open range country." There was no duty upon the owner to prevent the livestock from wandering even if the wandering took them onto the roads, streets and highways. The law of the "open range" continued until the courts and the state legislatures, sensitive to the changing social and economic pattern, began revising the law to what is known in many states as the General Stock Law. The General Stock Law, as you will see later, required the livestock to be fenced in rather than fenced out. This law was made necessary by the growth of population in the American West.

The structure of society and the economy changed as the people moved West. The demand for changes in the livestock law was recognized. Today, most of the "open range" territory is in the cattle country of the West. The basic difference between the "open range" law and the "General Stock Law" is that in "open range" territory the owner is not liable for damages caused by his livestock

67

if he is not negligent, whereas, under the "General Stock Law" the owner is held to strict liability for damages resulting from trespassing of livestock.

Open Range Liability

A leading case setting forth the law of the "open range" is *Bartsch v. Irvine Company* 427 P. (2) 302 decided by the Supreme Court of Montana in 1967.

In open range country, owner of livestock or one upon whose land such livestock is being pastured has no duty to prevent livestock from wandering and cannot be held negligent if livestock do wander, even if such wandering takes them onto highway right-of-way which runs through open range.

The facts of this case are these: On October 5, 1965, Mr. Bartsch was returning to his home in Bozeman, Montana, from a business trip to Whitehall, Montana. Mr. Bartsch's wife Deanna and his two-year-old son Steven were in the car with him. He was proceeding toward Bozeman on Highway 289 east from Norris, Montana. It was getting dark, and headlights were in use. Mr. Bartsch dimmed his lights as another vehicle approached from the other direction, and just as he passed the other vehicle, he got a split second glimpse of a horse in the roadway. The vehicle and the horse collided. The horse crushed in the top of the car.

Mrs. Bartsch was killed in the collision.

The horse was not owned by defendants, but was being pastured by them on land which they leased. The horse had wandered off defendants' leased pasture lands and along the highway right of way for some distance.

The testimony at the trial showed that the area in which the accident happened was open range country.

Plaintiff based his action on section 58–607, which provides in part: "Every one is responsible, not only for the

result of his willful acts, but also for an injury occasioned
to another by his want of ordinary care or skill in the
management of his property or person . . ." Plaintiff contends that allowing a horse to pasture in an area where
it wandered onto the highway right of way and remained
for some period of time resulting in a collision with plaintiff's car is lack of ordinary care or skill in the management of property and thus negligent. The court said:

> The issue presented by this appeal is whether it was negli-
> gent for defendant to pasture horses in an area of open
> range country in which such horses might wander onto the
> highway right of way during the course of their grazing.
> Montana has been open range country even before Mon-
> tana became a state. The law of the Territory provided that
> recovery for damages done by trespassing livestock could
> only be accomplished if the trespassed property was enclosed
> by a lawful fence, which the laws also defined.
> This state has long been a public range state wherein
> livestock of private ownership have been and now are per-
> mitted by license of the government to graze without hin-
> drance or restriction on the open, unoccupied, public do-
> main. Such stock are said to be "running on the range."
> The exception to this, of course, is willful or intentional
> herding or driving of livestock onto another's unfenced land
> or placing them so near that trespass is bound to occur.
> Such is not the law in *all* jurisdictions, but it has been the
> law for a long time in Montana.
> Thus, in open range country, the owner of livestock or
> one upon whose land such livestock is being pastured, has
> no duty to prevent the livestock from wandering. Since he
> has no duty to prevent such wandering, he cannot be said to
> be negligent if the livestock do wander—even if such wander-
> ing takes them onto a highway right of way which runs
> through the open range.
> The testimony at the trial did not show that there was
> any willful act or intention on the part of the defendant to
> drive the horse onto the highway right of way. For an ex-
> ample of what has been considered a negligent act by an
> owner of premises see *Hopkins v. Ravalli* County Electric
> Co-op, Inc., 144 Mont. 161, 395 P.2d 106. The Plaintiff's
> case failed to establish any duty on the part of the defendant
> which the defendant had violated.

General Stock Law

The midwest state of Ohio is a good example of the change in the control of livestock due to the change in the structure of society and the economy as the settlers moved West. In 1831 the problem of domestic animals running at large was presented to the Supreme Court of Ohio in the case involving the Town of Marietta. Marietta adopted an ordinance imposing a fine upon any person who permitted his horse to run at large on the streets of the town. The owner of a horse lived outside but adjacent to Marietta. His horse, while lawfully grazing on the highway outside of the town, strayed onto the corporate limits of Marietta. The owner was fined. He appealed and the court laid down this principle of law: "That an incorporated town within the state cannot subject stray animals, owned by persons not residents of such town, to its corporation ordinance." At that time, 138 years ago, the public use of highways was subservient to their use as pasture for horses.

But, by 1895, the court and General Assembly recognized that the growth of the population and the necessities of industry required animals to be kept fenced in, rather than fenced out. The court in *Morgan v. Hudnell*, 52 Ohio St. 552 held that if the animal breaks into the close of another, and there damages the real or personal property of the one in possession, the owner of the trespassing animal is liable, without reference to whether or not such animal was vicious, and without reference to whether such propensity was known to the owner.

The rule of strict liability reflected in *Morgan* was a natural development of the times:

> The legislation in Ohio with reference to fencing lands has advanced from time to time in the light of experience and to meet what the General Assembly regarded as the requirements of changing conditions.

Upon this state of the record, plaintiff relied for recovery on the theory of livestock trespass claiming the common-law rule of strict liability applied to this set of facts. Under that rule, possessors of livestock intruding upon the lands of other persons were held liable as for trespass, and the exercise of due care in keeping the animals confined did not affect the liability and the action was brought upon the theory of trespass *quare clausum fregit,* the gist of which was the breaking and entering of the close. The rule was held applicable to personal injury cases and available to the owner or occupier and members of his household.

Though not as agile as the cow in the Mother Goose rhyme, there was evidence that cows do jump fences and that this propensity is stimulated when the animal is in heat and particularly when a bull is in the vicinity. There was also evidence that the fence was 42 inches high, "chest high," and that the cow could not get back into Arnold's field through the fence. After the fence was examined, a staple pulling tool was procured, the staples securing the fence to two posts were pulled, the fence was pushed down and the cow passed into her proper enclosure.

The owner of a trespassing domestic animal is responsible for damages. We see no reason to disapprove or overrule *Morgan v. Hudnell.* It is sound law and consistent with changing conditions.

General stock laws in most states prohibit animals from running at large and provide strict liability of the owner whose animals cause damage while unlawfully on the lands of another. The language may differ to some degree in the different states having general stock laws but the general principle of law is the same. An example is the statute of West Virginia:

General Stock Law

Stock trespassing on enclosed grounds; damages

If any horse, mule, ass, jennet, cattle, sheep, swine, or goat shall enter into any grounds enclosed by a lawful fence, the owner or manager of any such stock shall be liable to the owner or tenant of such grounds for any damage he may sustain thereby, and the party so injured may, if he finds such stock on his premises, impound them, or a sufficient number thereof, subject to the provisions of sections eight, nine and ten of this article, until such damages and costs of keeping have been paid.

Unlawful running at large of stock on road or railroad right of way

It shall be unlawful for any horse, mule, ass, jennet, cattle, sheep or goat to run at large on any public road or highway or railroad right of way, and should any such stock injure or destroy the property of another while so running at large, the owner or manager thereof shall be guilty of a misdemeanor, and, upon conviction thereof, shall be fined not less than five nor more than ten dollars.

Unlawful Running at Large of Certain Male Animals and Swine

It shall be unlawful for any stallion, jack or bull over one year old, buck sheep over four months old, buck goat over six months old or swine, to run at large, and the owner or manager of any such stock running at large shall be guilty of a misdemeanor, and, upon conviction thereof, shall be fined not less than five nor more than ten dollars.

Unlawful Running at Large of Stock of Nonresidents of State

It shall be unlawful for any horse, mule, ass, jennet, cattle, sheep, swine, or goat owned by any person not a citizen of this State to run at large in this State.

Liability of Owner for Damage by Stock Unlawfully Running at Large

Should any stock, while running at large contrary to the provisions of sections two, three or four of this article, injure or destroy the property of another, the owner or manager of any such stock shall, notwithstanding any penalty imposed by said sections, be liable to the party whose property shall have been injured or destroyed for the amount of damage sustained by him by reason of such injury or destruction. And the party so injured may, if he find such stock on his premises, impound them, or a sufficient number thereof, subject to the provisions of sections eight, nine and ten of this article, until such damages and costs of keeping be paid.

Impounding Stock Unlawfully Running at Large

It shall be lawful for any person finding any stock running at large contrary to the provisions of sections two, three or four of this article, to impound such stock, subject to the provisions of sections eight, nine and ten of this article, until the costs of keeping such stock be paid.

The above Statutes make the owner of animals liable only for damages where there is injury or destruction to property, yet, the owner may be liable if he negligently permits his horse to run at large upon a highway and causes injury to a person. This was the ruling of the Supreme Court of West Virginia in *Smith vs. Whitlock*, 19 SE (2) 617:

> By his amended declaration, *the plaintiff alleged that while he was a passenger in an automobile being driven on a public highway in Fayette County, known as U. S. Route No. 19, the defendant was the owner of a certain horse, and that it thereupon became his duty* "to keep said horse from running at large on said public highway so as not to do damage or injury to the persons and property of others lawfully traveling thereon, and more especially to the person of this plaintiff then and there lawfully riding in said automobile as aforesaid." The alleged negligence of the defendant is charged in the following language: "Yet the defendant, not regarding his duty in that behalf, so carelessly, negligently and unlawfully suffered and permitted said horse to run at large upon said highway, that said horse ran into and against

the automobile in which this plaintiff was riding, with the result that said automobile was caused to be wrecked, and as the proximate result of said wreck, this plaintiff was thrown with great force and violence against the top and other parts of said automobile, * * *."

Today, the owner's permitting a horse to wander on a highway may or may not be actionable negligence, depending on the character of the highway and its traffic. To let such an animal range on a great automobile boulevard, there to become involved in the confusion of incessant traffic in both directions and at great speed, in which human intelligence is often unavailing, may be the grossest of negligence; while a horse browsing along a remote ,unimproved, unenclosed, little-used rural road, or mountain trail, may present no substantial risk of actual danger to travelers. This state has hundreds of miles of each of these types of road, with all kinds between. All these roads are equally "highways" under the law; all are subject to the same rules. Yet what would be dangerous on one road, may be perfectly safe on another; what would be legal negligence in one case, might be no evidence of want of care in another. These diverse conditions may account for the fact that the legislature has enacted no uniform statute to control in every case. Certain it is, that these considerations forbid that the courts shall, in the absence of action by the legislature, undertake to establish any universal rule applying to all highways in the state. Each case must stand on its own facts. The character of the road, the kind of traffic thereon, the time of day, and all other pertinent facts and the surrounding conditions, must be considered.

This status of the law is not as anomalous as might at first seem. While there is no statute creating any further liability for injuries caused by animals running at large on the highways of the state, there is not legal vacuum in this field. Although the owner may not, by virtue of any statute, be held liable for damages done to a person by the running at large of his horse on a highway, such owner should have no greater immunity from liability for injury by his beasts on a public road than for a like injury committed on his own premises, and no greater immunity than he would have from injury by his other property negligently used. An owner must so use all his property, animate or inanimate, on his premises or on a highway, so as not carelessly or purposely to injure another. Very plainly, an owner might be held liable, aside from any statute, for negligence in the care of his horse on his own premises, as, for example, by turning it loose, or permitting it to run unattended, in a field filled with children at play. He cannot unreasonably expose persons rightfully elsewhere to unnecessary danger, and he has no greater right to do so on a highway. His liability arises, not because the injury occurs on a highway, nor by reason of any statute, nor from the fact that it was inflicted by his horse, but from the very right of persons, wherever they lawfully are, to be free from careless, or purposeful injury by another—from the fundamental law, not necessary to be written, but inherent in any conception of justice, that the owner of property shall not intentionally, or negligently, so use it, or permit it to be used, as to injure another.

A case not wholly inapplicable is Walke v. Premier Pocahontas Collieries Co., 94 W. Va. 38, 117 S.E. 905, which involved a child injured by the negligent driving of defendant's unbridled horse, which escaped onto a private street between houses maintained by the defendant for its employees, and thereby injured the child playing thereon. This Court said, in syllabus 1 of that case: "It is negligence as a matter of law for a coal company, regardless of its custom or the custom of others, to hitch an untried horse, unaccustomed to such use, to steel rails, and without reins or lines attempt to drive him up a hill in the neighborhood of miners' houses built by such company in furtherance of its business, and by reason of such want of restraint the horse becomes scared and runs away through one of the streets or ways between such houses and does injury to an infant playing in the streets while residing with its parent, an employee of the company, in one of such houses."

If the owner of a horse is thus liable for negligently allowing it to escape and injure a person on a private way on the owner's premises, no possible reason appears why a like injury to a person on a highway would not also be actionable.

This conclusion has been reached in other states: "For any negligence in the keeping of an animal whereby injury is occasioned, the owner is always responsible. In determining the owner's liability for injuries inflicted, the criterion usually adopted is whether or not he could reasonably have anticipated the occurrence." 2 Am.Jur., Animals, sec. 59,

p. 737. An illustrative case is Drew v. Gross, 112 Ohio St. 485, 147 N.E. 757, 758, in which the syllabus by the court says:

"The owner of a domestic animal is responsible for negligence in its keeping whereby damage is occasioned. * * *

"It is a question of fact for the jury whether an owner of horses who turns them loose unattended into a field adjacent to a much-traveled highway in the nighttime, the fence of which field is in such defective condition that the horses may easily stray out onto the highway, could have anticipated that one of the horses would stray out onto the highway and collide with an automobile thereon."

In the opinion in this case, at page 491 of 112 Ohio St., at page 758 of 147 N.E., it is said that: "A statute is not always required to establish the duty of ordinary care. The duty may arise from statute, or it may arise from ordinance, from contract, or from the relation of the parties. Apart from specific statute the law imposes upon every person the duty of using his own property so as not to injure his neighbor. As conditions change and modes of life alter, the duty to observe ordinary care in the use of one's own property, while not altering in its essentials, will alter in its details. What ordinary care demands depends always upon the circumstances of the case, and a primary factor among those circumstances is the fact whether the injury could or could not have reasonably have been anticipated from the acts done or left undone by the defendant. When the state was established it was not in general unsafe to permit domestic animals to run at large in the highway outside of the confines of municipalities, and damage from so doing could not generally be reasonably anticipated. With the growth of traffic, particularly automobile traffic, the situation is changed, but the duty to observe ordinary care remains the same. This duty in modern times requires that the owner of livestock exercise ordinary care not to let his livestock stray out onto a much-traveled highway, because under our modern traffic conditions he can reasonably anticipate that, if the livestock stray onto such a highway, they are apt to damage persons or property."

An example of how serious a matter it is for the owner to negligently allow his animals, whether horses or hogs,

to trespass upon his neighbors' property is found in the
Iowa Case of *Leaders vs. Dreher*, 169 N. W. (2) 570,
decided in July 1969.

In negligence action for damages sustained when defendant's trespassing sow struck and injured plaintiff, trial
to jury resulted in a verdict of $13,350 for plaintiff.

Briefly stated the evidence discloses these two parties live
on adjoining farms, having been neighbors since 1946.

Among other farming operations defendant raises Wessex
Saddleback hogs. One of these animals, a 450 to 475 pound
sow, repeatedly escaped from its fenced enclosure and went
onto plaintiff's property. Plaintiff's witnesses testified defendant's hog had been found on plaintiff's premises each day
for about four to six weeks before the incident in question.
On these prior occasions plaintiff or the members of his
family, often chased the pig away. Other times they would
call defendant and request he remove it. But the record
discloses defendant usually arrived half an hour to an hour
after notification, during which time the animal continued
damaging plaintiff's property.

The hog was seen by plaintiff on his premises August 20,
1965, "up by the brooder house eating feed and upsetting the
water and feed stuff," also "in the brooder house scaring
the chickens." He then unsuccessfully attempted to remove
the unwanted invader. Failing this, he summoned his wife
and children to help. The children, with assistance of the
family dog, began chasing the swine toward a white gravel
lane leading to a country road. In the meantime, plaintiff
stationed himself on the lane between the brooder house and
hog pen in order to head the sow down the road toward
defendant's farm. With children and dog in pursuit the
animal approached the gravel lane where plaintiff was standing. At this point the unfortunate injury occurred. The sow
ran under plaintiff, catching his right leg and upsetting him.
He landed on his head and shoulders, causing a herniated
cervical disc at the interspace between the fourth and fifth
cervical vertebrae. A spinal fusion was performed and the
attending physican testified plaintiff suffered an injury connected partial permanent physical disability of 10–15 percent.
He was unable to do farm work for three months after the
operation.

There is evidence to the effect defendant's fence was not in good condition, a hole having been discovered in it after plaintiff's injury, through which livestock had apparently been escaping.

The negligence alleged in plaintiff's petition and submitted to the jury was, defendant failed to restrain his sow from running at large.

Under the law defendant in the case before us was prima facie responsible for the escape of his hog and its customary invasion of plaintiff-neighbor's premises. And, for reasons heretofore disclosed, the conduct of plaintiff, his wife and children, in a reasonable attempt to remove the damaging trespasser from their land, could not relieve defendant from liability for any act or omission on his part which may have permitted the sow to escape from her enclosure.

And as aforesaid, defendant should have realized plaintiff would attempt to remove the hog from his property, such being customary, not unusual or highly extraordinary.

The verdict is sustained by substantial evidence.

The measure of damages for wrongfully killing a horse is the market value, if any, and if the horse has no market value then actual or intrinsic value plus interest. If the horse is injured so that the horse can not be used for a time the damages for the use and hire of another animal are recoverable.

The Texas Supreme Court in ruling on the question of damages set forth the rule governing damages yet gave only poetic justice to the "one-eyed bay mare" in the case of *Guthrie vs. City of Canadian*, 87 SW (2) 316. The opinion was written by Chief Judge Hall:

Guthrie was engaged in hauling in the city of Canadian, in which occupation he used a wagon and team. One of the animals so used is described as a "bay mare, one-eyed, about 12 or 14 years old. That this mare, by reason of the loss of her said eye, which plaintiff alleges to be the left eye, was specially adapted to the work of teaming in connection with the other horse." It appears that on account of the dearth of vitamins from A to Z in her home cuisine, this particular mare was prone to spend her off nights prowling through the city, feasting upon the lawns, shrubbery, and gardens of her neighbors. Some days before the fatal day she had been placed in the city pound, plaintiff was duly notified and failed to pay her board bill, whereupon the city marshal employed one Jess, whose surname was Lemley, more familiarly known as "Panhandle Pete," who, at the direction of the mayor, ruthlessly took said mare's life by shooting her between the bad eye and the one not so bad. In other words, in the vernacular of gangland, when Panhandle Pete's pistol popped, she petered, for which the poundkeeper paid Pete a pair of pesos. The mayor testified that just before her execution he visited the city pound twice to see her and found her in bad shape, that she was sick and prostrate, and had hay and other provender in her nose. That he cleaned out her flues so she could breathe, but, nevertheless, he called out the militia and ordered Pete to put her out of her misery for humanitarian reasons. This established the corpus delicti. His honor testified that he knew nothing about mares, and the jury believed him.

There is testimony that she was thin in flesh, indicating that she had some fine points upon which her harness could be hung. From the record, we conclude that although she may not have had a skin you would particularly love to touch (though she had seen only fourteen joyous summers), yet she had a skin which clung like ivy to her rafters with a beautiful corrugated effect upon the sides of her lithe and spirituelle form.

Plaintiff immediately brought suit, fixing his actual damages at $50, alleging that his mare had no market value, and proudly averring that she was the only mare of her kind in Hemphill county, but that $50 was her actual and intrinsic value, and $100 was her sentimental value. He further sued for $350 for the loss of the services of said mare while pursuing his occupation of hauling, and claimed the further sum of $500 as exemplary damages on account of the malicious act of the city in having her killed. He averred that because of her loss his occupation, like Othello's, was gone and he "had been set out an empty." However, he concluded before the trial that a genial, brotherly-love city like Canadian, which had been converted into a one-horse town by Pete and the mayor, was incapable of harboring malice, and

the claim for exemplary damages was abandoned at the trial.
The record shows that upon at least two occasions

"When night drew her sable curtain down
And pinned it with a star,"
and
"Silence like a gentle spirit
Brooded o'er a still and pulseless world,"

the time lock on her corral mysteriously went off and so did
she, in search of tulips, dahlias, and gladioli in the neigh-
boring lawns and flower beds. It is clear from the record
that she had at least one eye for the beautiful, and was
excessively fond of flowers, but that the tender passion was
not reciprocated, for, as stated, he parted with her without
consideration. While her origin is shrouded in mystery, her
appetite for flora of the rarest and costliest varieties indicates
that somewhere back in the line of her ancestry there had
been injected a stream of royal blood. Although she had
only one eye, appellant contends she could find more edible
shrubbery in a single night than an experienced landscape
gardener could replant in thirty days. We may assume that
in her midnight excursions she had been thrown with porch
climbers, joy riders, orchard raiders, and other nocturnal
prowlers, which may account for her waywardness and utter
disregard for the property rights of others. But after her
midnight banquet upon orchids, delphiniums, and hyacinths,
the poundkeeper would take her in charge, and set before her
a bundle or two of mildewed sorghum of the vintage of 1927
in order to take the taste out of her mouth, but when he sent
the meal ticket to the plaintiff, the latter steadfastly refused
to pay. It was not denied that she had "went hence" and
was cut down in the heyday of her young and fitful life
because the mayor found some of the hay in her nose, and
he admitted that he was accessory before the fact and had
personally ordered her gentle soul sent to the great beyond
and the remainder to the municipal dump ground.

While, as bearing upon her sentimental value, it is sad-
dening to know that the beautiful flower beds and onion
patches of Canadians, over which she was wont to gambol
in the moonlight between the hour when

"Curfew tolled the knell of parting day,"
and some hours later,

"when greyeyed morn
Stood tiptoe upon the misty mountain height
And flecked the eastern hills with rays of golden light,"

would know her no more forever, nevertheless, in the cold unsympathetic eye of the law, sentimental value is not recognized as a basis for damages. 13 Tex. Jur. 155.

A jury was impaneled, who found: (1) That the mare had an intrinsic value; (2) of $25; (3) that plaintiff suffered special damages; (4) which were the proximate result of the city's unlawful act; (5) in the sum of $35. The court defined "proximate cause" in the stereotyped form, and charged the jury that special damages "are such consequences of an injury as are peculiar to the circumstances and conditions of the injured party." Judgment was rendered in favor of Guthrie for $60, with interest from the date of the judgment at 6 per cent.

Damages occasioned by the loss of the use and hire of an animal are recoverable where the animal is injured so that it cannot be used for a time, or where the possession is illegally detained; but no such damages are recoverable for the total loss or death of an animal. The measure of damages in the case of a wrongful killing of an animal is its market value, if it has one, and if not, then its actual or intrinsic value, with interest.

Guthrie's counsel suggested that this being the rule, it is cheaper to kill a mare in Texas than it is to cripple her. The same seems to be true with reference to men, but this court must declare the law as it exists.

After the item of $500 claimed as exemplary damages (which, of course, was not recoverable) had been abandoned by plaintiff, the trial court should have sustained the general demurrer to the item of $350 special damages, as the real amount in controversy is only $50, alleged to be the actual value of the mare.

In our original opinion, we held that because the actual damages fixed at $50 was an amount below the jurisdiction of the county court, that that court had no jurisdiction, and therefore this court acquired none by the appeal, and we dismissed the cause. We suggested that as the plaintiff's mare was wont to stray into the wrong curtilage for nourishment, likewise his attorneys had wandered into the wrong court in search of damages. In the light of the motion for rehearing, it appears that that was an unjust criticism of learned counsel, but it is far worse as a legal proposition, because, as counsel say in their motion for rehearing:

I.

"Comes now the plaintiff, appellee,
And moves this Honorable Court to see,
That House Bill Number 304
Threw open wide the Court House door,
Of County Court in Hemphill County
Where Guthrie sought relief and bounty,
And recompense and generous meed,
For his departed wayward steed,
Cut down in all her youthful pride,
When she was taken for a ride."

II.

"The court did hold, that as this mare,
To wrong curtilage did repair,
Likewise, these lawyers who here do pray,
Into the wrong court below did stray;
But this Honorable Court overlooked the fact,
That the Legislature passed an Act,
In Nineteen Hundred and Fifteen,
And Jurisdiction since has been,
In that Court whence this case came,
As in the Justice Court the same."

Reference to H. B. No. 304 (Laws 1915, c. 125) shows that the Legislature did extend the jurisdiction of the county court of Hemphill county, making it concurrent with the jurisdiction of justices' courts, a law which even this court did not know; but appellee's counsel have found too much law for his good, because section 3 of the act provides that no appeal shall be taken to the Court of Civil Appeals from any final judgment of said county court in civil cases of which said court has concurrent jurisdiction with the justices' court where the judgment or amount in controversy does not exceed $100, exclusive of interest and costs. The judgment as stated is $60. According to the allegations, the real amount in controversy is $50.

5

MOTORIST'S LIABILITY FOR INJURING HORSES ON HIGHWAYS

COURTS RECOGNIZE THAT THERE IS A RIGHT OF ACTION against one who negligently kills or injures a horse on the highway. As a general rule a motorist can be held liable for injuring or killing a horse upon a highway if the motorist is negligent in operating his motor vehicle. The owner of the horse who is claiming the loss must prove that the driver was negligent. Examples of negligence include operating a motor vehicle at a speed greater than what would be reasonable and safe, having due regard for the conditions then existing; operating a motor vehicle without proper brakes; operating a motor vehicle with defective front headlights; failing to keep a motor vehicle under proper control, so as to avoid endangering the property or persons or animals that might be in or upon a public highway; and failing to keep a proper lookout. There are many acts and omissions of negligence, depending upon the facts and circumstances of each case.

While a motorist is required to exercise reasonable care to avoid a collision with animals on a highway, he is not an insurer against injury. If an unavoidable injury occurs, he is not liable. The following cases indicate when a motorist is liable and when he is free of negligence. Even when there is a prohibition against permitting animals to run at large, this does not always relieve the motorist of responsibility for negligent injury to animals. The rule of liability for failing to use ordinary care applies to injury to animals drawn or led upon the highway by their keepers. If a motorist becomes aware of animals on the highway, it is his obligation to so operate his car so as to avoid striking the animals. Reduce speed, keep a safe distance while passing, or stop if necessary.

The Supreme Court of Maine in *O'Brien vs. Marston*, 74 A (2) 879 dealt with the rule of law governing motorists who observe horses upon the highway. The facts are as follows:

> The driver of the automobile observed some distance ahead at the top of a hill a run-away horse, and several people of whom at least one, carrying a bucket of grain, was endeavoring to catch the horse. Within seconds the accident took place on the motorist's right side of the traveled way. The Court found "It is an admitted fact, however, the motorist did not stop her car, but proceeded, at a rate which she estimated was probably not over twenty miles per hour, and whichever side the horse was on, the distance between the horse and the car was lessening, and the horse was not under control." The motorist not realizing that her continued driving of her car was fraught with peril to herself, her car, and the runaway horse, the probabilities are that the horse would not be likely to rush into a stationary object, while the continuing advance of the car was apt to excite it. She was unwittingly, yet legally negligent in not stopping her car. Surely it cannot be said that a runaway horse does not present a danger to the motorist. It is common knowledge that the course of a runaway horse is unpredictable and it may be further excited by a moving automobile. The reasonable prudent man may well consider the possibility of the horse bounding into the highway from a ditch.

In Neal B. Wailes, 346 OAC (2) 132, the Wyoming

Court found for the Motorist. The testimony disclosed the following fact:

The owner alleged that on or about July 1, 1955, at about 8:30 P.M., some fifteen head of horses were being drawn along the highway a short distance from the town of Jackson in Teton County, Wyoming, with the intention of driving the animals through a gate located on the north side of the highway and onto the property where the animals were being pastured; and at that time the motorist drove an automobile along the highway at an unlawful speed and negligently killed three of the plaintiff's animals, namely, a red sorrel registered quarter mare of the value of $1500, an Appaloosa horse of the value of $350 and a jenny burro of the value of $35. Judgement was asked for the sum of $1885. The motorist alleged that the owner was negligent in allowing his horses to wander along the highway in violation of 11–507, W. S. 1957 (56–1813, W. C. S. 1945) which forbids livestock to run at large in a fenced public road; that the owner was negligent in not providing some warning lights or signals to indicate the presence of animals on the highway; and that the owner knew or should have known with exercise of due care that automobiles traveling upon the highway could not have seen the horses, particularly when blinded by the lights of oncoming traffic. The Court said:

> The presence of the animals on the highway in the dark of the night is, to say the least, very unusual. A traveler along the highway in a car at night would hardly be expecting to find animals in his path. We cannot, we think, say that as a matter of law the motorist was negligent at the time of the accident heretofore mentioned.

A Colorado Case holds that a motorist is not an insurer against injuries to animals in Pevers vs Pierce, 103 PAC (2) 690. The owner kept about fifty saddle horses at

Estes Park. On the evening of July 5, 1938, about ten o'clock, two of his employees were driving the herd along the paved highway in an easterly direction from the village to the pasture. The horses were strung along the north side of the road (next to the pasture) for about one hundred yards. At the same time the motorist approached in his car, driving between forty and fifty miles an hour. He did not slacken his speed, he says, because he did not see the horses. He had passed all except the last one, which suddenly jumped in front of his car and was so badly injured that it had to be killed. The employees admitted they did nothing to get the horse off the shoulder of the road when they saw the car coming. The Court held that while a motorist is required to exercise reasonable care to avoid a collision with domestic animals on a highway, he is not an insurer against injury to such animals, and if injury occurs which is unavoidable he is not liable. Liability attaches in such cases only where the driver of the car is negligent, which negligence must be established by the owner of the animal injured or killed. Even where there is a sign "Cattle Crossing," a driver of an automobile on a public highway has no reason to anticipate stray animals rushing onto the highway, so held the Rhode Island Court in the case of Round vs Burns, 74 A (2) 861.

The motorist hit a stray cow that trotted from the barnyard onto the highway and collided with an automobile. The Court held that the sudden and unexpected appearance of the cow in front of the car and not the negligence of the driver was the sole proximate cause of the accident. The Court also found that the driver had no reason to anticipate stray animals rushing onto the highway merely because he was in part of the highway marked with "Cattle Crossing" signs. The Court then cited an older case which held that ordinarily the mere presence of a horse going loose and unattended on the highway is prima facia evidence of the negligence of the owner unless he rebuts it. That case was decided many years ago when the speed and volume of highway traffic was not to be compared with what it is today on a modern four-lane highway.

The ruling can be different if an unattended horse is struck by a motorist driving too fast in a heavy fog. A driver was operating his car on a highway in a heavy fog which greatly limited his range of vision so that he could see only seven feet ahead of him. Nevertheless he proceeded at a high speed and ran into a horse walking unattended on the highway. There the Court held the motorist failed to exercise due care commensurate with the circumstances created by the fog and blindly drove his car into hidden danger.

It is generally held by most Courts that it is negligent to drive too fast to stop within the range of vision limited by the headlights of the car or limited by atmospheric conditions.

The rule that a person is held to have seen an object which, by the use of ordinary care and prudence, he should have seen applies to motorists who should have seen horses upon the highway. In a Georgia Case the Court held that where the motorist drove down a straight and level road and ran into a mule which he did not see in the road until it was too late to avoid a collision, this was sufficient to submit to the jury the question of liability.

In most states motor vehicle laws provide that every person riding or driving or leading an animal upon a roadway should be subject to the provisions of the law applicable to the driver of a vehicle, except those provisions of the act which by their very nature can have no application.

A typical traffic law governing animal owners while on the highways with their animals is found in the West Virginia Code in Chapter 17 C Article 7, Section 6:

Every person riding an animal or driving an animal drawn Vehicle upon a roadway shall be granted all of the rights and shall be subject to all of the duties applicable to the driver of a Vehicle by this chapter, except those provisions of this chapter which by their very nature can have no application.

Should the owner while riding or driving a horse violate any of the traffic laws and should such an act cause an injury to the animal or the owner there can be no recovery.

For example if the owner rides a horse on the left side of the center line or fails to stop at a stop sign and is hit by a car and such negligent act of riding left of the center line or failure to stop at a stop sign was the proximate cause of the accident, the owner cannot recover. There is always a duty on the part of both the motorist and the animal owner to obey the law. To violate a traffic law is considered as a negligent act and if injury results to the one committing the negligent act he cannot recover.

6

CARRIER'S LIABILITY FOR INJURY AND LOSS OF HORSES

IN GENERAL IT IS THE DUTY OF A COMMON CARRIER, IN THE transporting of animals, to use that degree of care and prudence that an ordinary person would use under the same or similar circumstances to transport them to their destination; the carrier is liable for the failure to use such care to protect the animals from any form of violence or improper handling which would tend to injure them, but it is not liable for any injuries resulting merely from the ordinary and proper operation of the train, truck or transportation vehicle. By permitting animals to be exposed to excessive heat or cold for long periods of time, with the result that the animals suffer death or injury, the carrier would be liable.

If any animal injures itself without fault on the part of the carrier but the carrier fails to exercise the reasonable care necessary to prevent its subsequent death, the carrier is liable. The owner of an animal must prove that the carrier's negligent acts were the proximate cause of the injury or death of the animal. When animals are shown to have been delivered to the carrier in good condition, and to have been injured on the way, the burden then rests on the carrier to show that death or injury was not caused by the carrier's own negligence.

Where the owner of an animal gives directions to the express company's (the carrier's) messenger which are not special services and do not require an unreasonable degree of attention or service, and the animal dies, the carrier may be liable if the animal should die for failure of the carrier to carry out the instructions. The federal statute controlling the transportation of animals is known as the "Twenty-Eight Hour Law," enacted by Congress for the primary purpose of protecting animals shipped in interstate commerce. Common carriers are required to give the animals an "opportunity to rest" in 45 U.S.C. 71–74, where it is stated:

Care of Animals in Transit

Section 71. Transportation of animals—Time of confinement—Unloading for rest and feeding—Unloading sheep.— No railroad, express company, car company, common carrier other than by water, or the receiver, trustee, or lessee of any of them, whose road forms any part of a line of road over which cattle, sheep, swine, or other animals shall be conveyed from one State or Territory or the District of Columbia into or through another State or Territory or the District of Columbia, or the owners or masters of steam, sailing, or other vessels carrying or transporting cattle, sheep, swine, or other animals from one State or Territory or the District of Columbia into or through another State or Territory or the District of Columbia, shall confine the same in cars, boats, or vessels of any description for a period longer than twenty-eight consecutive hours without unloading the same in a humane manner, into properly equipped pens for rest, water, and feeding, for a period of at least five consecutive hours, unless prevented by storm or by other accidental or unavoidable causes which can not be anticipated or avoided by the exercise of due diligence and foresight: Provided, That upon the written request of the owner or person in custody of that

particular shipment, which written request shall be separate
and apart from any printed bill of lading, or other railroad
form, the time of confinement may be extended to thirty-six
hours. In estimating such confinement, the time consumed
in loading and unloading shall not be considered, but the
time during which the animals have been confined without
such rest or food or water on connecting roads shall be included, it being the intent of this Act [§§71–74 of this title]
to prohibit their continuous confinement beyond the period
of twenty-eight hours, except upon the contingencies hereinbefore stated: Provided, That it shall not be required that
sheep be unloaded in the nighttime, but where the time expires in the nighttime in case of sheep the same may continue
in transit to a suitable place for unloading, subject to the
aforesaid limitation of thirty-six hours. (June 29, 1906, c.
3594, § 1, 34 Stat. 607.)

**72. Animals unloaded to be fed and watered by or at
expense of owner—Lien—.**Animals so unloaded shall be
properly fed and watered during such rest either by the
owner or person having the custody thereof, or in case of his
default in so doing, then by the railroad, express company,
car company, common carrier other than by water, or the
receiver, trustee, or lessee of any of them, or by the owners
or masters of boats or vessels transporting the same, at the
reasonable expense of the owner or person in custody thereof,
and such railroad, express company, car company, common
carrier other than by water, receiver, trustee, or lessee of any
of them, owners or masters, shall in such case have a lien
upon such animals for food, care, and custody furnished,
collectible at their destination in the same manner as the
transportation charges are collected, and shall not be liable
for any detention of such animals, when such detention is of
reasonable duration, to enable compliance with section one
of this Act [§ 71 of this title], but nothing in this section
shall be construed to prevent the owner or shipper of animals
from furnishing food therefor, if he so desires. (June 29,
1906, c. 3594, § 2, 34 Stat. 608.)

73. Penalty for noncompliance—Exceptions.—Any railroad, express company, car company, common carrier other
than by water, or the receiver, trustee, or lessee of any of them,
or the master or owner of any steam, sailing, or other vessel
who knowingly and wilfully fails to comply with the pro-

visions of the two preceding sections [§§ 71, 72 of this title] shall for every such failure be liable for and forfeit and pay a penalty of not less than one hundred nor more than five hundred dollars: Provided, That when animals are carried in cars, boats, or other vessels in which they can and do have proper food, water, space, and opportunity to rest, the provisions in regard to their being unloaded shall not apply. (June 29, 1906, c. 3594, § 3, 34 Stat. 608.)

In *U.S. v. Powell*, 65 F.2d 793 (1933), the Court held that horses are included in the language "other animals." In this case, the shipping of horses, so loaded in box cars that they could not lie down for over eighty hours, was unlawful as depriving them of an "opportunity to rest" as required by 45 U.S.C.A. 71–74, even though there was some evidence that some horses do not lie down to rest but take their rest standing. The words "an opportunity to rest" clearly means that horses must be given an opportunity to lie down.

In the written decision the Court said:

To ship horses for this long period of time, so loaded as to prevent their lying down, is unquestionably to deprive them of a proper opportunity to rest and the shipper and carrier cannot by agreement set aside the statute.

Even when the railroad company receives a shipment of horses after they have already been confined without unloading for food, water and rest for a period in excess of that permitted by the "Twenty-Eight Hour Law," it is required to exercise diligence and to act with reasonable promptness in moving the car to its nearest unloading point and commence the unloading.

The "Twenty-Eight Hour Law" positively prohibits the confinement for a period of longer than twenty-eight consecutive hours, save only that by a special agreement and written request of the owner, the time of confinement may be extended to thirty-six hours. The extreme limit, therefore, to which the wishes of the owner may be recognized is thirty-six hours. In *Webster v. Union Pacific Railroad Company*, 200 Fed. 597, the Court held that an agreement for confinement beyond thirty-six hours is a contract to do that which the law says may not be done and is void and non-enforceable.

7

FEED AND MEDICINE—LIABILITY

AFTER IT BECAME COMMON FOR ARTICLES OF FOOD FOR human consumption to be manufactured and packaged, and by a series of transactions reached a retailer dealer who sold to the consumer, the Courts began to hold that the retailer seller impliedly warranted that such articles of food were wholesome and fit for immediate human consumption. The rationale for the Court's opinions were for reasons of public policy and for the preservation of life and health. The law deemed it wise that the person engaged in the business of selling provisions for domestic use should himself examine and know the fitness of his product for such use, and be liable for a lack of such knowledge.

When the question of animal food and medicine first came before the Courts they refused to follow the same rule of law as applied to food and medicine used by humans. Typical reasoning for such refusal is shown by the following language:

"If the preservation of human life and health be, as we think it is, the foundation of this exception, then it should not be extended to cases in which human life and health are in no wise endangered. Now the claim of

the plaintiff is simply of a property loss, that his estate
has been diminished and that alone is his cause of action.
His injury is similar to that which he would have sustained if he had purchased from a wagon maker a defective wheel, and thereby his wagon had broken down. No
matter of life or health of himself or family is involved."

The Kansas Supreme Court in 1967 began to have
second thoughts about applying one rule for human food
and medicine and a different rule for animal food and
medicine, in the case of *Chandler vs. Anchor Serum Company*, 426 P. (2) 82, 198 Kan. 571. Chandler owned 500
calves and in the Spring it had been his habit to vaccinate
them for Blackleg. On the occasion in question he purchased several bottles of vaccine from a local retailer and
vaccinated a group of calves. A few days later four dead
calves were discovered. On several different days he vaccinated several groups of calves and several of each group
died. A veterinarian who was called diagnosed Blackleg
as being the cause of death. Several days later approximately 250 more calves were vaccinated with vaccine
produced by another manufacturer. None of the last group
of calves developed Blackleg.

Chandler sued the manufacturer, distributor and retailer for the death of the calves. The Court said:

> Courts in other jurisdictions in which recovery has been
> sought against the manufacturer and seller of animal foods
> and medicines for breach of an implied warranty of fitness
> vary widely in their holdings and reasonings. We note, how-
> ever, that there has been a continuous eroding of the doctrine
> of *Caveat Emptor* in the area under consideration. We will
> mention only a few of the many cases that have come to our
> attention.
>
> In our neighboring state of Missouri an implied warranty
> of fitness attaches to the sale of food for animals where the
> food is not in its raw state but has been processed and pack-
> aged by the manufacturer.
>
> In *Burrus Feed Mills, Inc.* v. *Reeder*, 391 S.W. 2d 121

(Tex. Civ. App. 1965) the Court, in a well-reasoned opinion, extended an implied warranty to feed manufactured and processed for consumption by animals and advertised or labeled for such purpose, and held that the manufacturer as well as the retailer was liable to the ultimate purchaser, notwithstanding the absence of privity between the manufacturer and the purchaser. The Court cited *McAfee v. Cargill, Inc.*, 121 F. Supp. 5, which, applying California law, had reached a similar conclusion, saying:

". . . The same public policy considerations present for the protection of humans in the use of packaged and processed foods are also present where instead we deal with animals. . . ." (P. 6.)

Our research of decisions involving the manufacture and sale of drugs and medicines for treatment of animals has disclosed a dearth of cases dealing directly with an implied warranty of fitness. Cases in which recovery has been permitted against the manufacturer and seller have been under an express warranty in some instances and on negligence in others.

In *Brown v. Globe Laboratories, Inc.*, 165 Neb. 138, 84 N.W. 2d 151, the plaintiff purchased "Clostridium Perfringens Type D. Bacterin," a product designed for the prevention of Enterotoxemia in sheep, from a veterinarian who had, in turn, obtained it from the manufacturer. The manufacturer was held liable on both implied and express warranties regarding the fitness and quality of the bacterin.

In *Marxen v. Meredith*, 246 Iowa 1173, 69 N.W. 2d 399, the plaintiff sued for injury and death to his pigs from treatment with a hog spray purchased from the defendant retailer. Recovery was permitted on both express and implied warranty theories, the latter being an implied warranty of fitness for a particular purpose.

The foregoing cases amply illustrate a progressive step taken by many Courts away from the harsh doctrine of *Caveat Emptor* in the field of animal feeds and medicines. The trend is further hastened by the adoption of the new Uniform Commercial Code in many states including our own as of January 1, 1966. While this case arose before the code became effective, we note the provision therein that a warranty of merchantability is implied in a contract for the sale of goods if the seller is a merchant with respect to goods of that kind. As a part of the implied warranty of merchantability is the requirement that the goods be at least "fit for the ordinary purposes for which such goods are used."

In view of what has been said, we believe our holding in *Lukens* v. *Freiund Supra,* no longer represents the public policy of this state in regard to products intended for the feeding and caring of domestic animals. Indeed, the same public policy consideration necessary for the protection of human beings involving the manufacture and sale of food and drink for human consumption is likewise present in cases dealing with animal foods and medicines. Domestic animals constitute the backbone of farm economy in many of the agricultural areas of this country. In our system of enterprise where the potential purchaser is subjected to the advertising pressures of manufacturers, distributors and retailers in promoting the sale of a product, it is of necessity that the purchaser be provided a measure of assurance that the product is fit for the ordinary purposes for which it is sold. Medicines and vaccines for the treatment of domestic animals are manufactured and sold for the purpose and with the expectation they will be used as such, and public policy dictates that if such articles are unfit for the use contemplated by all parties in the chain of sale, then the purchaser must be protected. Accordingly, we are of the opinion there is no compelling reason in our modern-day system of merchandising to refuse to extend an implied warranty of fitness to include animal vaccines.

Further, we hold that the implied warranty of fitness runs not only from the manufacturer who created the defective product, but also from the distributor-wholesaler and the retailer as well.

In Tennessee the owner of a horse instituted a suit to recover for the death of his horse allegedly resulting from spoiled feed sold on expressed representation that the feed was good for the horse. The owner claimed that the loss of the horse was caused by the negligence of the manufacturer in selling unfit, spoiled horse feed. There was a verdict in favor of the owner of the horse for $1500.

The facts as presented by the owner were that he was a farmer raising Tennessee Walking Horses, and had a highbred, young horse, Little Go Boy, which he was preparing for the coming National Walking Horse Celebration. The company sent its field man and its salesman to the farm and the salesman represented to him that the particular horse feed was the best possible feed for this horse. Relying on their representation, he bought from the manufacturer's local dealer a 100-pound bag of feed.

He bought this bag August 6, 1951, and on the next day began to feed his horse. He fed the horse at about 5:00 P.M., August 8, and about two hours later he found the horse was violently ill, down, rolling in the stable. He called a veterinarian, who treated the horse for three or four hours, but to no avail. The horse died about midnight.

Plaintiff reported the matter and the salesman of the Company took samples of this bag of feed and of another bag of the same lot in the store. Both samples were found bad. The feed had gone through a heat and had spoiled. While the formula was not disclosed, it was shown that the feed contained No. 2 yellow corn, oats, blackstrap molasses, and other protein materials. The word "heat," as here used, is defined as "high temperature produced by fermentation or putrefaction"—Oxford Dictionary. The Court said:

> The rule now, in our opinion, is that where a product is such that, if negligently made, it may reasonably be expected to injure the person or property of an ultimate user of it, then, irrespective of contract, the manufacturer is under a duty to such user to make it carefully.
> This rule extends to a manufacturer of animal feeds, and such a manufacturer owes a duty to an ultimate user to use due care in making or supplying such feeds.
> We think on the evidence the jury could find the Company breached its duty and was negligent. It made and packed the feed in closed bags, and shipped some of them to its dealer, who kept them unopened and unaltered. This lot of feed was spoiled and dangerous to horses. These facts made a prima facie case of negligence against the Company.

It is urged for the Company, however, that it made this batch of feed one afternoon and shipped part of it to its dealer next morning; that by its tests this feed was in good condition when it left the Company's plant; that any deterioration it underwent was due to natural causes, and occurred after it left the Company's hands; and that therefore it is not chargeable with negligence therefor.

The Company's responsibility did not end with its sale of its product to its dealer, or with the condition of the product as it left the Company's hands if it knew, or by reasonable care could have known, that, due to natural causes, the product, before it could be used, would likely become unfit and dangerous for the use for which it was sold.

·It was shown by the evidence that the grain and the feed would quickly heat and "spoil" in hot, humid weather, especially when infested with grain mites; that all of these conditions prevailed and were known by the Company when it made the feed; and that it was experimenting on how to prevent its feed "going out of condition."

Thus it appeared that though the Company knew its feed would quickly spoil, like ice-cream, it nevertheless sold it, as fit for horses, without any warning of such a probable defect; that it put out a product which was apparently safe, but which to its knowledge would likely spoil and become dangerous before it could be used for the purpose for which it was sold.

Moreover, the Company, through its agents, represented to plaintiff that the feed was safe and fit and the best feed for his horse, and thereby induced him to buy and feed to his horse. Such conduct constituted negligence on the part of the Company.

Whether the feed would cause colic, and what caused the death of this horse, were questions of medical science which could not be answered by the Court or the jury without the aid of expert opinion; and the opinion of the two veterinarians referred to constituted substantial evidence to support the verdict of the jury.

Some states, such as Florida, have statutes making it a misdemeanor for any manufacturer to place in commerce any feed containing a substance injurious to the health of livestock. The Courts hold that where one violates a penal statute imposing upon him a duty designed to protect another he is negligent as a matter of law, and therefore responsible for such damages as is proximately caused by his negligence.

In the case involving a horse alleged to have died as a result of eating poisonous substance contained in feed, a Federal Court held that the manufacturer was liable where it was proven the poison had been in the feed sacks when the feed left the manufacturer's plant.

8

THE VETERINARIAN

Malpractice

A VETERINARIAN DOES NOT, IN THE ABSENCE OF A SPECIAL contract to do so, undertake to perform a cure of horses he treats. He only agrees to use such reasonable skill, diligence and attention as may be expected of the careful, skillful, ordinary attention possessed by a veterinarian in the community where he practices. In other words, a veterinarian does not undertake the treatment of a horse at the hazard of an action for damages if he fails to effect a cure or produce a perfect result. He is not an insurer of favorable consequences as the result of a particular treatment or operation which he has recommended or performed. The same rule that applies to medical doctors applies to veterinarians. *Rasmussen v. Shickle*, 41 Pac. (2) 184 contains the general rule:

"The law does not require that the advice, instructions and treatment given by a physician to a patient shall be at all events proper, or that his treatment should be such as to attain an approximate perfect result. It requires only, first, that he shall have the degree of learning and skill ordinarily possessed by physicians of good standing practicing in that locality; and, second, that he shall exercise reasonable and ordinary care and diligence in treating the patient and in applying such learning and skill to the case."

It will be noted that the above quotation requires a veterinarian to use reasonable and ordinary care, the same as a physician or surgeon. The same general legal principles apply to both the medical doctor and the veterinarian.

In the case of *Kerbow v. Bell*, 259 P. 317 (Okl)., damages were sought by the owner of a dog for the loss of his pet, which died soon after being dipped by the defendant (veterinarian) in a lye solution as a cure for mange. In the trial another veterinarian testified the solution used was too strong and death could have resulted therefrom. The Court held a person professing and undertaking to treat animals is bound to use, in performing the duties of his employment, such reasonable skill, diligence and attention as may ordinarily be expected of careful, skillful and trustworthy persons in his profession, and if he does not possess and exercise these qualities, he is answerable for the result of his want of skill and care.

In *Carson v. City of Beloit*, 145 N.W. 2d 112 (Wis., Oct. 7, 1966) the Court held a veterinarian not liable for death of puppies. "Damages could not be recovered in a suit against a veterinarian for the death of five pedigreed puppies, where the evidence failed to show that the veterinarian was negligent in his treatment of them," a Louisiana intermediate appellate court ruled.

Incorrect Diagnosis and Treatment

In making examinations to diagnose the ailment of an animal the question for the Court to determine is whether the veterinarian did the things necessary to conform to the standards of his profession in his community.

A veterinarian, once he has undertaken to examine a horse who is apparently sick, is under duty to exercise the ordinary care as established by the standards of veterinary medicine in his community. The gist of such action is the failure to properly diagnose the sickness.

Often the question may be one of judgment, and liability should not follow a mistake of judgment. If two or more veterinarians have different opinions as to the ailment, it is a matter of judgment; there can be no negligence. A veterinarian will be liable for gross ignorance and want of skill. He does not contract to use the highest degree of skill nor an extraordinary amount of diligence.

The Nebraska Supreme Court set forth the degree of care required by veterinarians in the treatment of animals in an early case involving the death of a mare after being treated by a veterinarian. The Court held that a veterinarian in his practice is bound to use in the performance of his duties such reasonable skill, diligence, and attention as may ordinarily be expected of a person in that profession. He does not contract to use the highest degree of skill nor an extraordinary amount of diligence, but to exercise a reasonable degree of knowledge, diligence and attention. No doubt an action will lie against a veterinarian for gross ignorance and want of skill as well as for negligence.

Once a veterinarian undertakes to treat an animal he can not abandon the treatment without liability should the animal die as a result of his failure to continue the treatment. A New York case involved a veterinarian who, after treating a very sick horse, failed to return the next morning as promised. The Court found that he had abandoned the treatment by his failure to return and that the same rules are applicable to the case of a veterinarian as have been applicable to other physicians.

A veterinarian who undertakes to render professional

services must meet these requirements: (1) He must possess the degree of professional learning, skill and ability that others similarly situated ordinarily possess; (2) he must exercise reasonable care and diligence in the application of his knowledge and skill to the patient's case; and (3) he must use his best judgment in the treatment and care of his patient. If the veterinarian lives up to the foregoing requirements he is not civilly liable for the consequences. If he fails in any one particular, and such failure is the proximate cause of injury and damage, he is liable.

A veterinarian who undertakes to treat an animal may be liable for negligence in treatment notwithstanding the fact that such undertaking was gratuitous. He does not absolve himself of responsibility merely by not charging for his services.

Liability for Acts of Agent or Employees

A veterinarian may be liable for the negligent acts of his agent or employees. In the case of *Acherman v. Robertson,* 3 M.W. (2) 723 (Wis.), the owner of 89 hogs brought suit for damages after they died due to being sprayed with lysol, which was mistaken for mange oil. The owner alleged that the lysol was negligently delivered to him by the veterinarian's son in place of the mange oil he had ordered. The veterinarian's son, who had two years training in veterinary practice, helped his father in and about the office. The veterinarian had told the owner about the mange oil and that they could get some any time at his office. The owner called while the veterinarian was away, and the son got a can labeled *Liquor Cresolis Sepanetus.* The son thought the *Liquor Cresolis Sepanetus* was the Latin term for "mange oil." The son delivered the can to the owner. The owner sprayed his hogs without reading the label. Soon the hogs were dead.

The Court held that the son was the agent of his father. The son was negligent in delivering the can of lysol instead of the mange oil. The veterinarian, therefore, was liable for the act of his agent.

It is a fundamental rule of agency law that the principal is bound by, and liable for, those acts which his agent does within the actual or apparent authority of the principal, and those acts which the agent does within the scope of his employment. When a veterinarian permits another to act for him and a third party justifiably relies upon the care and skill of such agent or employee and the third person is harmed by the lack of care or skill of the servant, agent or employee, the veterinarian is liable.

Employment Contract Between Veterinarians

Professional people such as veterinarians often enter into partnership agreements and employment contracts which provide that in the event of the termination of the contract, one of the parties agrees not to engage in the practice of their profession for a certain period of time and not to practice within certain areas. The provisions of the agreement are known as restrictive covenants. The Courts have held that public policy favors enforcement of contracts intended to protect legitimate interests and frowns upon unreasonable restrictions. The following two cases will help to illustrate these two views.

The case of *Brecher v. Brown*, 17 N.W. (2) 377, involved a suit for injunction to restrain the defendant from the practice of veterinary medicine and surgery and the operation of a veterinary hospital in violation of the terms of a contract of employment.

On March 25, 1943, the parties executed a written agreement by which the plaintiff employed the defendant as a veterinary assistant in Storm Lake, Iowa, for an indefinite period of time at a salary of $200 per month until changed by further agreement. Defendant agreed not to engage in any other type of work and to devote all his working hours to plaintiff's service. The controversy involved the following paragraph of the contract:

"It is further stipulated and agreed that upon the termination of the second party's employment by the first party that the second party will not engage in the practice of veterinary medicine or surgery, or any competing business of that of first party, in Storm Lake, Iowa, or a territory within a radius of twenty-five miles of Storm Lake, Iowa, without the expressed written consent of first party." Both parties were licensed veterinarians. Plaintiff operated a veterinary hospital in connection with his practice.

They operated under the agreement until December 27, 1943, when defendant quit and soon thereafter opened a veterinary office and hospital about 100 feet from plaintiff's office and hospital.

Under earlier decisions, the Courts held that restrictions unlimited as to both time and space were invalid; those limited as to time but unlimited as to space were also held invalid; while those limited as to space but unlimited as to time and those limited as to both time and space were ordinarily upheld.

It has been held that restrictive stipulations in agreements between employer and employee are not viewed with the same indulgence as such stipulations between a vendor and vendee of a business and its good will.

We are constrained to agree with the trial court that the area attempted to be reserved by the appellant (plaintiff) is much greater than reasonably necessary to his protection. The fact he has a patron twenty-six miles away and others somewhat less remote does not fix the area of his practice as a circle with a twenty-five mile radius.

The restriction is entirely unlimited as to time and has no relationship to duration of the employment which the contract expressly made indefinite.

The indefiniteness in the time and employment does not

render the contractual restriction without consideration, but
it is to be taken into account in appraising the reasonableness of the restriction which was entirely unlimited in duration.

In the case of *Beam v. Rutledge*, 9 S.E. (2) 476. Beam,
in a civil action against Rutledge to enjoin him from
practice of medicine in violation of an agreement entered
into by the parties in which the following clause was in
the partnership agreement, is the one causing the controversy:

In the event of a dissolution of the co-partnership
herein created, it is agreed by Dr. H. M. Rutledge, one
of the parties, that he will not engage in the practice of
the profession of medicine in the Town of Lumberton,
Robeson County, North Carolina, or within 100 miles of
said Town of Lumberton, Robeson County, North Carolina, for a period of five years from the date of said
dissolution.

Partnership was dissolved and Rutledge opened an
office in the Town of Lumberton. There was but a single
question for the Court to decide. Whether the restrictive
covenant in the partnership agreement was valid and
enforceable.

The application of two principles was involved here:
freedom to contract and public policy. The plaintiff
invoked the one, the defendant the other.

Speaking of public policy, the Court said that this contract is not forbidden by any principle of policy or law.
A doctor can be useful to the public at any other town
as in the town where he is now presently practicing, and
the lives and health of persons in other villages are as
important as they are there. Communities are, therefore,
not injured by any stipulation of this kind between two
practicing and eminent physicians.

The Court discussed freedom of contract by saying the
right of the parties to decide upon what terms and condi-

tions they are willing to form a partnership, or to enter into a contract of the character here disclosed, is not to be lightly abridged. Indeed, it is no small part of the liberty of citizens. The parties themselves, when the contract was made, regarded the restriction as reasonable. They were dealing with a situation of which both were familiar. The defendant insisted on having the contract signed and did not object to the restrictive covenant. It was limited both as to time and place.

The important thing to remember is that the restrictive covenant must be limited in time and place. If the contract is unlimited as to years, the Court will hold it void and of no effect. The same thing is true if there is no limit as to the territory the party is restricted to in the practice of his profession.

Even though the contract is limited as to time and place, it can be void because of unreasonableness as to time and place. The Court held in the above case that five years was not unreasonable, nor the restriction of 100 miles. Reasonableness of these two important principles depend upon the facts of each case. If a physician's patients were limited to 100 mile radius, it would be unreasonable for the agreement to provide a restrictive covenant limiting the practice within 200 miles.

Action for Services Rendered

Whenever it becomes necessary for a veterinarian to bring action to collect his fee for services rendered, he must allege that he is a veterinarian and that he held himself out as such, also that he is a licensed veterinarian under the laws of the state where he is practicing. As one Court said: "It requires education to be able to treat diseases of dumb animals, as well as diseases of men. There is no presumption of qualification. It is equally essential that he should establish it by proof. If he were simply a 'quack' without education or experience, and were employed by the owner of the horse upon the representation that he was a qualified veterinarian, he could not recover. Proof that the services were reasonable and necessary to treat the horse is a necessary item of proof. A Court in New York said: "Doubtless the same rules are applicable to the case of a veterinary surgeon bringing an action to recover the value of his services, as have been applicable to other physicians and surgeons. He must possess and exercise a reasonable degree of learning and skill. He must use reasonable and ordinary care and diligence in the exercise of his skill and the application of his knowledge." Otherwise he could not recover.

9

HORSES AND INCOME TAXES

IN DETERMINING WHETHER THE TRAINING, SHOWING AND breeding of horses will be considered a business or a hobby in the eyes of the Internal Revenue Service will depend upon several factors. If it is considered a business, expenses are deductible as in any other business. If it is a hobby, expenses are not deductible. Yet, profits are taxable. Therefore, it is most important to be able to prove you intend to produce a profit and that such enterprise should be considered a trade or business. There can be a very thin line separating a hobby from a business. Some hobbies become profitable. They become a business. There are certain guidelines to distinguish those qualifying for expense and loss deductions. The courts have held that raising and breeding animals may well be an enterprise entered into as a business for profit. The burden is on the taxpayer to prove it is a trade or business and not a hobby.

Documentation of all your records is most important for evidence that you have entered into the breeding, showing or training of horses with a sincere effort to make a profit. Here the intent of the taxpayer is of paramount importance. Some of the factors in determining if the breeding, showing, or training of horses is a business rather than a hobby are as follows: (1) Taxpayer's personal attention to phases of the operation and a practical and common sense managing such as would be expected in any other business enterprise. (2) Serious study and acquired knowledge going into the operation. (E.g.: Functional barn design with no attempt to make it a show place.) (3) Advertisement and promotion of Stallions and marketing horses in horse magazines. (4) A farm or ranch of such size that there is a reasonable opportunity to gain a profit. (5) A well planned program of breeding and marketing that will show a profit in four or five years. (6) The operation of the horse farm and showing and the breeding of horses is the only occupation. (7) The keeping of complete records of all transactions. (8) After a reasonable time there must be a profit.

It requires time to build up any kind of business. The horse business is not unlike the beginning orchardist who plants trees and waits several years for even the first crop to be harvested.

In the case of Charles B. Pennington, T.C. Memo 1967 —111, Pennington was engaged in a horse breeding business; even though he had lost money, he expected a profit. The Court found that Pennington was "engaged in a business in which profit can be reasonably anticipated after an operating period of eight to ten years."

A federal court set forth several points for determining if the enterprise is a hobby or a business: (1) The taxpayer's intention is the determining factor as to whether the enterprise's losses are deductible as a business entered into for profit. (2) Whether the horse business is a hobby or a business depends upon the circumstances of each case. The seven factors listed above are some of the circumstances which will help to prove if the enterprise is business or trade. (3) If the taxpayer has independent income and the amount of money expended each year would put the average horse farm owner or the average handler out of business, this fact tends to show that his business is actually a hobby. (4) Last, but the most important rule governing such cases, is that the burden of proof that the taxpayer is carrying on a business enterprise for a profit is upon the taxpayer. This fact tends to show a hobby. This means that you must come forth with sufficient facts, records and evidence to convince the court of your intent. Each case must be treated on its own merits since no two cases are identical.

Section 61 of the United States Internal Revenue Code defines taxable income as gross income minus deductions and Section 162 provides for deductions of ordinary and necessary expenses of a trade or business. The question is how the courts define "business." The courts endeavor to find out from the evidence the taxpayer presents if the enterprise is for a personal pleasure or an undertaking established for a profit.

In the event a taxpayer is questioned as to his deductions and losses in operating a horse farm business he should be prepared to show from his own records and testimony that there is a reasonable expectation of making a profit. This requires tax planning from the beginning of the business. There is no substitute for well documented records. Professional handlers will have very little difficulty in showing they are in the business of handling and showing horses for a profit. The difficulty arises most often when a businessman operates a horse farm as a sideline while spending full time in his business or profession.

Sometimes the intent and motive of the tax payer becomes important in determining if he is operating a business or a hobby. *Imbest vs Commissioner of Internal Revenue*, 361 F (2) 640 illustrates this point.

The taxpayer has been engaged in the manufacture, bot-

tling and promotion of a soft drink popularly known as
"7-Up" in the Philadelphia-New Jersey area since the 1930s.
His initiative and skill has promoted the soft drink into a
highly successful product. In the years involved—1955
through 1959—he was the president of three and a partner in
four "7-Up" bottling companies. He was also an active director in an advertising agency which dealt with the "7-Up"
product, and was an officer and director in a realty company
and in an apartment building venture. His salaries, director's fees and partnership distributions from the "7-Up"
bottling companies during the years involved were large and
his director's and management fees from the advertising
agency, the realty company and the apartment house were
substantial.

The taxpayer had owned and been interested in English
Setter dogs since childhood. He considered the English Setter
a beautiful, intelligent and "noble" animal and feared that
the breed was declining in popularity as a sporting dog. He
therefore determined sometime in 1934 that he would pre-
serve and enhance the English Setter. This, in his own words,
was the primary reason for his undertaking to breed them.
While he was engaged in the breeding and selling of dogs,
sometime in 1945 he decided to raise cattle for money-making
purposes. He continued in this for about three years, but
abandoned the enterprise because it was not profitable. In
1955 he realized that his dog breeding activities were likely
to continue unprofitable and decided to enter the thorough-
bred horse breeding and racing fields which he thought
would yield large profits. At the time he had no familiarity
with the sport, but he thought he would put to use in horse
breeding and racing the knowledge he had acquired in his
breeding and racing of dogs. During the years involved he
owned twenty-five or thirty horses which were trained for
racing by a public trainer. In 1960 he obtained a full-time
trainer. In 1957 or 1958 he purchased property in New Jersey where he established his home and apparently his stables
and kennels as well.

During the years involved the taxpayer kept no detailed
books and records of the income and expenses relating to his
dog and horse activities, and commingled the income from
these sources with his general personal income in a single
bank account from which he also paid out all expenses. At

the end of each taxable year an accountant, who was the controller of the "7-Up" bottling companies, made up worksheets of the income and expenses of the taxpayer's dog and horse activities taken from the taxpayer's bank statements and checkbooks. On the basis of these worksheets, which lumped together the dog and horse activities, a certified public accountant prepared the taxpayer's federal income tax returns. This record keeping was in marked contrast to the careful and detailed records kept by the "7-Up" bottling companies in which the taxpayer was interested, each of which had its separate bank account and detailed records of income, expenses, inventories, etc.

Beginning in 1943 to and including the years in issue the taxpayer claimed losses from cattle, dog and horse operations in generally increasing magnitude. Until 1960 these activities showed no profit. There were small profits in 1960 and 1963 and large losses in 1961 and 1962.

The Tax Court found that the taxpayer's dog and horse operations were not carried on for profit but as personal hobbies and therefore disallowed the losses during the years involved. It is this conclusion which the taxpayer attacks as clearly erroneous.

The Tax Court based its ultimate finding that the taxpayer's dog operation was not carried on for profit but as a personal hobby on his long-standing interest in English Setters, his admission that it was for this reason that he initially undertook their breeding, which he continued despite uninterrupted substantial losses, and on his informal accounting methods. We have carefully reviewed the record and cannot say that the Tax Court's conclusion was clearly erroneous.

The decision regarding the horse operation, however, is not free from clear error. Absent here, of course, was the important element which motivated him to undertake the breeding and exhibition of dogs—his childhood love of English Setters. Despite this difference, the Tax Court relied on the reasoning which it followed in regard to the taxpayer's dog operation with the added findings that the taxpayer had failed to cull his unprofitable horses and had received no winnings from racing. The two findings regarding culling and race winnings are clearly erroneous.

The Tax Court found that the taxpayer made no attempt to "cull" or dispose of unprofitable horses during the years involved. It considered this failure to be "inconsistent with the existence of a profit motive." This was a significant item in the Tax Court's ultimate decision. An examination of the record shows, however, that there is evidence, apparently not called to the Tax Court's attention, which makes it clear that the taxpayer did engage in culling. His income tax returns for the years in issue disclose that he sold ten horses at cost or less, which clearly indicates that he was reducing his losses by selling unprofitable horses. The Tax Court's finding that there was no culling of horses during the years involved must therefore be set aside.

The error in this refusal was serious. The primary intent or motive of the taxpayer has always been the ultimate test for determining whether losses are deductible because incurred in a trade or business or in transactions for profit, or on the other hand are not deductible because they are personal expenses.

It is true that motive ordinarily is not put in issue. This is because the usual enterprise is surrounded by the conventional characteristics of a business or profession, and profit motive, therefore, is taken for granted. Indeed, it would seem an invasion of privacy to inquire whether a physician or a lawyer loved his work and engaged in it for pleasure, although cases may readily be called to mind of physicians and lawyers who remain devoted to their profession despite the greater financial reward their talents would bring them in commercial or industrial activities. Men of wealth may continue a business out of consideration of the welfare of their employees, or to carry on a family name, rather than to continue the accumulation of profits. In such cases the customary indications of a business enterprise so surround the activity that little thought arises of penetrating from the external appearance to the taxpayer's intention and motive in order to determine whether at its core there may lie a pleasure-seeking or philanthropic motive which made the profit-seeking motive secondary. The reason for this, however, is not that motive is irrelevant, but that a predominant profit motive simply is assumed. Thus, the profit motive will be inquired into even though the activity has all the surface appearance of a business, if it is shown to have been arranged in a manner which fundamentally contradicts a profit-making purpose.

**The
Tax Reform Act
of
1969**

Subtitle B—Farm Losses, Etc.

Sec. 211. Gain From Disposition of Property Used in Farming Where Farm Losses Offset Nonfarm Income.

(a) IN GENERAL.—Part IV of subchapter P of chapter 1 (relating to special rules for determining capital gains and losses) is amended by adding at the end thereof the following new section:

"Sec. 1251. Gain From Disposition of Property Used in Farming Where Farm Losses Offset Nonfarm Income.

" (a) CIRCUMSTANCES UNDER WHICH SECTION APPLIES.— This section shall apply with respect to any taxable year only if—

" (1) there is a farm net loss for the taxable year, or

" (2) there is a balance in the excess deductions account as of the close of the taxable year after applying subsection (b) (3) (A) .

" (b) EXCESS DEDUCTIONS ACCOUNT.—

" (1) REQUIREMENT.—Each taxpayer subject to this section shall, for purposes of this section, establish and maintain an excess deductions account.

" (2) ADDITIONS TO ACCOUNT.—

" (A) GENERAL RULE.—There shall be added to the excess deductions account for each taxable year an amount equal to the farm net loss.

" (B) EXCEPTIONS.—In the case of an individual (other than a trust) and, except as provided in this subparagraph, in the case of an electing small business corporation (as defined in section 1371 (b))), subparagraph (A) shall apply for a taxable year—

"(i) only if the taxpayer's nonfarm adjusted gross income for such year exceeds $50,000, and
"(ii) only to the extent the taxpayer's farm net loss for such year exceeds $25,000.
This subparagraph shall not apply to an electing small business corporation for a taxable year if on any day of such year a shareholder of such corporation is an individual who, for his taxable year with which or within which the taxable year of the corporation ends, has a farm net loss.

"(C) MARRIED INDIVIDUALS.—In the case of a husband or wife who files a separate return, the amount specified in subparagraph (B) (i) shall be $25,000 in lieu of $50,000, and in subparagraph (B) (ii) shall be $12,500 in lieu of $25,000. This subparagraph shall not apply if the spouse of the taxpayer does not have any nonfarm adjusted gross income for the taxable year.

"(D) NONFARM ADJUSTED GROSS INCOME.—For purposes of this section, the term 'nonfarm adjusted gross income' means adjusted gross income (taxable income, in the case of an electing small business corporation) computed without regard to income or deductions attributable to the business of farming.

"(3) SUBTRACTIONS FROM ACCOUNT.—If there is any amount in the excess deductions account at the close of any taxable year (determined before any amount is subtracted under this paragraph for such year) there shall be subtracted from the account—

"(A) an amount equal to the farm net income for such year, plus the amount (determined as provided in regulations prescribed by the Secretary or his delegate) necessary to adjust the account for deductions which did not result in a reduction of the taxpayer's tax under this subtitle for the taxable year or any preceding taxable year, and

"(B) after applying paragraph (2) or subparagraph (A) of this paragraph (as the case may be), an amount equal to the sum of the amounts treated, solely by reason of the application of subsection (c), as gain from the sale or exchange of property which is neither a capital asset nor property described in section 1231.

"(4) EXCEPTION FOR TAXPAYERS USING CERTAIN ACCOUNTING METHODS.—

"(A) GENERAL RULE.—Except to the extent that the taxpayer has succeeded to an excess deductions account as provided in paragraph (5), additions to the excess deductions account shall not be required by a taxpayer who elects to compute taxable income from farming (i) by using inventories, and (ii) by charging to capital account all expenditures paid or incurred which are properly chargeable to capital account (including such expenditures which the taxpayer may, under this chapter or regulations prescribed thereunder, otherwise treat or elect to treat as expenditures which are not chargeable to capital account).

"(B) TIME, MANNER, AND EFFECT OF ELECTION.— An election under subparagraph (A) for any taxable year shall be filed within the time prescribed by law (including extensions thereof) for filing the return for such taxable year, and shall be made and filed in such manner as the Secretary or his delegate shall prescribe by regulations. Such election shall be binding on the taxpayer for such taxable year and for all subsequent taxable years and may not be revoked except with the consent of the Secretary or his delegate.

"(C) CHANGE OF METHOD OF ACCOUNTING, ETC.— If, in order to comply with the election made under subparagraph (A), a taxpayer changes his method of accounting in computing taxable income from the business of farming, such change shall be treated as having been made with the consent of the Secretary or his delegate and for purposes of section 481 (a) (2) shall be treated as a change not initiated by the taxpayer.

"(5) TRANSFER OF ACCOUNT.—

"(A) CERTAIN CORPORATE TRANSACTIONS.—In the case of a transfer described in subsection (d) (3) to which section 371 (a), 374 (a), or 381 applies, the acquiring corporation shall succeed to and take into account as of the close of the day of distribution or transfer, the excess deductions account of the transferor.

"(B) CERTAIN GIFTS.—If—

"(i) farm recapture property is disposed of by gift, and

"(ii) the potential gain (as defined in subsection (e) (5)) on farm recapture property disposed of by gift during any one-year period in which any such gift occurs is more than 25 percent of the potential gain on farm recapture property held by the donor immediately prior to the first of such gifts,

each donee of the property shall succeed (at the time the first of such gifts is made, but in an amount determined as of the close of the donor's taxable year in which the first of such gifts is made) to the same proportion of the donor's excess deductions account (determined, after the application of paragraphs (2) and (3) with respect to the donor, as of the close of such taxable year), as the potential gain on the property received by such donee bears to the aggregate potential gain on farm recapture property held by the donor immediately prior to the first of such gifts.

" (6) JOINT RETURN.—In the case of an addition to an excess deductions account for a taxable year for which a joint return was filed under section 6013, for any subsequent taxable year for which a separate return was filed the Secretary or his delegate shall provide rules for allocating any remaining amount of such addition in a manner consistent with the purposes of this section.

" (c) ORDINARY INCOME.—

" (1) GENERAL RULE.—Except as otherwise provided in this section, if farm recapture property (as defined in subsection (e) (1)) is disposed of during a taxable year beginning after December 31, 1969, the amount by which—

" (A) in the case of a sale, exchange, or involuntary conversion, the amount realized, or.

" (B) in the case of any other disposition, the fair market value of such property,

exceeds the adjusted basis of such property shall be treated as gain from the sale or exchange of property which is neither a capital asset nor property described in section 1231. Such gain shall be recognized notwithstanding any other provision of this subtitle.

" (2) LIMITATION.—

" (A) AMOUNT IN EXCESS DEDUCTIONS ACCOUNT.—The aggregate of the amounts treated under paragraph (1) as gain from the sale or exchange of property which is neither a capital asset nor property described in section 1231 for any taxable year shall not exceed the amount in the excess deductions account at the close of the taxable year after applying subsection (b) (3) (A).

" (B) DISPOSITIONS TAKEN INTO ACCOUNT.—If the aggregate of the amounts to which paragraph (1) applies is limited by the application of subparagraph (A), paragraph (1) shall apply in respect of such dispositions (and in such amounts) as provided under regulations prescribed by the Secretary or his delegate.

"(C) SPECIAL RULE FOR DISPOSITIONS OF LAND.— In applying subparagraph (A), any gain on the sale or exchange of land shall be taken into account only to the extent of its potential gain (as defined in subsection (e) (5)).

"(d) EXCEPTIONS AND SPECIAL RULES.—

"(1) GIFTS.—Subsection (c) shall not apply to a disposition by gift.

"(2) TRANSFER AT DEATH.—Except as provided in section 691 (relating to income in respect of a decedent), subsection (c) shall not apply to a transfer at death.

"(3) CERTAIN CORPORATE TRANSACTIONS.—If the basis of property in the hands of a transferee is determined by reference to its basis in the hands of the transferor by reason of the application of section 332, 351, 361, 371 (a), or 374 (a), then the amount of gain taken into account by the transferor under subsection (c) (1) shall not exceed the amount of gain recognized to the transferor on the transfer of such property (determined without regard to this section). This paragraph shall not apply to a disposition to an organization (other than a cooperative described in section 521) which is exempt from the tax imposed by this chapter.

"(4) LIKE KIND EXCHANGES; INVOLUNTARY CONVERSION, ETC.—If property is disposed of and gain (determined without regard to this section) is not recognized in whole or in part under section 1031 or 1033, then the amount of gain taken into account by the transferor under subsection (c) (1) shall not exceed the sum of—

"(A) the amount of gain recognized on such disposition (determined without regard to this section), plus

"(B) the fair market value of property acquired

with respect to which no gain is recognized under subparagraph (A), but which is not farm recapture property.

"(5) PARTNERSHIPS.—

"(A) IN GENERAL.—In the case of a partnership, each partner shall take into account separately his distributive share of the partnership's farm net losses, gains from dispositions of farm recapture property, and other items in applying this section to the partner.

"(B) TRANSFERS TO PARTNERSHIPS.—If farm recapture property is contributed to a partnership and gain (determined without regard to this section) is not recognized under section 721, then the amount of gain taken into account by the transferor under subsection (c) (1) shall not exceed the excess of the fair market value of farm recapture property transferred over the fair market value of the partnership interest attributable to such property. If the partnership agreement provides for an allocation of gain to the contributing partner with respect to farm recapture property contributed to the partnership (as provided in section 704 (c) (2), the partnership interest of the contributing partner shall be deemed to be attributable to such property.

"(6) PROPERTY TRANSFERRED TO CONTROLLED CORPORATIONS.—Except for transactions described in subsection (b) (5) (A), in the case of a transfer, described in paragraph (3), of farm recapture property to a corporation, stock or securities received by a transferor in the exchange shall be farm recapture property to the extent attributable to the fair market value of farm recapture property (or, in the case of land, if less, the adjusted basis plus the potential gain (as defined in subsection (e) (5)) on farm recapture property) contributed to the corporation by such transferor.

" (e) Definitions.—For purposes of this section—

"(1) Farm recapture property.—The term 'farm recapture property' means—

"(A) any property (other than section 1250 property) described in paragraph (1) (relating to business property held for more than 6 months), (3) (relating to livestock), or (4) (relating to an unharvested crop) of section 1231 (b) which is or has been used in the trade or business of farming by the taxpayer or by a transferor in a transaction described in subsection (b) (5), and

"(B) any property the basis of which in the hands of the taxpayer is determined with reference to the adjusted basis of property which was farm recapture property in the hands of the taxpayer within the meaning of subparagraph (A).

" (2) Farm net loss.—The term 'farm net loss' means the amount by which—

"(A) the deductions allowed or allowable by this chapter which are directly connected with the carrying on of the trade or business of farming, exceed

"(B) the gross income derived from such trade or business.

Gains and losses on the disposition of farm recapture property referred to in section 1231 (a) (determined without regard to this section or section 1245 (a)) shall not be taken into account.

" (3) Farm net income.—The term 'farm net income' means the amount by which the amount referred to in paragraph (2) (B) exceeds the amount referred to in paragraph (2) (A).

" (4) Trade or business of farming.—

"(A) Horse racing.—In the case of a taxpayer engaged in the raising of horses, the term 'trade or business of farming' includes the racing of horses.

"(B) Several businesses of farming.—If a taxpayer is engaged in more than one trade or business of farming, all such trades and businesses shall be treated as one trade or business.

" (5) POTENTIAL GAIN.—The term 'potential gain' means an amount equal to the excess of the fair market value of property over its adjusted basis, but limited in the case of land to the extent of the deductions allowable in respect to such land under sections 175 (relating to soil and water conservation expenditures) and 182 (relating to expenditures by farmers for clearing land) for the taxable year and the 4 preceding taxable years."

(b) CONFORMING AMENDMENTS.—

(1) Section 301 (b) (1) (B) (ii) (relating to corporate distributions of property) is amended by striking out "or 1250 (a) " and inserting in lieu thereof "1250 (a) , 1251 (c) , or 1252 (a) ".

(2) Section 301 (d) (2) (B) (relating to the basis of property distributed by a corporation) is amended by striking out "or 1250 (a) " and inserting in lieu thereof "1250 (a) , 1251 (c) , or 1252 (a) ".

(3) Section 312 (c) (3) (relating to adjustment to corporate earnings and profits) is amended by striking out "or 1250 (a) " and inserting in lieu thereof "1250 (a) , 1251 (c) , or 1252 (a) ".

(4) Section 341 (e) (12) (relating to nonapplication of section 1245 (a) with respect to collapsible corporations) is amended by striking out "and 1250 (a) " and inserting in lieu thereof "1250 (a) , 1251 (c) , and 1252 (a) ".

(5) Section 453 (d) (4) (B) (relating to distribution of installment obligations under certain liquidations) is amended by striking out "or 1250 (a) " and inserting in lieu thereof "1250 (a) , 1251 (c) , or 1252 (a) ".

(6) Section 751 (c) (relating to unrealized receivables in partnership transactions) is amended by strik-

ing out "and section 1250 property (as defined in section 1250 (c)) " and inserting in lieu thereof "section 1250 property (as defined in section 1250 (c)), farm recapture property (as defined in section 1251 (e) (1)), and farm land (as defined in section 1252 (a)) "; and by striking out "1250 (a) " and inserting in lieu thereof "1250 (a), 1251 (c), or 1252 (a) ".

(7) The table of sections for part IV of subchapter P of chapter 1 is amended by adding at the end thereof the following:

"Sec. 1251. Gain from disposition of property used in farming where farm losses offset nonfarm income."

(c) EFFECTIVE DATES.—The amendments made by this section shall apply to taxable years beginning after December 31, 1969.

Sec. 212. Livestock.

(a) DEPRECIATION RECAPTURE.—

(1) GENERAL RULE.—Section 1245 (a) (2) (relating to recomputed basis with respect to gain from disposition of certain depreciable property) is amended by striking out "or" at the end of subparagraph (A), and by inserting immediately after subparagraph (B) the following:

"(C) with respect to livestock, its adjusted basis recomputed by adding thereto all adjustments attributable to periods after December 31, 1969, or".

(2) CONFORMING AMENDMENT.—Section 1245 (a) (3) (relating to section 1245 property) is amended by striking out " (other than livestock) ".

(3) EFFECTIVE DATE.—The amendments made by paragraphs (1) and (2) shall apply with respect to taxable years beginning after December 31, 1969.

(b) LIVESTOCK USED IN TRADE OR BUSINESS.—

(1) AMENDMENT OF SECTION 1231.—Section 1231 (b) (3) (relating to property used in a trade or business) is amended to read as follows:

"(3) LIVESTOCK.—Such term includes—

"(A) cattle and horses, regardless of age, held by the taxpayer for draft, breeding, dairy, or sporting purposes, and held by him for 24 months or more from the date of acquisition, and

"(B) other livestock, regardless of age, held by the taxpayer for draft, breeding, dairy, or sporting purposes, and held by him for 12 months or more from the date of acquisition.

Such term does not include poultry."

(2) EFFECTIVE DATE.—The amendments made by paragraph (1) shall apply to livestock acquired after December 31, 1969.

(c) EXCHANGES OF LIVESTOCK OF DIFFERENT SEXES.—

(1) NOT TO BE TREATED AS LIKE KIND EXCHANGES.— Section 1031 (relating to exchange of property held for productive use or for investment) is amended by adding at the end thereof the following new subsection:

"(e) EXCHANGES OF LIVESTOCK OF DIFFERENT SEXES.— For purposes of this section, livestock of different sexes are not property of a like kind."

(2) EFFECTIVE DATE.—The amendment made by paragraph (1) shall apply to taxable years to which the Internal Revenue Code of 1954 applies.

Sec. 213. Deductions Attributable to Activities Not Engaged in for Profit

(a) GENERAL RULE.—Part VI of subchapter B of chapter 1 (relating to itemized deductions for individuals and corporations) is amended by adding at the end thereof the following new section:

"Sec. 183. Activities Not Engaged in for Profit

"(a) GENERAL RULE.—In the case of an activity engaged in by an individual or an electing small business corporation (as defined in section 1371(b)), if such activity is not engaged in for profit, no deduction attributable to such activity shall be allowed under this chapter except as provided in this section.

"(b) DEDUCTIONS ALLOWABLE.—In the case of an activity not engaged in for profit to which subsection (a) applies, there shall be allowed—

"(1) the deductions which would be allowable under this chapter for the taxable year without regard to whether or not such activity is engaged in for profit, and

"(2) a deduction equal to the amount of the deductions which would be allowable under this chapter for the taxable year only if such activity were engaged in for profit, but only to the extent that the gross income derived from such activity for the taxable year exceeds the deductions allowable by reason of paragraph (1).

"(c) ACTIVITY NOT ENGAGED IN FOR PROFIT DEFINED.— For purposes of this section, the term 'activity not engaged in for profit' means any activity other than one with respect to which deductions are allowable for the taxable year under section 162 or under paragraph (1) or (2) of section 212.

"(d) PRESUMPTION.—If the gross income derived from an activity for 2 or more of the taxable years in the period of 5 consecutive taxable years which ends with the taxable year exceeds the deductions attributable to such activity (determined without regard to whether or not such activity is engaged in for profit), then, unless the Secretary or his delegate establishes to the contrary, such activity shall be presumed for purposes of this chapter for such taxable year to be an activity engaged in for profit. In the case of an activity which consists in major part of the breeding, training, showing, or racing of horses, the preceding sentence shall be applied by substituting the period of 7 consecutive taxable years for the period of 5 consecutive taxable years."

(b) TECHNICAL AMENDMENT.—Section 270 (relating to limitation on deductions allowable to certain individuals) is repealed.

(c) CLERICAL AMENDMENTS.—

(1) The table of sections for part VI of subchapter B of chapter 1 is amended by adding at the end thereof the following new item:

"Sec. 183. Activities not engaged in for profit."

(2) The table of sections for part IX of subchapter B of chapter 1 is amended by striking out the item relating to section 270.

(3) Section 6504 (relating to cross references) is amended by striking out the item relating to section 270.

(d) EFFECTIVE DATE.—The amendments made by this section shall apply to taxable years beginning after December 31, 1969.

Sec. 214. Gain From Disposition of Farm Land.

(a) IN GENERAL.—Part IV of subchapter P of chapter 1 (relating to special rules for determining capital gains and losses) is amended by adding after section 1251 (added by section 211 of this Act) the following new section:

"Sec. 1252. Gain From Disposition of Farm Land.

"(a) GENERAL RULE.—

"(1) ORDINARY INCOME.—Except as otherwise provided in this section, if farm land which the taxpayer has held for less than 10 years is disposed of during a taxable year beginning after December 31, 1969, the lower of—

"(A) the applicable percentage of the aggregate of the deductions allowed under sections 175 (relating to soil and water conservation expenditures) and 182 (relating to expenditures by farmers for clearing land) for expenditures made by the taxpayer after December 31, 1969, with respect to the farm land or

"(B) the excess of—

"(i) the amount realized (in the case of a sale, exchange, or involuntary conversion), or the fair market value of the farm land (in the case of any other disposition), over

"(ii) the adjusted basis of such land,

shall be treated as gain from the sale or exchange of property which is neither a capital asset nor property described in section 1231. Such gain shall be recognized notwithstanding any other provision of this subtitle, except that this section shall not apply to the extent section 1251 applies to such gain.

"(2) FARM LAND.—For purposes of this section, the term 'farm land' means any land with respect to which deductions have been allowed under sections 175 (relating to soil and water conservation expenditures) or 182 (relating to expenditures by farmers for clearing land).

"(3) APPLICABLE PERCENTAGE.—For purposes of this section—

"If the farm land is disposed of—	The applicable percentage is—
Within 5 years after the date it was acquired	100 percent.
Within the sixth year after it was acquired	80 percent.
Within the seventh year after it was acquired	60 percent.
Within the eighth year after it was acquired	40 percent.
Within the ninth year after it was acquired	20 percent.
10 years or more years after it was acquired	0 percent.

"(b) SPECIAL RULES.—Under regulations prescribed by the Secretary or his delegate, rules similar to the rules of section 1245 shall be applied for purposes of this section."

(b) CLERICAL AMENDMENT.—The table of sections for part IV of subchapter P of chapter 1 is amended by adding at the end thereof the following:

"Sec. 1252. Gain from the disposition of farm land."

(c) EFFECTIVE DATE.—The amendments made by this section shall apply to taxable years beginning after December 31, 1969.

Sec. 215. Crop Insurance Proceeds.

(a) YEAR IN WHICH INCLUDED IN INCOME.—Section 451 (relating to general rule for taxable year of inclusion) is amended by adding at the end thereof the following new subsection:

"(d) SPECIAL RULE FOR CROP INSURANCE PROCEEDS.— In the case of insurance proceeds received as a result of destruction or damage to crops, a taxpayer reporting on the cash receipts and disbursements method of accounting may elect to include such proceeds in income for the taxable year following the taxable year of destruction or damage, if he establishes that, under his practice, income from such crops would have been reported in a following taxable year. An election under this subsection for any taxable year shall be made at such time and in such manner as the Secretary or his delegate prescribes."

(b) EFFECTIVE DATE.—The amendment made by subsection (a) shall apply to taxable years ending after the date of the enactment of this Act.

10

HORSE AND LIVESTOCK INSURANCE

INSURANCE IS A CONTRACT BY WHICH ONE PARTY, FOR CON-
sideration, promises to make a certain payment in money
upon the destruction or injury of property, such as a
horse, in which the other party has an interest. The insurance contract requires that the insurer pay a sum of
money upon the occurrence of certain particular events
named in the policy contract. Since insurance is a contract,
the parties are bound by the terms just as are parties to
other contracts. As the Supreme Court of Georgia said:
"Contracts of insurance, like other contracts, must be
construed according to the terms which the parties have
used . . ." It is a voluntary contract and the parties may
incorporate such provisions and conditions as they choose
so long as the terms are not prohibited by law.

Insurance on horses and other livestock is a contract
by the insurer (insurance company) to indemnify the
insured (owner of the horse or livestock) against loss
sustained by reason of injury or death of the horse or
livestock occurring or resulting from specific causes or
risks set forth in the policy. It is, therefore, most important
for the owner of a horse who desires to obtain insurance

on his animal to read carefully the specified causes or risks covered by the policy. Particularly, it is important to know what the insurance company is not liable for as set out in the insurance contract. Do not take the statement of the agent as to the provisions of the contract, as his statements may be contrary to the provisions of the policy. Most agents insist that the insured read and become acquainted with the terms of the policy to prevent any misunderstanding later on. So the question facing the horse owner is when and under what circumstances is his horse covered. To answer this question it is necessary to see what the courts say about the provisions of insurance policies covering horses and livestock.

In the case of *Abraham v. Insurance Company of North America,* 117 Vt. 75, 84 A (2) 670, the owner of a horse sought to recover under a policy of insurance on his horse. The policy covered destruction, in the case of incurable illness or injury, providing that a written certificate from a qualified veterinarian were first obtained certifying that such destruction was necessary in order to immediately relieve incurable suffering. The veterinarian based his opinion on his findings that the mare was totally blind in both eyes, due to periodic ophthalmia (moon blindness) which condition rendered her useless as a saddle mare. But he also found she was not suffering acute pain. The horse was destroyed upon advice of the veterinarian. The issue before the court was whether or not the insurance company was liable under the policy. The insurance company claimed that the veterinarian's certificate did not state that the destruction was necessary in order to immediately relieve incurable suffering as provided in said policy. The court had this to say:

> *Insurance on livestock is regarded as a contract by which the insurer* agrees to indemnify the insured against such loss as he may sustain by reason of injury to or the death of livestock by the happening of specified risks or causes.
> *In order that there may be a recovery on the policy, the*

loss of or injury to the insured livestock must result from the particular peril against which the insured is indemnified. The burden is on the plaintiff to prove this fact.

The only question in the instant case is: Does the certificate furnished comply with the terms of item (f)? This presents the question: What is meant by the words "necessary in order to immediately relieve incurable suffering" so that destruction is justified?

There are some general rules applicable to the construction of insurance policies. The language of the policy is to be strictly construed against the insurer, although the entire contract is to be construed together for the purpose of giving force and effect to each clause. Equivocation and uncertainty are to be resolved in favor of the insured and against the insurer.

If clear and unambiguous the provisions must be given force and effect. The construction must be reasonable and not such as to deprive the insurer of the benefit of an unambiguous provision placed therein for its protection. It is the general rule that when the terms of a contract of insurance are ambiguous or fairly susceptible of two different constructions, that construction will be adopted that is most faborable to the insured; however, it is equally well settled that contracts of insurance, like other contracts, are to be construed according to the sense and meaning of the terms which the parties have used, and if they are plain and unambiguous, their terms are to be taken in their plain, ordinary and popular sense.

The key words in the instant case in ascertaining the meaning of the provision under consideration are, "necessary," "immediately" and "suffering." They must all be given effect. We spend no time on "incurable" as the parties are in agreement that the illness or affliction of the horse was incurable.

The word "necessary" must be construed in the connection in which it is used. It is a word susceptible of various meanings. The word "necessary" has different significations, meaning sometimes, indispensably requisite, at others, needful, requisite, incidental or conducive to. The ordinary definition of the word "necessary" indicates something indispensable and which cannot be disregarded or omitted. For various definitions of its meaning, depending upon the context with which it is used.

When a pivotal word is not defined either in the policy

or the application it is permissible for the court to take judicial notice of its meaning as given in standard works, such as dictionaries. Webster's New International Dictionary defines "Necessary" as "Unavoidable, impossible to be otherwise or to be dispensed with." Funk & Wagnalls New Standard Dictionary defines it as "that which cannot be otherwise, impossible to avoid, inevitable, as a necessary event; indispensably requisite or absolutely needed to accomplish a desired result." The word "necessary" is defined by lexicographers as synonymous with "indispensable," "unavoidable" or "that which must be."

In the instant case the word "necessary" is qualified by the phrase "in order to immediately relieve." Webster's New International Dictionary defines "immediately" as "without interval of time, without delay, straightway, instantly, at once." Funk & Wagnalls New Standard Dictionary defines it as "Without lapse of time, instantly, at once." Thus qualified by the context with which it is used, we hold that "necessary" as used in item (f) means indispensable, unavoidable or impossible to be dispensed with.

"Suffering" is defined in Webster's New International Dictionary as "the bearing of pain, inconvenience or loss; also a pain endured, a distress, loss or injury incurred, as sufferings by pain or sorrow, sufferings by want or sorrow." Funk & Wagnalls New Standard Dictionary defines it thus, "a state of anguish or pain, misery or loss; also the pain thus borne, distress, injury, misery, loss. Syn. agony, pain." The New Century Dictionary defines it thus, "The undergoing of pain or distress or a particular instance of this."

In National Live Stock Ins. Co. v. Elliott, 60 Ind App 112, 108 NE 784, 785, the veterinarian described the horse in the following terms, "her intestines were torn into. . . . She was bleeding to death, and suffering great pain . . . and in great misery . . . in the sun." He killed her. The court in holding the killing justified and the insurance collectible used this language, "The animal was in a suffering, dying condition, and there was no possibility of [her] recovery. Under such circumstances every instinct of humanity dictated that the veterinary surgeon and the owner of the animal should do exactly what they did—end the suffering. . . . The act . . . was but humane."

In Live Stock Ins. Ass'n of Huntington County v. Edgar, 56 Ind App 489, 105 NE 641, it appeared that the horse had a broken leg, the bone was splintered and shattered and parts of it protruded through the flesh and skin of the leg. It was suffering great pain and misery. It was held the killing was justified and the insurance collectible.

In Tripp v. Northwestern Livestock Ins. Co. 91 Iowa 278, 59 NW 1, 2, the horse had a disease from which it could not recover and the plaintiff claimed that as an act of mercy and to prevent its suffering a veterinary surgeon sent by the company to treat the horse directed that it be killed which was done. It appeared that this veterinarian told the plaintiff that the horse was worthless and never would be worth anything and could not recover and he thought it best to kill him, that the disease would prove fatal, that he was liable to drop dead at any time and would die within a few days at the furthest and he would advise taking the horse out and shootng him. The horse was killed. Death occurred a short time before the policy expired. The court in denying liability said, "It is not shown that the horse was in pain, nor that its death was required as an act of mercy, to relieve his sufferings."

In New York Life Ins. Co. v. Calhoun, 8 Cir, 97 F2d 896, 898, in discussing the meaning of the word "suffered" and after quoting the meaning of the word from various dictionaries the court said, "Plainly the customary use of the word indicates some experience of conscious pain." This Court is of the opinion that it is true when the word is applied to the condition of a horse.

The word "suffering" as here used in the expression under consideration must be construed with the context with which it is used. To justify the destruction of the animal it must be such suffering that destruction is indispensable for immediate relief. We hold that means there must be conscious suffering. In other words the condition must be so acute as to demand action at once and without delay in order to put the horse out of misery.

Does the certificate of the veterinarian comply with the requirements of item (f)? We think not. It negatives acute pain. If we give any effect, which we must do, to what is said about not keeping the horse for breeding purposes because of the inherent tendency toward transmission of the weakness to offspring it somewhat negatives the necessity of immediate destruction. If immediate destruction was necessary then there is no place for any thought of keeping for breeding purposes. Again, all he says is that in his opinion the animal should be destroyed. That is some distance from saying that destruction is necessary. Furthermore, the certificate shows that he examined the horse on February 10 and the certificate was not made until two days later, on February 12. That does not indicate that he felt at the time of the examination the condition was such as to necessitate immediate destruction to relieve suffering. As we construe the certificate as a whole it does not show that "destruction is necessary in order to immediately relieve incurable suffering" within the meaning of those words in the policy.

The plaintiff has failed to show that the death of the horse was from a cause covered by the policy.

As can be seen by the above, in cases involving horse and livestock insurance the general rule followed by the court is that under such policies losses may be recovered when the risks and losses are covered by the policy.

There are other collateral problems of horse and livestock insurance which face the horse owner who carries insurance on his animals. An example is the effect of changing the location of the animal after obtaining the insurance. The courts have held that animals may be moved in the usual and ordinary course of using them. A farmer in Iowa drove his team of horses to town hauling grain to market. He stopped over night at a hotel and during the night the hotel and barn were destroyed by fire. His horses perished. The court held that the team was covered by the policy and that the farmer was not limited to the use of horses on his farm but extended to the ordinary use in the pursuit of his business. Also where the owner is required to temporarily board his horses in a barn approximately seven miles from his farm, the Court held in Wisconsin that the loss was covered by the policy which provided for coverage "on the farm."

In a case in 1895 in Iowa the court held that the policy which provides that coverage against loss or damage by fire of horses, mules and colts while "on premises only" did not cover the loss where the horses moved temporarily some twenty miles for the purpose of plowing. The court stressed the terms in the policy relating to loss "while on the premises only."

If a horse dies as a result of abuse, mistreatment, overwork, or failure of the owner to use ordinary care, the insured cannot recover. This is based on the theory of the law that a person cannot take advantage of his own wrong. The law presumes that the owner of an animal will use the care the ordinary prudent owner would use under same or similar circumstances. An interesting case involves the "firing" of a race horse after which the horse died, as reported in *Hartford Live Stock Ins. Co. v. McMillen,* 9 F (2d) 961.

Wheaton was a two year old colt and was purchased by McMillen for $12,000 at New Orleans in January 1924. Shortly thereafter he was insured for $15,000.

The insurance policy did not cover loss due to operations of any kind.

In April he was shipped to Havre de Grace, Md., and on April 29th was subjected to the treatment known on the race track as firing. This treatment, according to plaintiff's contention, is to be regarded as prophylactic or therapeutic, as distinguished from an operation in a surgical sense. The veterinary surgeon who administered it, testifying as to his reasons for so doing, said: "I went over his knees and fetlock; . . . there were symptoms of exostosis (a bony growth), what is commonly known as osselet by the general racing community. The knees were in a bulky, loose condition, and I told him by firing I thought that would be rectified, and in my opinion it was the proper thing to do. . . .
. . . The legs were, of course, swollen as the result of this operation, and in that condition the horse was shipped to the Maple Heights race track in Ohio. Prior to the shipment lime was placed on his legs, to dry out the raw places. Soon after his arrival at Maple Heights, he was treated by a veterinarian, his legs bathed in an antiseptic solution. He

was also given an injection of anti-tetanic serum. On May 21st he died of septicaemia, which, as the post mortem showed, had fastened itself upon some of his vital organs.

Some of the veterinarians who testified thought the firing of the horse a major operation, while others did not consider it an operation at all, or at most a minor one. The facts as to what was done are beyond dispute, and we think it was for the court to determine whether it was within the inhibition against subjecting the animal to an "operation of any kind." The parties to an insurance policy have the right to contract as to risks the company will or will not assume, and if the facts are admitted it is the province of the court to determine whether they come within the clear and unambiguous terms of the policy, having in mind, as it is its duty to do, that the terms are ordinarily to be construed in their popular sense and according to common understanding.

In its broadest meaning "operation" would include the loading of a horse into a car, the unloading of one, or any act or series of acts by which some result is accomplished. But the usual and popular conception is restricted to its surgical sense; i.e., it is popularly understood to refer to a surgical operation, and clearly it was in that sense that it was used by the parties to this suit, in which it is an act or series of acts performed upon the body of a patient to produce a curative or remedial effect. The act performed on Wheaton was not one usually performed by any one but a veterinary surgeon. Certainly it required skill in surgery to puncture the skin in many places and thus properly start a counter irritant that would neutralize or destroy an incipient exostosis. The policy did not prohibit the performance of a major operation without the company's consent or one that involved hazard, but the performance of an "operation of any kind." This clause, as every other in the policy, should, of course, receive a reasonable construction. In the opinion of a majority of the court, such construction includes the operation in question,

and the insurance company is relieved of liability.

Some insurance policies contain provisions that the owner of a horse can not recover for loss caused by voluntary destruction unless the owner first obtains the writ-

ten consent of the insurance company and the written
consent of a veterinarian. The destruction of a race horse
on advice of a veterinarian obtained by the owner was not
sufficient for the owner to recover where the insurance
company refused to give its consent to such destruction.
So held a Federal Court in the case of *Wilson v. Hartford
Livestock Ins. Co.*, 193 F (2d) 752.

The owner of Floral, a race horse, was insured for
$20,000. The material provision of the policy provided
coverage of loss caused by the voluntary destruction when
destroyed for humane consideration under two circumstances: (1) Where the company consents to such destruction in writing signed by its general agent and (2) where
a licensed veterinarian certifies that the destruction was
immediately necessary because of its having been acci-
dentally crippled or maimed.

From the evidence it appears that the horse Floral partici-
pated in a race at Hawthorne Race Track, Stickney, Illinois,
on September 10th, 1949. He was examined by Dr. Kent,
a veterinarian employed by the Illinois Racing Board, prior
to the running of the race and was found to be "fit for
racing." At the completion of the race Floral pulled up lame.
Subsequent examinations of Floral, together with study of
x-ray pictures of the injured member, disclosed that he was
suffering a lineal fracture of the left front coffin bone, known
also as the os pedis bone, which is the most distal bone in the
leg and is encased by the hoof.
The insurance company was notified of the injury either
on September 12th, or on September 15th, by Dr. Kent, who
had examined Floral after the race on September 10th, and
on September 12th. Timmons, one of the insurance company's managers, in response to this notice, caused Dr. Hew-
itt to x-ray Floral on September 15th and Dr. Cameron, a
veterinarian, to examine Floral on September 16th.

On September 24th, the owner requested consent to
destroy Floral because "the horse had been suffering with
severe pain." The insurance company refused.

The owner, who had been sick when the injury occurred, first learned of the injury on October 16th. At that time, he directed that Dr. Proctor be asked to examine Floral. Dr. Proctor examined the horse on October 17th and recommended that it be destroyed. On October 22nd, Dr. Proctor was again called at owner's request and on that date painlessly destroyed Floral in the presence of four witnesses, two of whom were veterinarians. After destroying the animal, Dr. Proctor removed the injured member and prepared it for exhibit. He notified the owner by telegram that Floral had been destroyed "for humane consideration because of incurable injury."

Both Dr. Kent and Dr. Proctor testified at the trial as witnesses for the insurance company. They were in agreement that Floral was suffering pain at the times they examined him and would never have been able to walk without pain. Dr. Kent testified the injury was healing, and Dr. Proctor stated that the healing was remarkable, but that it was a bad form of healing. Dr. Proctor also testified that at the time he destroyed Floral the animal was in "good flesh" and was eating all his feed, which is not normal for a sick horse, or one that was suffering great pain. Both doctors agreed that the horse should have been destroyed for humane consideration. Kent had given a certificate to this effect on September 26th.

Dr. Cameron, who had examined Floral on September 16th and September 27th, testified that the horse was in pain on September 16th, but was considerably improved on September 27th, although he was still sore. He thought the destruction of the horse on October 22nd was an unusual act, considering his examinations and the degree of healing that had taken place since the date of the injury. In his opinion the injury would have healed and the horse "could walk and go along and live a normal life."

The horse continued in good flesh, with good appetite, and was not destroyed until 42 days after the injury and 22 days after refusal of the insurer to grant consent to such destruction, at a time less than one week prior to the expiration of the policy.

The Court held that since the contract unequivocally required prior consent of the insurance company for the destruction of Floral and such consent was not granted, but, to the contrary, was specifically denied, there can be no recovery.

Of course the insurance company cannot arbitrarily withhold consent such as in the case where the owner of a valuable horse known as Palatine King insured him for $19,200. The policy provided that no liability should attach in the event of destruction without the consent of the insurance company's veterinarian. Palatine King suffered an injury of such nature as to require immediate destruction. The owner of Palatine King alleged that the withholding of consent was arbitrary, deliberate and with the sole purpose of prolonging the life of the horse beyond the terms of the policy. He also alleged that the veterinarian knew the animal could not recover and should be destroyed. The Court held that where an insurance company withholds its consent to the destruction of an animal and the insurance company's veterinarian knew or should have known the animal could not recover, the owner is entitled to recover.

If the insurance policy prohibits recovery for any animal destroyed by public authority or society for the prevention of cruelty to animals the owner cannot recover. In a case where the owner was denied recovery for the loss of a mare which was shot by a veterinarian of the state board of health, the court relied on the state statute requiring the owner of any animal infected with a disease which might be communicated to other animals to notify the health department and that it was the power of the state to destroy such animals. Most states have statutes which place a duty on the owners of animals infected with a communicable disease. However, the liability may be different where an animal is injured and it becomes necessary to destroy it because it cannot recover and a veterinarian of the health department destroys the animal not in the official capacity of a state official but as a veterinarian acting humanistically.

Insurance policies insuring the owner against loss from causes of disease, accidental injury or hazards of transportation cover loss in transit. An example is the case of the owner of race horses who shipped them by railroad car and while the car was crossing a trestle the horses forced the door open in such a manner as to cause the horses to fall through the door and die. The court held the policy covered such loss.

The death of animals as a result of serious injuries due to the rolling of a ship in a violent storm was covered by a policy insuring livestock shipped by water. In an early Kentucky case (1868), the owner shipped several mules by steamboat down the Mississippi River. The mules were killed by steam escaping from the boat. The Kentucky Supreme Court held that even though the insurance company could not explain how the steam escaped, the terms of the policy covered perils of the sea or of the river, and this meant dangers incident to the vessel used for the transportation of the mules.

As indicated in the beginning of this chapter, it is most important to know the terms of the policy covering the risks and losses of horses and livestock and that the unambiguous terms are taken in their plain, ordinary and popular sense. Construction of policies must be reasonable and not such as to deprive the owner of the benefit of an unambiguous provision in the policy for the protection of the insurance company. In interpreting an insurance contract the courts must construe the entire contract together for the purpose of giving force and effect to each paragraph and clause.

It is the duty of the owner of an animal suing on a policy of livestock insurance to prove compliance with all the terms and conditions of the policy. So, if the policy requires a veterinarian's certificate that the destruction of the horse was necessary, the burden is on the owner to show he complied.

APPENDIX I:

USEFUL FORMS YOU WILL ENCOUNTER AS A HORSE OWNER

Agreement to Train and Show Horses
Agreement to Train and Show a Horse at Specific Shows
Stallion Service Contract
Stallion Service Agreement
Bill of Sale Stallion With Warranty
Bill of Sale Without Warranty
Lease Agreement With Option to Buy
Installment Sales Under Uniform Commercial Code, Security
  Agreement
Co-Owner Agreement for Stallion
Co-Owner Agreement for Mare
Lease Agreement for Stallion
Lease Agreement for Mare
Notice of Breeder's Lien
Boarding Stable Agreement
Horse Farm Manager Contract

About These Forms

The old saying that a man's word is his bond is as out of date as the horse and buggy on a federal super highway. The complex and fast-moving world today demands more from the

147

average person than his grandfather would ever have dreamed possible. In the old days grandfather sold a horse to his neighbor and his word was sufficient. Today most sales are made to strangers who live far from the neighborhood of the seller. Many transactions are carried on by mail and telephone. With the number of transactions involved in the modern-day horse business it is possible that memory may fail to correctly record the small but important details in the negotiations and the closing of the agreement. If a contract is worth entering into it is worth the time and effort to put it into writing. Most misunderstandings involve those things the parties failed to say or failed to remember. Either may cause an expensive law suit. Written agreements are important to reduce the gamble of becoming involved in litigation. The following forms are designed to meet the everyday transactions of the average horse owner. It is apparent there are no syndication agreements included. Such agreements are involved, complicated and technical and involve a number of persons and large sums of money. Such agreements should not be prepared from a general form but should be prepared by an attorney selected especially for his skill in such matters.

The following forms are drafted so the user may expand them to include any agreement he and the other party desire. One of the simplest yet most important agreements is the bill of sale. If a bill of sale is used with the proper description, correct age and a clear statement of the terms and conditions, the parties will reduce the chance of misunderstanding to a minimum and make the business of owning and raising horses more enjoyable.

The fact that a person has gotten by for many years without the use of written contracts and agreements is no guarantee that he has alleviated the future problem of misunderstanding and disagreements leading to litigation.

Agreement to Train and Show Horses

THIS AGREEMENT, made and entered into this ＿＿＿ day of ＿＿＿, 19＿＿, by and between ＿＿＿, of ＿＿＿, hereinafter called the "Trainer," and _____, of _____, hereinafter called the "Owner,"

WITNESSETH:

WHEREAS, the Owner owns a certain _____ (sex), _____ (breed) horse, named _____, Registration No. _____, age _____ years and is desirous of having the said horse trained and shown, and

WHEREAS, the Trainer is experienced in training and showing pure-bred horses and is desirous of showing said horse,

NOW, THEREFORE, in consideration of the mutual covenants and agreements herein contained, the parties agree as follows:

1. The Owner agrees to deliver one registered _____ (sex), _____ (breed) horse named _____, Registration No. _____, to the Trainer at _____ (address) to be trained and shown.

2. The Trainer shall have the right to select horse shows where the said horse is to be shown. The Trainer shall notify the Owner when the horse is entered in a show either by mail, wire or telephone and shall notify the Owner the results of same by the same method.

3. The Owner shall, during the term of this agreement, pay the Trainer as follows:

   (a) $_____ each show.
   (b) $_____ a day board.

In addition the Owner shall pay for all long distance telephone calls, wires, entry fees and all medical bills. Payment shall be made within ten (10) days after billing (or on the _____ day of each month beginning on the _____ day of _____, 19_____.)

4. The Trainer agrees to train and show the above described horse and to feed and care for it in a good and proper manner as is necessary in preparing and maintaining the said horse in show shape.

5. Transportation of the horse to and from horse shows shall be provided by the Trainer.

6. It is agreed that the horse shall be listed in the name of the Owner and handled in the name of the Trainer.

7. In the event the horse becomes ill or in need of major medical attention or hospital attention, the Trainer shall notify the Owner by telephone or wire for instructions.

8. Either party may terminate this agreement by notifying the other in writing or by wire as first above written. The Trainer shall return the horse to the Owner or his agent and in accordance with instructions of the Owner. They shall pay to the Trainer the amount due at time of redelivery of the horse to the Owner or his agent.

9. All prize money shall belong to (Trainer) (Owner) and the ribbons and trophies shall belong to the Owner.

10. The Trainer shall use his best efforts in training and showing said horse.

This agreement is signed and executed on this the _____ day of _____, 19____, in duplicate.

_____ (Trainer)
_____ (Owner)

Agreement to Train and Show a Horse at Specific Shows

THIS AGREEMENT, made and entered into this _____ day of _____, 19____, by and between _____, of _____, hereinafter called the "Trainer," and _____, of _____, hereinafter called the "Owner,"

WITNESSETH:

WHEREAS, the Owner owns a certain _____ (sex) , _____ (breed, horse named _____, Registration No. _____, age _____ years and is desirous of having the said horse trained and shown, and

WHEREAS, the Trainer is experienced in training and showing horses and is desirous of showing said horse,

NOW, THEREFORE, in consideration of the mutual covenants

and agreements herein contained, the parties agree as follows:

1. The Owner agrees to deliver one registered _____ (sex),
_____ (breed), horse named _____, Registration No.
_____ to the Trainer at _____ (address) to the trained
and shown.

2. The Trainer shall show the said horse at the following
shows:

    (a)
    (b)
    (c)
    (d)

and at such other shows as the Owner shall select in writing
to the Trainer.

3. The Owner shall, during the term of this agreement, pay
the Trainer as follows:

    (a) $_____ each show.
    (b) $_____ a day board.

In addition the Owner shall pay for all long distance telephone calls, wires, entry fees and all medical bills. Payment
shall be made within ten (10) days after billing (or on the
_____ day of each month beginning on the _____ day of
_____, 19_____.

4. The Trainer agrees to train and show the above described horse and to feed and care for it in a good and proper
manner as is necessary in preparing and maintaining the said
horse in show shape.

5. Transportation of the horse to and from horse shows shall
be provided by the Trainer.

6. It is agreed that the horse shall be listed in the name of
the Owner and handled in the name of the Trainer.

7. In the event the horse becomes ill or in need of major
medical attention or hospital attention, the Trainer shall
notify the Owner by telephone or wire for instructions.

8. Either party may terminate this agreement by notifying
the other in writing or by wire as first above written. The
Trainer shall return the horse to the Owner or his agent and

in accordance with the instructions of the Owner. They shall pay to the Trainer the amount due at time of redelivery of the horse to the Owner or his agent.

9. All prize money shall belong to (Trainer) (Owner) and the ribbons and trophies shall belong to the Owner.

10. The Trainer shall use his best efforts in training and showing said horse.

This agreement is signed and executed on this the _____ day of _____, 19_____, in duplicate.

_____ (Trainer)
_____ (Owner)

Stallion Service Contract

I hereby agree to breed a mare by the name of _____, Description _____, Age _____ Registration No. _____ Sire _____ Dam _____ to the Stallion _____ (name) standing at _____ (farm), _____ (address, and to pay you the sum of $_____, $_____ of which is payable with this contract, and $_____ will be paid before the mare leaves the farm.

It is further agreed that:

1. Your veterinarian may check my mare for normal breeding condition.

2. Should the above stallion die or become unfit for service, or if my mare should die or become unfit to breed, then this contract shall become null and void.

3. It is understood that you will not be responsible for accident, sickness or death to my mare or foal, and that you will exercise your judgment in caring for and supervising my mare.

4. That you guarantee a live foal. For this purpose, a live foal is defined as one that stands and nurses after foaling. Notice of the death of a foal must be accompanied by a statement from a licensed veterinarian.

5. If the mare proves not to be in foal in the year bred, or

loses her foal, as stated in paragraph 4 above, the stallion owner has the option to rebreed the mare the following year.

6. Board for Mares:

Pasture & hay	$_____
Grain	$_____
Individual lots with hay and grain	$_____

All boarding fees and veterinary fees must be paid when the mare leaves the farm.

7. Should mare owner fail to deliver said mare on or before _____, 19____, to the premises where said stallion is standing for the purpose of breeding said mare, the stallion owner shall be under no further obligation under this contract.

8. This contract shall not be assigned or transferred by the mare owner.

9. This contract is not valid unless completed in full.

Signed, in duplicate, this _____ day of _____, 19____.

_____ (Name of Stallion owner)
_____ (Address)

_____ (Name of Mare owner)
_____ (Address)

Stallion Service Agreement

Date _____

To _____ (Owner of mare)
_____ (Address)

I hereby agree to use my stallion, named _____, Registration No. _____, to breed your _____ (breed) mare named _____, Registration No. _____, for the sum of $_____, payable on the _____ day of _____, 19____.

In the event your said mare does not deliver a live foal, you shall have one free service within one year from date of breeding at your option.

It is understood and agreed that your mare is free from infectious, contagious or transmissible disease or unsoundness.

It is understood by delivering the said mare to me that you agree to the above and that you will pay all transportation costs and $_____ per day during the time the mare is kept by me.

If you accept this agreement, sign the original and one copy and return the original to me.

_____ (Owner of Stallion)

_____ (Address)

Date _____

I accept the above agreement.

_____ (Owner of Mare)

Bill of Sale: Stallion with Warranty

KNOW ALL MEN BY THESE PRESENTS:

That I, _____, of _____, have this day sold to _____, of _____, a _____ (sex) , _____ (breed) stallion foaled on _____ (date foaled) , registered with the _____ Horse Club, Registration No. _____, for the sum of _____ Dollars ($_____) , the receipt whereof is hereby acknowledged.

In the event that the above named stallion is properly used, and with mares in good health and condition, I warrant that he has breeding capacity; but it is expressly provided, as a condition of this warranty, that the purchaser shall keep a list of all mares bred with the date of each service and name of owner for one year from date of purchases.

In the event the above conditions are not performed or should the above named stallion hereafter become injured or disabled through accident or disease, this warranty shall be null and void and of no effect, and all obligations incurred by me herein shall be considered fulfilled and ended.

This bill of sale contains all the agreements of warranty or guaranty made by me in this sale.

IN WITNESS WHEREOF, I have hereunto set my hand and seal this _____ day of _____, 19_____.

_____ (Seller)   (SEAL)

Bill of Sale Without Warranty

TO WHOM IT MAY CONCERN:

Know all men by these presents: That I, _____, of
_____ (address), have this day sold to _____ (name), of
_____ (address), a _____ (sex), _____ (breed) horse, foaled
_____ (date), _____ (color), for the sum of _____ Dollars ($_____), the receipt whereof is hereby acknowledged.

IN WITNESS WHEREOF, I have hereunto set my hand and seal
this _____ day of _____, 19_____, at _____ (city),
_____ (state).

_____ (Seller) (SEAL)

Lease Agreement with Option to Buy

THIS LEASE, executed this _____ day of _____, 19_____,
by and between _____, hereinafter referred to as "Owner,"
and _____, hereinafter referred to as "Lessee,"

WITNESSETH: Owner does hereby lease to Lessee and Lessee
does hereby lease from Owner for a period of _____ months,
approximately, beginning on the _____ day of _____,
19_____, and ending on the _____ day of _____, 19_____,
the following animal:

RENTAL: The Lessee agrees to pay Owner a total sum of
$_____ for the use of the above horse for the lease period to be
paid, _____. In addition, the Lessee agrees to pay the Owner
the sum of $_____ on or before the _____ day of _____,
19_____, which will be refunded to the Lessee when he returns
the horse to the Owner at his _____ at the termination of
this lease period providing the horse is in good condition
(approximately the same condition as when accepted by the
Lessee at the beginning of the lease period). Owner also hereby
grants the Lessee the option to lease the horse for a second
lease period to commence the day following the expiration
date of this lease and the second lease period to end on or

before the _____ day of _____, 19_____, for a total sum of
$_____, to be paid $_____ the day second lease period starts
(_____) and $_____ on or before the _____ day of _____,
19_____. Owner also grants Lessee option to purchase this
horse for a total sum of $_____ and if Lessee does purchase
horse, the lease fee which has already been paid, (will) (will
not) apply against the total of $_____. To exercise either of
these options, Lessee must notify Owner in writing to that
effect on or before the _____ day of _____, 19_____.

Lessee warrants that he (has) (has not) inspected said horse
and agrees to accept this horse in his present condition. Lessee
shall pay and provide for the transportation of the horse from
Owner to the Lessee and for the return of said horse to Owner
at _____ (address) at the expiration of the lease.
Lessee shall not obligate Owner for any expense of any kind
whatsoever in connection with the leased horse unless authorized in writing by the Owner.

CARE OF HORSE: The Lessee, at his expense, shall provide
feed, service, equipment and other necessary services for the
proper care, maintenance, handling and protection of the
leased horse, also veterinary services if needed, all according to
the rules of good animal husbandry and reasonable standards
and methods of the horse breeding industry. Owner shall have
the right at any time, in person or by authorized agent, to go
upon the Lessee's premises to inspect the horse, and to determine if it has been properly cared for and is in good health.

It is not necessary that Lessee provide death and injury insurance on the leased horse providing he provides good and
reasonable care and precautions at all times to prevent injury
or death of the horse, and providing if horse becomes sick or
injured that Lessee immediately provides for proper veterinary
care and attention at Lessee's expense. Owner will not hold
Lessee liable for any serious injury or death of the horse while
in the custody of the Lessee.

Owner will supply Lessee with such pedigree and registration information as may be needed for registration of future
produce of this horse resulting from breeding him to mares by
the Lessee during this lease period.

Lessee shall hold Owner harmless for any injury to persons

or damages to any property caused by this leased horse. Lessee shall not permit the leased horse to be seized or impounded by anyone because of damages to property of others. Lessee shall pay when due any taxes which may be levied by any city, township, county, state or other taxing body wherein said leased horse may be located during the term of said lease. Lessee shall not assign this lease nor sublease this horse covered hereby.

The title and ownership of the leased horse shall be and remain in the name of Owner. Lessee shall not sell, mortgage or encumber this leased horse in any manner whatsoever.

If the leased horse should at any time become missing, lost, estrayed, seriously injured, sick, or dead, the Lessee shall immediately notify Owner by telephone and subsequently by mail. There shall be no abatement of rental paid due to death of leased horse if the horse dies during the period for which the rental has already been paid.

MODIFICATION OF LEASE: No modification of this lease shall be binding unless in writing and executed by the parties hereto.

BINDING ON HEIRS: It is further agreed that this lease and all covenants and agreements herein contained shall accrue to and be binding upon the parties hereto, their heirs, successors, administrators, executors and assigns.

IN WITNESS WHEREOF, the Owner and Lessee have executed this the day and year first above written.

_____ (Owner)
_____ (Lessee)

STATE OF _____,
COUNTY OF _____, to-wit:

BE IT REMEMBERED, that on this ____ day of _____, 19____, before me, the undersigned, a Notary Public in and for the County and State aforesaid, came _____, who is personally known to me to be the same person who executed the within instrument of writing and such person duly acknowledged the execution of the same.

IN WITNESS WHEREOF, I have hereunto set my hand and affixed my notarial seal the day and year last above written.

_____ (Notary Public)
(Notarial Seal)
My commission expires _____.

Installment Sales Under Uniform Commercial Code

SECURITY AGREEMENT

_____ (Date)

_____ (Name) _____ (No. and Street) _____ (City or Town) _____ (County) _____ (State) , hereinafter called Buyer-Debtor, for valuable consideration, receipt of which is hereby acknowledged, does hereby purchase from or grants to _____ (Name) _____ (No. and Street) _____ (City or Town) _____ (State) , hereinafter called Seller-Secured Party, a security interest and agrees to pay for the described horse (s) being hereinafter called Collateral for a total price and upon subject to the terms stated below.

DESCRIPTION OF HORSES:

_____ (sex) , _____ (breed) , horse foaled _____ (date) , Reg. No. _____

_____ (sex) , _____ (breed) , horse foaled _____ (date) , Reg. No. _____

TERMS AND PAYMENT:

1. Cash price $_____
2. Down payment $_____
3. Unpaid balance $_____
4. Principal balance owing $_____
5. Finance charge $_____
6. Time balance—amount of note $_____

Time balance payable in ___ consecutive monthly payments of $_____. (State the number of payments and amounts of other than monthly payment.) First payment due _____ day of _____, 19_____.

The conditions of this security agreement are such that Buyer has executed and delivered to Seller his certain promissory note of even date herewith and hereinafter referred to as the "Note" in the principal amount equal to the time balance shown above, payable as set forth above.

If the obligation hereby secured, or any part thereof, is not paid at the maturity hereof, whether such maturity be caused by lapse of time or by acceleration, such entire obligation, or the part thereof which has matured, as the case may be, shall thereafter draw straight interest at the rate of ____% per annum until paid. Time is of the essence.

In the event there is a default in the payment or conditions of this agreement, the Seller or Secured Party shall have the right to take possession of the said Collateral without notice or at the option of the Seller or Secured Party to take such action as is available under the law.

The Collateral shall be kept at _____ (Address where horses are to be kept) and the Buyer shall have the right to transport the said Collateral in the usual course of business of owning, showing, training and exhibiting horses. However, the Buyer will notify Seller of any permanent change in location of the Collateral and will not remove the Collateral from the State of _____ without first giving the Seller ten (10) days written notice by registered mail of his intent to change the location and such notice will state the new address in the same detail as above.

Seller warrants that he has good title to said horse (s) and that it is free of all liens and encumbrances.

The Seller will execute all necessary registration certificates and will comply with all requirements of the _____ Horse Club relating to the transfer of ownership of the said horse (s) to the Buyer.

_____ (Seller-Secured Party)   _____ (Buyer-Debtor)

NOTE: The Security Agreement need not be filed. The Financing Statement is filed in the county where the Debtor resides and where the horses are to be permanently located if at a different location than the residence of the Buyer. In some states there is a central filing. Each state's Uniform Commercial Code provides for filing officers. Consult the Code of the state where the horses are to be located.

Installment credit comes within the "Truth in Lending" law enacted on May 29, 1968, as Title I of the Federal Consumer Credit Protection Act. All horse owners selling horses on installment should consult the "Truth in Lending Act" before entering into such sales. It is sufficient here to point out that the creditor must disclose the amount of credit to be paid to him; all charges must be individually itemized, the total amount to be financed, finance charge expressed as an annual percentage rate, the number, amount, and the due date or period of payments scheduled to repay the indebtedness, and the description of the security interest held or to be retained or acquired by the creditor must also be disclosed.

Co-Owner Agreement for Stallion

To _____ (Name of Co-Owner)
_____ (Address)

I hereby convey and transfer to you a one-half interest in a _____ (sex), _____ (breed) stallion foaled on the _____ (date), Registration No. _____ for the sum of $_____, the receipt whereof is hereby acknowledged. On and after this date we shall be co-owners and I shall make application to the _____ Horse Club for the certificate of registration to be issued in the names of _____ and _____, as co-owners.

Expenses and care of the stallion shall be divided as follows: (Here set forth the arrangements for all expenses, care and showing of the stallion.)
Stud fees shall be divided as follows: (Here set forth agreement as to the breeding arrangements and stud fees.)

You agree to sign all necessary applications for the registration of all offspring as required by the _____ Horse Club.
The co-ownership of the stallion shall continue (until the _____ day of _____, 19_____) (or for the life of the stallion).
Upon the termination of the co-ownership of said stallion other than by death of the stallion, you shall sign the certificate of registration authorizing the _____ Horse Club to issue a certificate of registration to me as the sole owner.
Signed this _____ day of _____, 19_____, in duplicate.

_____ (Owner)

The undersigned accepts the above co-ownership of said stallion in accordance with the terms set forth.
Signed this _____ day of _____, 19_____, in duplicate.

_____ (Co-Owner)

Co-Owner Agreement for Mare

To _____ (Name)
  _____ (Address)
  I hereby convey and transfer to you a one-half interest in a
_____ (sex) , _____ (breed) mare foaled on _____ (date) , Registration No. _____, for the sum of $____, the receipt whereof
is hereby acknowledged. On and after this date we shall be co-
owners and I shall make application to the _____ Horse
Club for the certificate of registration to be issued in the names
of _____ and _____, as co-owners.

  Expenses and care of the mare shall be divided as follows:
  (Here set forth the arrangements for all expenses, care and
  showing of the mare.)
  Breeding arrangements shall be as follows: (Here set forth
  the arrangements for breeding and dividing the offspring.)

  You agree to sign all necessary applications for the registration of all offspring as required by the _____ Horse Club.
  The co-ownership of the mare shall continue (until the _____
day of _____, 19____) (or for the life of the mare) .
  Upon termination of the co-ownership of said mare, other
than by death of the mare, you shall sign the certificate of registration authorizing the _____ Horse Club to issue a certificate of registration to me as the sole owner.
  Signed this _____ day of _____, 19____, in duplicate.
                                     _____ (Owner)
  The undersigned accepts the above co-ownership of said mare
in accordance with the terms set forth.
  Signed this _____ day of _____, 19____, in duplicate.
                                     _____ (Co-Owner)

Lease Agreement for Stallion

  THIS LEASE, executed this _____ day of _____, 19____, by
and between _____, hereinafter referred to as "Owner" and
_____, hereinafter referred to "Lessee,"
  WITNESSETH: Owner does hereby lease to Lessee and Lessee

does hereby lease from Owner for a period beginning the _____ day of _____, 19____, and ending on the _____ day of _____, 19____, the following stallion:

Breed _____
Registration No. _____
Name _____
Date foaled _____

RENTAL: The Lessee agrees to pay Owner a total sum of $_____ for the use of the above stallion for the lease period to be paid, _____. In addition, the Lessee agrees to pay the Owner the sum of $_____ on or before the _____ day of _____, 19____, which will be refunded to the Lessee when he returns the stallion to the Owner at his _____ at the termination of this lease period providing the stallion is in good condition (approximately the same condition as when accepted by the Lessee at the beginning of the lease period). Owner also hereby grants the Lessee the option to lease the stallion for a second lease period to commence the day following the expiration date of this lease and the second lease period shall end on or before the _____ day of _____, 19____, for a total sum of $_____ to be paid, $_____ the day second lease period starts (____) and $_____ on or before the _____ day of _____, 19____. To exercise the option, the Lessee shall notify the Owner in writing at least sixty (60) days prior to the termination of the agreement.

Lessee warrants that he (has) (has not) inspected said stallion and agrees to accept this stallion in his present condition. Lessee shall pay and provide for the transportation of the stallion from Owner to the Lessee and for the return of said stallion to Owner at _____ upon the expiration of the lease. Lessee shall not obligate Owner for any expense of any kind whatsoever in connection with the leased stallion unless authorized in writing by the Owner.

CARE OF STALLION: The Lessee, at his expense, shall provide feed, service, equipment and other necessary services for the proper care, maintenance, handling and protection of the leased stallion, also veterinary services if needed, all according to the rules of good animal husbandry and reasonable standards and

methods of the horse breeding industry. Owner shall have the
right at any time, in person or by authorized agent, to go upon
the Lessee's premises to inspect the stallion and to determine
if said stallion is being properly cared for and in good health.

It is not necessary that Lessee provide death and injury insurance on the leased stallion providing he provides good and
reasonable care and precautions at all times to prevent injury
or death of the stallion, and providing if stallion becomes sick
or injured that Lessee immediately provides for proper veterinary care and attention at Lessee's expense. Owner will not
hold Lessee liable for any serious injury or death of the stallion
while in custody of the Lessee.

The Lessee agrees to provide proper veterinary care immediately at his expense if the stallion becomes sick or injured.

Owner will supply Lessee with such pedigree and registration
information as may be needed for registration of future produce of this stallion resulting from breeding him to mares by the
Lessee during this lease period. Any stud fees collected by the
Lessee during the lease period will be the property of Lessee.

Lessee shall hold Owner harmless for any injury to persons
or damages to any property caused by this leased stallion. Lessee
shall not permit the leased stallion to be seized or impounded
by anyone because of damages to property of others. Lessee
shall pay when due any taxes which may be levied by any city,
township, county, state or other taxing body wherein said
leased stallion may be located during the term of said lease.
Lessee shall not assign this lease nor sublease this stallion covered hereby.

The tilte and ownership of the leased stallion shall be and
remain in the name of Owner. Lessee shall not sell, mortgage
or encumber this leased stallion in any manner whatsoever.

If the leased stallion should at any time become missing, lost,
estrayed, seriously injured, sick or dead, the Lessee shall immediately notify Owner by telephone and subsequently by mail.
There shall be no abatement of rental paid due to death of
leased stallion if the stallion dies during the period for which
the rental has already been paid.

MODIFICATION OF LEASE: No modification of this lease shall be
binding unless in writing and executed by the parties hereto.

BINDING ON HEIRS: It is further agreed that this lease and all covenants and agreements herein contained shall accrue to and be binding upon the parties hereto, their heirs, successors, administrators and executors.

IN WITNESS WHEREOF, the Owner and Lessee have executed this lease on the day and year first above written.

_____ (Owner)

_____ (Lessee)

Lease Agreement for Mare

THIS LEASE, executed this _____ day of _____, 19____, by and between _____, hereinafter referred to as "Owner," and _____, hereinafter referred to as "Lessee,"

WITNESSETH: Owner does hereby lease to Lessee and Lessee does hereby lease from Owner for a period of _____ months, approximately, beginning the _____ day of _____, 19____, and ending the _____ day of _____, 19____, the following mare:

Name_____

Registration No. _____

Breed_____

RENTAL: The Lessee agrees to pay Owner a total sum of $_____ for the use of the above mare for the lease period to be paid upon the execution of this agreement. In addition, the Lessee agrees to pay the Owner a deposit in the sum of $_____ before delivery of said mare, which deposit will be refunded to the Lessee when he returns the mare to the Owner at the termination of this lease period providing the mare is in good condition (approximately the same condition as when accepted by the Lessee at the beginning of the lease period).

Lessee warrants that he (has) (has not) inspected the mare and agrees to accept said mare in her present condition. Lessee shall pay and provide for the transportation of the mare from Owner to the Lessee and for the return of said mare to Owner at _____ upon the expiration of the lease. Lessee shall not obligate Owner for any expense of any kind whatsoever in connection with the leased mare unless authorized in writing by the Owner.

CARE OF MARE: The Lessee, at his expense, shall provide feed, service, equipment and other necessary services for the proper care, maintenance, handling and protection of the leased mare, also veterinary services if needed, all according to the rules of good animal husbandry and reasonable standards and methods of the horse breeding industry. Owner shall have the right at any time, in person or by authorized agent, to go upon the Lessee's premises to inspect the mare and to determine if said mare is being properly cared for and in good health.

The Owner shall assign the registration certificate to the Lessee for the purposes of permitting the Lessee to register the offspring of this mare resulting from breeding her. Upon the termination of this lease the Lessee shall assign the registration certificate to the Owner.

The title and ownership of the leased mare shall be and remain in the name of the Owner. Lessee shall not sell, mortgage or encumber this leased mare in any manner whatsoever.

Lessee shall hold Owner harmless for any injury to persons or damages to any property caused by this leased mare. Lessee shall not permit the leased mare to be seized or impounded by anyone because of damages to property of others. Lessee shall pay when due any taxes which may be levied by any city, township, county, state or other taxing body wherein said leased mare may be located during the term of said lease. Lessee shall not assign this lease nor sublease this mare covered hereby.

If the leased mare should at any time become missing, lost, estrayed, seriously injured, sick or dead, the Lessee shall immediately notify Owner by telephone and subsequently by mail. There shall be no abatement of rental paid due to death of leased mare if the mare dies during the period for which the rental has already been paid.

In the event the mare does not foal from the first breeding season, the Lessee may breed her at the next breeding season and return the mare after the offspring is weaned. If the mare does not produce offspring within twelve months after the second season breeding, this lease shall terminate and the Lessee shall return the mare to the Owner as hereinabove provided.

MODIFICATION OF LEASE: No modification of this lease shall be binding unless in writing and executed by the parties hereto.

BINDING ON HEIRS: It is further agreed that this lease and all covenants and agreements herein contained shall accrue to and be binding upon the parties hereto, their heirs, successors, administrators, executors and assigns.

IN WITNESS WHEREOF, the Owner and the Lessee have executed this lease on the day and year first above written.

_____ (Owner)
_____ (Lessee)

Notice of Breeder's Lien

Notice is hereby given that I, _____, the undersigned owner of a certain _____ (breed) stallion, named _____, Registration No. _____, on or about the _____ day of _____, 19_____, did use said stallion for propagating purposes on a _____ (breed) mare by the name of _____, Registration No. _____, agreeing to pay _____ ($_____). Payment for the breeding service has not been made and I, _____, the undersigned, hereby claim a lien in the amount of _____ ($_____) upon said mare and offspring of such service.

Signed this _____ day of _____, 19_____.

_____ (name)
Stallion owner

A lien for breeding fees may be created by agreement between the owner of the stallion and the owner of the mare. In some states statutes provide for such liens.

Boarding Stable Agreement

NAME OF OWNER _____
ADDRESS _____
HOME PHONE _____   BUSINESS PHONE _____
BREED OF HORSE _____   AGE _____   SEX _____
APPROXIMATE WEIGHT _____ POUNDS.   SPECIAL

MARKS OR SCORES _____. OBVIOUS DEFECTS _____
VET'S NAME _____   PHONE _____
SPECIAL SERVICE ORDERS _____
DISPOSITION OF HORSE _____

The owner agrees to:

1. Pay in advance $____ per (day) (week) (month) as board.

2. Pay all medical, hospital and veterinarian expenses.

3. If the animal becomes ill or is injured, the owner shall be notified at once at owner's expense for instructions, and if owner cannot be informed or does not answer the notice or the horse's health requires immediate action, the stable owner shall have the right to use his best judgment in regarding measures to be taken for the welfare and health of the horse.

4. The stable owner shall not be liable for any damage which may accrue from any cause growing out of or as a result of the boarding of the said horse including, but not limited to, loss by fire, theft, running away, death, injury to person, horse or property, except gross negligence of the stable owner, his agents, servants and employees and then the liability of the stable owner shall not exceed the sum of $____.

5. The stable owner shall have and is hereby granted a lien on the aforesaid amount for any and all unpaid boarding and other charges resulting from boarding of said horse. The owner shall pay for the boarding charges within ____ days after they become due and payable.

6. Stable owner may exercise his lien rights and ____ days after written notice to the owner at the address above set out may dispose of said horse for the unpaid charges at private or public sale and the owner waives all other legal notice. In the event sale does not secure a price sufficient to pay costs and charges, the owner shall be liable for the difference. Any sum realized over and above costs and charges shall belong to the owner.

7. Owner agrees to abide by all the rules and regulations of the stable.

8. In the event some one other than the owner calls for the horse, such person shall have written authority signed by the owner to obtain the horse.

9. It is understood that the word "owner" means the owner of the horse and the word "stable" or term "stable owner" means the owner and operator of the boarding stable. No person is authorized to change or alter the terms of this agreement signed in duplicate this _____ day of _____, 19_____.
_____ (Owner or authorized agent)

Boarding Stable
By _____

Horse Farm Manager Contract

THIS AGREEMENT, made this _____ day of _____, 19_____, by and between _____, hereinafter called the "Owner," and _____, hereinafter called the "Manager,"

WITNESSETH: _____ owns and operates a horse farm known as _____, which is located at _____, and is desirous of employing a full time Manager, and _____ is experienced in the management of horse farms and the care of horses.

NOW, THEREFORE, for and in consideration of the mutual covenants herein contained, the parties hereto agree as follows:

1. The Manager, after inspecting the _____ Farm and understanding the work involved, agrees to manage the Farm for a period of _____ years, beginning on the _____ day of _____, 19_____, and terminating on the _____ day of _____, 19_____.

2. The Manager shall devote his full time and best efforts in managing the said horse farm.

3. Manager shall contract no debts on account of the Owner without first obtaining the sanction of the Owner.

4. All sums received from services performed by the Manager and employees shall belong to the Owner and adequate records shall be kept at all times.

5. Manager shall comply with all rules and regulations set forth in writing by the Owner for the operation of the farm.

6. In the event the Manager is required to travel on behalf of the farm, he shall be reimbursed for his actual expenses.

7. All records shall be open and available for examination at any time by the Owner.

8. The Owner shall furnish the Manager the following:
(Here set forth living quarters, cars, etc., to be furnished to the Manager by the Owner.)

9. The Owner shall pay the Manager the sum of $_____ per (week) (month), payable on:

    (a) _____ day of each week.
    (b) First and fifteenth day of each month.
    (c) First of each month.
    (d) Any other time as agreed upon between the parties.

10. Manager shall be entitled to __ weeks vacation with pay each year, beginning after one year's employment.

Signed, in duplicate, this _____ day of _____, 19_____.

                _____ (Owner)
                _____ (Manager)

APPENDIX II:

STATUTORY REGULATIONS

Each of the fifty states of the United States have found it necessary to enact laws controlling livestock running at large. These laws were intended to protect agricultural crops from the ravages of stray domestic animals. As more and more land was used for crops the more demanding farmers became for the legislature to enact laws for their protection. Thus each state passed acts regulating and restraining trespassing animals. Each state statute must be examined to determine when an animal is trespassing and the extent of liability for damages. All the statutes are similar in their general intent but may vary as to when an animal is actually trespassing. For instance, in Nebraska the statute defines trespassing of animals as cattle, horses, mules, swine and sheep causing damage upon the cultivated lands of another. But in Indiana the animal is trespassing when it breaks into an enclosure or wanders upon the land of another. Alaska statute says the owner of an animal is liable for all damages done by cattle or animals to the land or crops of another enclosed by a legal fence.

Each state statute must be consulted as to the damages the injured party may collect and for the authority and procedure necessary to impound the trespassing animal.

When animals are impounded and the owner does not appear to claim them, most state statutes define the animals as "strays." An animal becomes a "stray" when the owner is unknown and no one claims it within a certain number of days. West Virginia requires the owner to appear within three days and claim the stock, or the cattle may be advertised for sale at public auction.

In New Mexico a "stray" is defined as any bovine animal—horse, mule or ass—whose owner is unknown in the section where found or which is fifty miles or more from the limits of its usual range or pasture or which is branded with a brand not of record.

Liens for boarding, feeding and pasturing animals are statutory laws in all states. Again, all the statutes are similar in their general terms and purposes but differ as to specific grounds for a lien. Some states provide for a lien only for boarding, feeding and pasturing. Yet others, such as Oklahoma, provide for a lien for keeping, boarding, pasturing or training any animal. A lien on an animal means the person furnishing the food, board and pasture has the right to keep the animal until the owner has paid for such services in full. Where a person furnishes feed and board, it is defined as a livery stable lien. Where a person furnishes pasture, it is called an agister's lien. However, the terms are used interchangeably. Such liens are purely statutory. The rights, liabilities and priorities must be obtained from the statutes.

Statutes controlling stallions and jacks are important. These statutes prohibit male animals from running at large. In Rhode Island the owner is absolutely liable for damages caused by a stallion over one year of age. Whereas in Missouri the statute prohibits stallions, male mules or jackasses over two years of age from running at large.

Since the modern day horse owners and trainers travel from one state to another, it is important to know the requirements, not only of their home states but of each state where they are traveling. For that reason the statutes of all fifty states are included alphabetically.

Statutory Regulations Governing Horses and the Legal Obligation of the Owner in Each of the 50 States

Alabama

Trespass by stock.—Every owner of cattle, horses, mules, hogs, sheep, jacks, jennets, or goats, shall be liable in damages for all injuries and trespass committed by such animals by breaking into the inclosure or grounds of another inclosed by a lawful fence, or running at large in a common inclosure within which more persons than one are cultivating land without the consent of all such persons; and the person injured shall have a lien on the animal trespassing for the damages, and for every subsequent trespass double damages.

No trespass, if fence not a lawful one; penalty for injury to cattle.—If any trespass or damage is done by any animal breaking into lands not inclosed by a lawful fence as defined in this article, the owner is not liable therefor; and if any person injures or destroys any such animal, he is liable to the owner for five times the amount of injury done, to be recovered before any court of competent jurisdiction.

Unlawful for stock to run at large on public property.—On and after March 1, 1941 it shall be unlawful for the owner of any livestock or animal, as hereinafter defined, to knowingly, voluntarily, negligently, or wilfully permit any such livestock or animal to go at large in the state of Alabama either upon the premises of another or upon the public lands, highways, roads, or streets in the state of Alabama. Nothing in this section or elsewhere in this article shall be construed to make it unlawful for livestock or other animals to run at large on the premises of another when the owner or person in charge of the premises has consented in writing to let livestock or other animals run at large on the same, or to subject the owner of such livestock or other animals to criminal prosecution therefor.

Owner liable for damage done by stock running at large; exception.—The owner of such livestock or animal being or running at large upon the premises of another or upon the public lands, roads, highways or streets in the state of Alabama shall be liable for all damages done to crops, shade or fruit trees or ornamental shrubs and flowers of any person, to be recovered before any court of competent jurisdiction; and the judgment of the court against the owner of such livestock or animal so depredating shall be a lien superior to all other liens on the livestock or animal causing the injury, except as to taxes. Provided, however, that the owner of any stock or animal shall not be liable for any damages to any motor vehicle, or any occupant thereof, suffered, caused by, or resulting from a collision with such stock or other animal, unless it be proven that such owner knowingly or wilfully put or placed such stock upon such public highway, road or street, where such damages were occasioned.

"Open range counties" abolished; unlawful for livestock to go at large.—There shall be no "open range counties" as defined in section 90 of Title 3 of the Code of Alabama (1940), and after the effective date of this section it shall be unlawful for horses, mares, mules, jacks, jennies, colts, cows, calves, yearlings, bulls, oxen, sheep, goats, lambs, kids, hogs, shoats, and pigs to go at large in any county in the state.

Livery Stable Keepers.

Lien declared.—Any keeper, owner, or proprietor of a livery stable, or other place for feeding and caring for stock for pay, shall have a lien on all stock kept and fed by him, for the payment of his charges, for keeping and feeding such stock, and he shall have the right to retain the stock, or so much thereof as may be necessary for the payment of such damages; and said lien shall continue for six months on any stock so kept, fed and cared for in possession of persons with notice of such lien.

Stock Breeder's Protection against Bogus or Fraudulent Pedigrees.

Stock breeder's lien; how secured.—In order to protect farmers of this state against damage resulting from breeding to sires advertised with bogus or fraudulent pedigrees, and to secure to the owners of sires payment for service, the following provisions are enacted: That every owner of a sire charging a service fee, in order to have a lien upon the get of any such sire under the provisions of this subdivision for said service, shall file a statement verified by oath or affirmation to the best of his knowledge and belief, with the commissioner of agriculture and industries, giving the name, age, description and pedigree, as well as the terms and conditions upon which such sire is advertised for service.

Lien.—The owner or owners of any sire receiving such certificate by complying with the provisions of this subdivision, shall obtain and have a lien upon the get of any such sire for the period of one year from the date of birth of get.

Estrays may be taken up.—Any person in this state, finding any horse, mare, mule, jack or jennet, any neat cattle, hog, sheep, or goat, running at large about his residence or plantation or the residence or plantation of which he has charge, the owner of which is unknown, may take up such animals as an estray.

Oath of taker.—Every person taking up an estray must, within three days thereafter make oath before some justice of the county in which such estray was found, that the same was taken up about his plantation or residence, or about the plantation or residence in his charge, and that the marks or brands have not been defaced or altered since taking up.

Alaska

Liability of owner of animals damaging enclosed land or crops.—The owner of cattle or other domestic animals or a person having possession and control of them is liable for all damage done by the cattle or animals to the lands and crops of another enclosed by a legal fence as defined in this chapter. A person bringing an action for damages has a lien on the cattle or other domestic animals for damage done by them.

Impounding animals breaking into enclosed area. (a) If a domestic animal breaks into an enclosure surrounded by a legal fence, the owner or occupant of the enclosure may take the trespassing animal into his possession, and keep it until all damages, together with reasonable charges for keeping and feeding the animal, are paid. Within 24 hours after taking the animal into his possession, the owner or occupant shall give notice to the owner or claimant of the animal that he has taken up the animal or, if the owner or claimant is unknown, he must post a like notice at some public place near the enclosure. If the owner fails to claim the animal and pay the reasonable charges incurred for keeping and feeding it within five days after the receipt or posting of the notice the animal shall be dealt with as in the case of an estray.

Estrays

Record of estrays. District magistrates and deputy magistrates shall keep a record of estrays, showing claims, notices, awards, orders, affidavits and proceedings relative to estrays.

Who may impound. Any person, or his agent, upon whose premises any estray is running at large, may impound the estray in a reasonably safe place.

Surrender of estray to owner upon payment of expenses and damages. If the owner or person entitled to the possession of the estray proves prior to the expiration of the 10-day period, his ownership of or possessory right to the estray, the impounder shall immediately surrender possession to him upon his paying the impounder $1 for the impounder's services, a reasonable rate for keeping the animal and payment for any damages the estray has caused to the property of the impounder. If at the time of impounding the estray, the impounder knows the owner or person entitled to the possession but fails to notify him as required by this chapter, the impounder may not recover for impounding, posting or keeping the estray.

Transportation, Storage and Agistment.

Persons entitled to carrier, warehouse, and livestock liens. The following persons shall have liens upon personal property for their just and reasonable charges for the labor, care, and attention bestowed and the food furnished, and may retain possession of the property until the charges are paid:

(1) a person who is a common carrier, or who, at the request of the owner or lawful possessor of personal property, carriers, conveys, or transports the property from one place to another;

(2) a person who safely keeps or stores grain, wares, merchandise, and personal property at the request of the owner or lawful possessor of the property; and

(3) a person who pastures or feeds horses, cattle, hogs, sheep, or other livestock, or bestows labor, care, or attention upon the livestock at the request of the owner or lawful possessor of the livestock.

Brands and marks. Any person having cattle, sheep, horses, mules or asses, may adopt a brand or mark. After recording the brand or mark as provided in this chapter, the person has the exclusive right to its use.

Record of ownership. The owner may brand or mark an animal on either side with his brand or mark. The animal shall be branded or marked so that the brand or mark shows distinctly. Sheep may be marked distinctly with a mark or device to distinguish them readily when they become intermixed with other flocks of sheep owned in the state. No evidence of ownership by brand or mark may be permitted in any court in this state unless the brand or mark is recorded as provided in this chapter.

Recording. (a) to adopt a brand or mark, a person shall forward to the commissioner of natural resources a facsimile of the brand or mark, together with a written application, and the recording fee of $2. Upon receipt, the commissioner shall record the brand or mark unless it is of record or conflicts or closely resembles that of some other person, in which case the commissioner shall return the facsimile and fee to the applicant. No brand described as being on either side of the animal shall be accepted or recorded.

(b) The commissioner shall file all brands or marks offered for record pending examination. The commissioner shall make an examination as promptly as possible, and if the brand or mark is accepted, ownership thereof vests from the date of filing. The recording of the brand or mark gives the applicant ownership thereof until the next renewal period. A renewal period occurs every five years, beginning with January 1, 1960. At least 90 days before the expiration of each renewal period, the commissioner shall notify every owner of a recorded brand or mark of the renewal period and the owner shall pay to the commissioner a renewal fee of $1 and furnish other information as may be required. The renewal fee is due and payable on or before January 1 of the renewal year, and if an owner fails, refuses or neglects to pay the renewal fee by March 1, of the renewal year, the brand or mark is forfeited and becomes available for issuance to another applicant.

Copy of record; procurement; fee. Upon the recording of a brand or mark, the commissioner shall furnish the owner with a certified copy of the record. Additional certified copies of the record may be obtained by anyone upon the payment of $1 for each copy.

Use without certificate prohibited. It is unlawful to brand any horse, cattle, mule or ass, unless the person using the brand holds a written certificate of acceptance from the commissioner.

Penalty for use without certificate. Any person who violates § 50 of this chapter is guilty of a misdemeanor, and upon conviction is punishable by a fine of not less than $50 nor more than $300.

Brand is personal property. Any recorded brand or mark is the property of the person causing the record to be made, and is subject to sale, assignment, transfer, devise and descent, as personal property. Instruments of writing evidencing the sale, assignment or transfer of the brand or mark shall be recorded by the commissioner, and the fee for recording the sale, assignment or transfer is $1. The recording of the instrument is notice to all persons of the matter recorded. Certified copies are admissible in evidence.

Record is evidence of ownership. In all actions and proceedings in which the title to animals is an issue, the certified copy provided for in this chapter is prima facie evidence of ownership of the animal by the person whose brand or mark it may be.

Arizona

*Civil and criminal liability of person allowing
stock to run at large within no-fence district*

The owner or person in charge of livestock, who knowingly, wilfully, carelessly or negligently allows or permits livestock to run at large within a no-fence district is guilty of a misdemeanor, and in addition is liable for damages for any trespass as provided for the collection of damages by owners of land enclosed within lawful fences.

Garages and livery stables

A. Proprietors of public stables shall have a lien on all animals placed with them for feed or care and upon vehicles or other equipment placed in their care for the amount of the charges against them.

B. Proprietors of garages, repair and service stations shall have a lien upon motor vehicles of every kind, and the parts and accessories placed thereon, for labor, materials, supplies and storage for the amount of the charges, when the amount of the charges is agreed to by the proprietor and the owner.

C. The lien shall not impair any other lien or conditional sale of record at the time the labor, materials, supplies and storage were commenced to be furnished, unless furnished with the knowledge and consent of the record lienor or vendor.

Lien for service charges of stallion

Upon filing the statement and posting the certificate, the services of the stallion, from the date of such service, shall be a lien on each mare served, together with the foal of the mare resulting from the service, for the amount agreed upon between the parties at the time of service, or if there is no agreement, then in an amount specified in the statement. Notice of the lien shall be filed within six months after the service in the office of the county recorder of the county in which the stallion is owned or stands, giving the date of service, description of mare, name of owner and amount for which a lien is claimed. The lien shall expire at the end of one year from the date of filing the notice, unless within that time an action is commenced to foreclose the lien.

Owner of stallion in service to file statement and post certificate

Every person having the custody or control of a stallion for service, before advertising or offering such service to the public for compensation, shall file with the county recorder of the county in which he resides, or in which the stallion is kept for service, a written statement giving the name, age, pedigree and record, if known, and if not known, that they are unknown, the description, terms and conditions upon which the stallion will serve. The recorder shall record the statement upon payment of a fee in a book kept for that purpose, and issue a certificate that the statement has been filed in his office. A copy so filed and recorded shall be posted in a conspicuous place in each locality in which the stallion is kept for service.

Giving false pedigree; penalty

Any person who files or publishes a false pedigree, record or statement regarding a stallion, or who neglects or refuses to comply with the provisions of above section, shall forfeit all fees for services of the stallion, and is guilty of a misdemeanor. The person deceived or defrauded may sue and recover damages sustained by reason of false representation.

Allowing poor-bred stallion to run at large; penalty

A person who permits a stallion over two years old to run at large upon the range, unless the stallion is of some recognized good breed of horses, is guilty of a misdemeanor punishable by a fine of not less than twenty-five nor more than three hundred dollars.

Arkansas

Running at large unlawful when prohibited by initiated act —Liability for damage to crops—Lien for crop injury.—In all counties of this State where there has been, or may be, submitted to the people by Initiative Petition a proposed act prohibiting horses, mules, cattle, hogs, sheep and goats, or any of them, from running at large in said county or counties and at an election held pursuant thereto the electors voting thereon have enacted, or shall enact, such act, it shall be unlawful from the effective date of such act for any such animals, at any time during the year, to run at large and enter in and upon the fields and lands of said county or counties either enclosed or unenclosed; and in every such case of trespass by animals described and prohibited by such Initiated Act, the owner of such animal or animals shall be liable in damages for all damages they may do, to the person or persons owning such crops to be established and recovered in a civil action, and a lien shall exist against such animal or animals in favor of the person whose crops may have been damaged or destroyed and they may be sold under an order of the court rendering judgment for such damages to which shall be added any and all costs of taking up, feeding and caring for such animal or animals and the costs.

Stallion or jack running at large—Penalty.—If any seed horse or any unaltered mule or jack, over the age of two [2] years, be found running at large, the owner shall be fined, for the first offense, three dollars [$3.00]; and for every subsequent offense not exceeding ten dollars [$10.00], to be recovered by action (of debt) in the name of any person who shall sue for the same; one-half [½] to his own use, and the other to the county's; which action may be prosecuted before any justice of the peace of the county where the offense is committed, and shall also be liable for all damages that may be sustained by the running at large of any such seed horse, jack or mule, to be recovered by an action (of debt), before any court having jurisdiction thereof.

Right of person taking up.—Any person may take up any such seed horse, mule or jack found running at large, and if not claimed within two [2] days, may castrate him; for which service he shall be entitled to recover of the owner of any such horse, mule or jack, three dollars [$3.00], which may be recovered in an action (of debt), before any justice of the peace of the county.

Method of castration.—Such castration shall be done in the usual manner, so that the life of the animal shall be endangered as little as possible.

Right to kill stallions and jacks—Notice.—If any such horse, mule or jack be running at large, and cannot be taken up, he may be killed, if notice be first put up at the courthouse, and at three [3] other of the most public places in the county, for ten [10] days, describing the color, marks and brands, as near as practicable, of the animal, and that he will be killed unless taken away and secured.

Livery stable keepers', agistors', and wagon yard keepers' liens.—Hereafter all persons in this state, keepers of livery, sale or feed stables or wagon yards, shall have a lien on all horses, mules or other stock, or other property, left in their charge to be kept, fed, sold or otherwise cared for and sheltered, for all their reasonable costs and charges for feeding, keeping and otherwise taking care of the same; for which lien such stable or wagon yard keeper are hereby authorized to keep possession of any of the aforementioned property until such reasonable

charges are paid or tendered to them or their agents by the
owner of the same, or his or her agent; and in case any such
property shall be left with such stable or wagon yard keeper,
and not be called for by the owner thereof, and the charges
and costs paid thereon to such keeper before such charges and
costs shall amount to the value thereof, and the cost of selling
the same, as hereinafter provided, it shall be lawful for such
stable or wagon yard keeper to cause the same to be sold in the
manner prescribed in section two [§ 51-904] of this act.

*Lien for service of male animal—Penalty for disposing of
female or offspring without consent.*—The owner of any male
animal, kept for the propagation of his species, shall have a lien
upon any female animal and her offspring to which such male
is let for the sum contracted therefor, which lien shall attach
at the time of service of such male and shall not be lost by
reason of any sale, exchange or removal from the county or
other disposition without consent of the person holding the
lien [in which case] the same may be immediately enforced.
Provided, also, upon the sale, exchange removal or disposition
of such female animal without consent of person holding the
lien or with intent to defraud him, the owner of such female
animal shall be guilty of a misdemeanor and, upon conviction
thereof shall be fined in any sum not less than twenty-five
[$25.00] dollars nor more than fifty [$50.00] dollars.

California

*Lien for services: Manufacture, alteration, or repair of prop-
erty: What persons to have liens.*—Every person who, while
lawfully in possession of an article of personal property renders
any service to the owner thereof, by labor or skill, employed
for the protection, improvement, safekeeping, or carriage
thereof, has a special lien thereon, dependent on possession, for
the compensation, if any, which is due to him from the owner
for such service; a person who makes, alters, or repairs any
article of personal property, at the request of the owner, or

legal possessor of the property, has a lien on the same for his reasonable charges for the balance due for such work done and materials furnished, and may retain possession of the same until the charges are paid; and livery or boarding or feed stable or feed yard proprietors, and persons pasturing horses or stock, have a lien, dependent on possession, for their compensation in caring for, boarding, feeding, or pasturing such horses or stock; and foundry proprietors and persons conducting a foundry business, have a lien, dependent on possession, upon all patterns in their hands belonging to a customer, for the balance due them from such customers for foundry work; and laundry proprietors and persons conducting a laundry business, and dry cleaning establishment proprietors and persons conducting a dry cleaning establishment, have a general lien, dependent on possession, upon all personal property in their hands belonging to a customer, for the balance due them from such customer for laundry work, and for the balance due them from such customers for dry cleaning work, but nothing in this section shall be construed to confer a lien in favor of a wholesale dry cleaner on materials received from a dry cleaning establishment proprietor or a person conducting a dry cleaning establishment; and veterinary proprietors and veterinary surgeons shall have a lien dependent on possession, for their compensation in caring for, boarding, feeding, and medical treatment of animals; and keepers of garages for automobiles shall have a lien, dependent on possession for their compensation in caring for and safekeeping, and for making repairs and performing any labor upon or furnishing supplies or materials for such automobiles; and keepers of trailer parks shall have a lien, dependent on possession, for their compensation for rental of parking space for trailers, and for such other services as are furnished to the owners or legal possessors of trailers at their request; provided, however, that where the possession of, or lien upon, any automobile or trailer held under a claim of lien hereunder is lost by reason of fraud, trick or device, the repossession of said automobile or trailer by said garage keeper or trailer park keeper shall revive the lien so lost; provided, further, that any lien thus revived shall be subordinate to any sale, lien, encumbrance, right, title or interest in such automobile or trailer acquired or exercised in good faith and for value by any person between the time of loss of possession and the time of repossession.

Advertising animal as having pedigree other than true pedigree thereof: Forfeiture of right to collect for animal's services.— Every person who wilfully advertises any cattle, horse, sheep, swine, or other domestic animal for purposes of copulation or profit as having a pedigree other than the true pedigree of such animal shall forfeit all right by law to collect pay for the services of such animal.

Breeding of mares or jennies within municipality

A person shall not let to mares or jennies any stallion or jack within the limits of any city, town, or village, or within 400 yards of it, except in an inclosure which is sufficient to obstruct the view of all the inhabitants within such limits.

Running at large of stallions, etc.

A person in charge of any stallion, bull, boar, ram, or male goat shall not turn out or permit such animal to be turned out or to run at large.

Misdemeanor: Fine: Imprisonment

A violation of any provision of this chapter is a misdemeanor punishable by a fine of not less than five dollars ($5) or more than twenty dollars ($20), or by imprisonment in the county jail not less than 30 days, or by both such fine and imprisonment.

Brands

Any person that desires to use a brand on horses, mules, burros, or sheep shall be governed *by the same provisions and procedures with reference to such animals* as are made applicable to the branding of cattle in Chapter 4.

Liability of owner, etc., of animal killing or injuring animals or poultry: Scienter unnecessary: Killing of such animal: Acci-

dental killing or injury.—The owner, possessor, or harborer of any dog or other animal, that shall, on the premises of any person other than the owner, possessor, or harborer of such dog or other animal, kill, worry, or wound any bovine animal, swine, horse, mule, burro, sheep, angora goat, or cashmere goat, or poultry, shall be liable to the owner of the same for the damages and costs of suit, to be recovered in any court of competent jurisdiction:

Colorado

Owner may recover for trespass.— (1) Any person maintaining in good repair a lawful fence as described in section 8-13-1, may recover damages for trespass and injury to grass, garden or vegetable products or other crops of such person from the owner of any livestock which break through such fence. No person shall recover damages for such a trespass or injury unless at the time thereof such grass, garden or vegetable products or crops were protected by such a lawful fence. Even though such land, grass, garden or vegetable products or other crops were not at such time protected on all side by a lawful fence, if it is proved by clear and convincing evidence that livestock have broken through a lawful fence on one side of such land to reach such land, grass, products or crops, recovery and the remedies under this section may be had the same as if such land, grass, products or crops had been at such time protected on all sides by a lawful fence.

(2) Whenever any person stocks land, not enclosed by a lawful fence, on which such person has a lawful right to pasture or forage livestock, with a greater number of livestock than such land can properly support or water and any of such livestock pasture, forage or water on the lands of another person in order to obtain the proper amount of pasture, forage or water, or whenever any person stocks with livestock land on which such person has no lawful right to pasture or forage livestock and such livestock pasture, forage or water on such land or on other land on which such person has no right to pasture or forage livestock, any such person so stocking land

shall be deemed a trespasser, liable in damages and subject to injunction.

(3) All damages sustained on account of the foregoing trespasses may be recovered, together with costs of court and arbitration, and the livestock so trespassing may be taken up by the person damaged and held as security for the payment of such damages and costs. A court of competent jurisdiction in any proper case may issue an injunction to prevent further trespasses. In any action for trespass where the injury complained of shall have been aggravated and attended by a willful or reckless disregard of the injured person's rights, the board of arbitration, court or jury may in addition to awarding actual damages include reasonable exemplary damages. Recovery may be had under this section either in a court of law, or by arbitration as provided in section 8-13-3.

Grazing on roads and in municipalities—penalty.— (1) It shall be unlawful for the owner or any person in charge of any livestock knowingly to cause or permit such livestock to graze or run at large in any incorporated or unincorporated municipality, lane, road or public highway provided the same is separated from the land or range of such owner or person in charge by a fence or other barrier sufficient to keep livestock from reaching such municipality, lane, road or public highway. In case any such livestock so running at large shall be killed or injured by any vehicle of whatsoever nature, the owner, driver or person in charge of such vehicle shall not be liable therefor, provided the killing or injury shall not be malicious, willful or wanton. Nothing in this section shall be ap-

Stallions and jacks licensed.—It shall be unlawful for any person, company or corporation to stand any stallion or jack for public service in the state of Colorado without first having obtained from the state board of stock inspection commissioners a license authorizing such public service. Such license shall be issued by the state board of stock inspection commissioners, who shall charge and collect a fee of five dollars for such license, and shall authorize the public service of such stallion or jack for the calendar year of the year issued and shall state whether the stallion so licensed is a purebred registered stallion or a grade stallion, as the case may be. All such fees shall be deposited with the state treasurer and by him credited to the general funds of the state to be used for the general purposes of the state pursuant to appropriations made by law.

Application for license.—Before any license shall be issued for the public service of any stallion or jack, an application shall be made therefor upon suitable blanks to be provided by the state board of stock inspection commissioners, and in case of a purebred stallion or jack, the application shall be accompanied by the certificate of registration and in case of a grade stallion or jack the application shall be accompanied by an affidavit sworn to by either owner or breeder on suitable blank form provided by the state board of inspection commissioners, giving all necessary information regarding the breeding of said grade stallion or jack, including the registry number of either parent and name of breeder. For the purpose of this article, a purebred stallion or jack is one that is registered in a book, recognized by the national registry board, and a grade stallion or jack is one whose either parent is registered in a book recognized by the national registry board. A stallion or jack whose parents are purebred but of different breeds shall be licensed as a grade. The license shall state in large type that the animal licensed is a purebred stallion or jack, or that it is a grade stallion or jack, as the case may be, and it shall give the breed, age, color, marking and name or names of breeder and owner.

Veterinarian's certificate—fee.—There shall accompany each application for a license a certificate from some licensed veterinarian of the state of Colorado or federal veterinarian, stating that the stallion or jack sought to be licensed is not afflicted with any of the diseases or unsoundnesses known as roaring, ringbone, chorea, St. Vitus dance, crampiness, shivering, string halt, bone spavin, bog spavin, specific ophthalmia, moon blindness, curb, when accompanied with curby conformation, or any form of venereal or other contagious diseases. Any stallion or jack that is a ridgling or that is deformed or afflicted with any of the diseases or unsoundnesses above mentioned shall not be imported into Colorado to be used for breeding purposes or if in the state, shall not be licensed for service in the state, and it shall be unlawful for any person, company or corporation to stand any such stallion or jack for public service in this state; provided, that in securing the certificate from any licensed veterinarian on the examination of any such stallion or jack sought to be licensed, it shall be unlawful for any licensed veterinarian to charge more than three dollars and actual expenses as fee for such service.

Revocation of license.—Should the attention of the state agricultural commission be called to the fact that any stallion or jack being stood for public service under a license is afflicted with any of the diseases named in section 8-9-3, it shall be the duty of the state agricultural commission to make an examination of such animal, and if the animal is found to be afflicted, it shall be the duty of the state agricultural commission to report the same to the state board of stock inspection commissioners, who shall revoke the license of said animal and cancel the same, and thereafter such stallion or jack so afflicted shall not be allowed to stand for public service in this state.

Posting and exhibition of licenses.—Any person who shall offer the breeding services of any stallion or jack to the public in this state, or make a charge for such service, shall have a license and shall keep such license posted in a prominent place on or near the stall where the said stallion or jack is kept or if the stallion or jack is upon the road being vended for service, then the person in charge of said stallion or jack shall carry or exhibit such license to the owner in charge or care of any mare to be served by said stallion or jack, and such license must be shown for the inspection of any person desiring the service of the stallion or jack, or who may for any reason desire to see such license.

Offenses—penalty.—Any person, company or corporation, who shall violate any of the provisions of sections 8-9-1 to 8-9-7, or who shall change the color markings of any stallion or jack, or give false verbal or written statements regarding the breeding of any stallion or jack with the intent to deceive, shall be deemed guilty of a misdemeanor and upon conviction thereof in any court of competent jurisdiction shall be fined a sum not to exceed one hundred dollars or may be imprisoned in the county jail not to exceed thirty days, or both such fine and imprisonment, at the discretion of the court.

Lien of agistor and landlord.—Any ranchman, farmer, agistor, herder of cattle, livery stable keeper, veterinarian or other person to whom horses, mules, asses, cattle, sheep, hogs, dogs, cats or other domestic animals shall be entrusted for the purpose of feeding, herding, pasturing, keeping, ranching, boarding or medical care, shall have a lien upon such horses, mules, asses, cattle, sheep, hogs, dogs, cats or other domestic animals for the amount that may be due for such feeding, herding, pasturing, keeping, ranching, boarding or medical care, and for all costs incurred in enforcing such lien. The keeper of any hotel, tavern, or boarding house, or trailer court, or any person who rents furnished or unfurnished rooms, or trailer space, or any owner or operator of any apartment house consisting of rooms or suites of rooms rented, furnished for the housekeeping purposes of the tenant shall have a lien upon all the personal property of any kind then being upon the rental premises belonging to his patrons, boarders, guests, or tenants, for such boarding, lodging, or rent, and for all costs incurred in enforcing such lien. The provisions of this section shall not apply to stolen livestock. The lien hereby given shall secure obligations contracted for rent due in advance for thirty days in like manner with obligations for the past use and occupation.

Agistor's contract to be recorded.—All contracts, or copies thereof, made by the owner of any animals, such as sheep, bovine cattle, horses, or of any other kind, with any other person for the herding or caring for the same for pay, or on shares, or in any other manner, may be filed with the county clerk of the county where the owners or either of them reside, if they reside in the state, and if the owners, or either of them, do not reside in the state, then the copies may be filed with the county clerk of the county in which the contract may have been made.

Brands on livestock—evidence.—It shall be lawful to mark cattle and horses with the owner's brand. When animals are brought into this state from another state or territory, in transit beyond the boundaries of this state, the brand, or a copy thereof, duly certified to by the proper officer in each state or territory, shall be received in evidence, with like force and effect as a brand duly recorded in this state.

Connecticut

Damage by animals

All damage done within enclosures by cattle, horses, asses, mules, sheep, swine or goats, when the fence is sufficient, shall be paid by the owner of the animals. No person shall recover for damage done within his enclosure by reason of the insufficiency of his fence, unless done by animals at large contrary to law, or by unruly cattle that are not restrained by ordinary fences; or unless the owner of animals puts them into or voluntarily trespasses on such enclosure; or unless they entered through a part of the fence which was sufficient; in all of which cases the owner of the land may impound them and recover poundage and damages.

Lien on animals, birds and fish for their keep

When a special agreement has been made between the owner of any animals, including birds and fish, and any person who keeps and feeds such animals, regarding the price of such keeping, such animals shall be subject to a lien, for the price of such keeping, in favor of the person keeping the same; and such person so keeping such animals may detain the same until such debt is paid; and, if it is not paid within thirty days after it is due, he may sell such animals, or so many thereof as are necessary, at public auction, upon giving written notice to the owner of the time and place of such sale at least six days before such sale, and apply the proceeds to the payment of such debts, returning the surplus, if any, to such owner.

Trespasser's act; proceedings; penalty

If the animal so seized has been running at large or trespassing through the wilful act of any third person or without negligence or the knowledge or permission of its owner, such owner shall be entitled to its possession, upon paying to the party aggrieved all just damages occasioned by such animal and to the town clerk and constable their legal fees and disbursements, and without paying any other charges. Any person committing such wilful act shall be fined twenty dollars or imprisoned not less than thirty days or both and shall be liable to the person making the seizure for all damages sustained by him through such act.

Animals not to go at large on highway

Any person entitled to the custody of any horse, ass, mule, neat cattle, sheep, goat, swine or goose, who permits the same to be at large upon any highway or common without a keeper, shall be fined not more than seven dollars.

False pretenses as to pedigree of animal

Any person who, by any false pretense, device or representation, obtains from any club, association, society or company for improving the breed of cattle, horses, sheep, swine or other domestic animals the registration of any animal in the herd register or other register of any such club, association, society or company or the transfer of any such registration or who knowingly gives a false pedigree of any such animal shall be imprisoned not more than one year or fined not more than five hundred dollars or both.

Delaware

Liability for trespasses; fence-viewers to assess damages

If any horse, cattle, goat, sheep, or hog, trespasses on any grounds enclosed with lawful fence, the owner of the animal, so trespassing, shall pay such damages as shall be awarded by the fence-viewers. Any person having unruly horses, goats, sheep, hogs, or cattle, which break through lawful fences, shall, after notice thereof, be liable for double damages for any trespass committed by such animal, after such notice, to be awarded by the fence-viewers.

Collection of lien by public sale; notice of sale; warrant for seizure; disposition of proceeds; loss of lien

(a) Any hotel-keeper, inn-keeper, garage owner or other person who keeps a livery or boarding stable or garage, and for price or reward at such stable or garage, furnishes food or care for any horse, or has the custody or care of any carriage, cart, wagon, sleigh, motor vehicle or other vehicle, or any harness, robes, or other equipments for the same, shall have a lien upon such horse, carriage, cart, wagon, sleigh, motor vehicle or other vehicle, harness, robes or equipments, and the right to detain the same to secure the payment of such price or reward.

(b) The lienor may, subject to the provisions hereinafter contained, after the expiration of 30 days from the time the same or any part thereof became due and payable, the same remaining unpaid in whole or in part, sell the property, upon which he has such lien at public sale, at such livery or boarding stable or garage, to the highest and best bidder or bidders therefor, first giving at least 10 days' notice of such sale by hand-bills posted in 5 or more public places in the county in which the sale is to be had and by advertisement in a newspaper published in the County, describing the property to be sold and naming the day, hour and place of sale thereof.

(c) The lienor may apply the money arising from the sale to the payment of the amount then remaining due, including therein compensation at the same rate as such stipulated price or reward for food, care or custody furnished or bestowed up to the time of sale, together with the costs and expenses of sale.

(d) In case either before or after the price or reward has become due and payable, the keeper of such stable or garage has parted with the possession or custody of the property subject to such lien, he may, if the contract for food, care or custody was made with the owner of the aforementioned property, at any time within the space of 10 days from the time of such parting with the possession or custody thereof, make an affidavit, to be filed in the office of a justice of the peace of the county in which such stable or garage is situated, describing such property and stating the amount of such price or reward then remaining due and payable, from whom owing, and that the same is justly and truly due. Thereupon, the justice of the peace shall forthwith issue to a constable a warrant for the seizure of such property and for the delivery thereof to the keeper of such stable or garage. The constable shall forthwith, at any place within such county, seize and deliver such property pursuant to such warrant. Thereafter the keeper of such stable or garage may, unless there has been a previous execution and levy, for an amount exceeding the value of the property, or unless such property has been sold fairly for a valuable consideration and delivered to the purchaser after the keeper of such stable or garage has parted with its possession or custody and before such seizure thereof, sell the same in manner aforesaid, after giving notice as aforesaid, and may apply the money arising from such sale in manner aforesaid.

(e) The balance, if any, of the proceeds of sale shall be paid to the owner or owners of the property sold; but in case such owner or owners cannot be found such balance shall be deposited in the Farmers' Bank of the State of Delaware, for the county in which such sale has been had, to the credit of such owner or owners.

False registration of animals; penalty

Whoever, by any false pretense, obtains from any club, association, society, or company for improving the breed of cattle, horses, sheep, swine or other domestic animals, a certificate of registration of any animal in the herd register or other register of any club, association, society or company, or a transfer of any registration, or knowingly gives a false pedigree of any animal, shall be fined not more than $500 or imprisoned not more than one year, or both.

Lien upon colts and mule-colts for service of sire

(a) Every colt and mule-colt in this State shall be liable for the service of the stallion or jack that sires it. In any cases where the pedigree or qualities of the stallion or jack are misrepresented by the owner or agent thereof, the foal shall not be liable for the services.

(b) In order for the owner of any stallion or jack to avail himself of the benefits of this section, the owner shall have printed and posted, at ten of the most public places in the county in which the stallion or jack is to stand or travel, a full description and pedigree of his stallion or jack, and exhibit a copy to the owner of any mare to be served by the stallion or jack. After 60 days from the day the foal was dropped, and a refusal to pay by the then owner of the mare or colt or mule-colt, as the case may be, the owner of the stallion or jack, the sire of the colt or mule-colt, shall bring an action for the service of the stallion or jack, as per agreement.

(c) Any justice of the peace of the county shall have full and complete jurisdiction to hear and give judgment in any such action. If the justice of the peace is satisfied of the correctness of the claim and gives judgment in favor of the owner of the stallion or jack, as the case may be, the owner may at once take out execution on the judgment, and when so executed, the lien shall revert back to the day of the foaling of the colt or mule-colt and shall be a paramount and prior lien upon the colt or mule-colt, as the case may be, paramount and prior to any other execution or mortgage upon the same.

Liability for stallions at large

The owner, or keeper, of a stallion over eighteen months old, shall be liable for any damages happening in consequence of his being at large, and if such owner, or keeper, after being admonished to confine the horse, suffers him to go at large out of his enclosed ground, he shall forfeit and pay, to anyone who will sue, the sum of five dollars.

District of Columbia

Lien of liverymen.

It shall be lawful for all persons keeping or boarding any animals at livery within the District, under any agreement with the owner thereof, to detain such animals until all charges under such agreement for the care, keep, or board of such animals shall have been paid: *Provided, however,* That before enforcing the lien hereby given notice in writing shall be given to such owner in person or by registered mail at his last-known place of residence of the amount of such charges and the intention to detain such animal or animals until such charges shall be paid.

Florida

Duty of owner

No owner shall permit livestock to run at large on or stray upon the public roads of this state.

Liability of owner

Every owner of livestock who intentionally, willfully, carelessly or negligently suffers or permits such livestock to run at large upon or stray upon the public roads of this state shall be liable in damages for all injury and property damage sustained by any person by reason thereof.

Definitions.—In construing this act the following words, phrases or terms shall be held to mean:

(1) "Livestock" shall include all animals of the equine, bovine or swine class, including goats, sheep, mules, horses, hogs, cattle and other grazing animals.

(2) "Owner" shall include any person, association, firm or corporation, natural or artificial, owning or having custody of or in charge of livestock.

(3) "Running at large" or "straying" shall mean any live-

stock found or being on any public roads of this state and not under manual control of a person.

(4) "Public roads" as used herein shall mean those highways within the state which are, or may be, maintained by the state road department, including the full width of the right of way.

Liens for care and maintenance of animals

In favor of all persons feeding or caring for the horse or other animal of another, including all keepers of livery, sale or feed or feed stables, for feeding or taking care of any horse or other animal put in their charge; upon such horse or other animal.

Liens for feed, etc., for raising horses, polo ponies and race dogs

In favor of any person who shall furnish corn, oats, hay, grain or other feed or feed stuffs or straw or bedding material to or upon the order of the owner, or the agent, bailee, lessee, or custodian of the owner, of any race horse, polo pony or race dog, for the unpaid portion of the price of such supplies upon every race horse, polo pony or race dog which consumes any part of such supplies.

Lien for service of stallions and other animals

In favor of owners of stallions, jackasses or bulls, upon the colt or calf of the get of said stallion, jackass or bull, and also upon the mare, jenny or cow served by said stallion, jackass or bull in breeding thereof for the sum stipulated to be paid for the service thereof, by filing at any time within eighteen months after the date of service a statement of the account thereof, together with the description as to color and markings of the female served, and the name of the owner at the date of service, in the office of the county clerk of the county wherein the owner of the said female resided at the time of service. Neither the mare, jenny or cow, nor the get thereof, shall be sold within eighteen months after the date of service, unless the service fee shall be paid, unless such sale shall be agreed to and approved in writing by the owner of the stallion, jackass or bull at the time of the sale or transfer of the mare, jenny or cow, or offspring thereof. At any time after such mare, jenny or cow shall conceive, any one having the lien herein provided, may enforce the same in the same manner as is now provided by law.

Stud-horse or ass running at large may be gelded by permission of justice of peace

It shall not be lawful for any stud-horse or ass to run at large, and if any such shall be found running at large, any person may take up the same, and having taken him before the justice of the peace of the district, may geld the same stud-horse or ass, with the permission of the justice, taking care that the operation be performed by a person usually doing such business, for which the person so gelding shall receive five dollars, to be paid by the owner of the horse or ass, to be recovered from him by summary proceedings before a justice of the peace. But if any person shall take up and geld such stud-horse or ass contrary to this section, or without fully pursuing the directions of this section, he shall for every such offense forfeit to the party injured double the value of such horse or ass, to be recovered in a court of competent jurisdiction.

Georgia

Trespass by animal upon inclosure not protected by lawful fence.—In any county which has not adopted the stock law if any trespass or damage shall be committed in any inclosure, not protected by lawful fence, by the breaking in of any animal, the owner of such animal shall not be liable to answer for the trespass; and if the owner of the inclosure shall kill or injure such animal in any manner, he shall be liable in three times the damage.

Landowner prohibited from killing trespassing animal. Liability of owner of animal.—When fences are made pursuant to law and any animal shall break in, the owner of the inclosure shall not kill or injure him for the first breaking, and not until after notice shall be given to the owner or agent, if possible, but said last-mentioned owner shall be liable for double the damages done by his stock.

Animals to be confined.—In any county which shall adopt the stock law no horse, mule, cow, or hog, or any other animal or animals, used or fit either for food or labor, shall be permitted to run at large beyond the limits of the lands of its owner or manager.

Impounding permitted, when.—If any of the animals enumerated in the foregoing section shall commit any trespass or damage, or shall be found going at large on the premises of any person other than the owner of such animals or stock, whether inclosed or uninclosed, and whether such animals wandered from the premises of the owner in the county in which the trespass was committed or from another county, the owner of such premises may impound such animals and retain them until the owner thereof shall make full satisfaction or reparation for the damages committed by such animals, including all costs and expenses, unless disposed of according to the provisions of the following sections.

How impounded animals disposed of; damages, how assessed. —In case any of the said animals shall be impounded under the provisions of the preceding section, the person so impounding them shall give all necessary care, feed, and attention, for which he shall have such compensation as is allowed sheriffs for like care, feed, and attention to stock. It shall also be his duty to give the owner, if known, notice of the fact of such impounding in 24 hours, and if not known or ascertained within three days from the taking up and impounding, such animals shall be disposed of as provided by law in cases of estrays.

Liens on get of stallions, etc; record; priorities.—The owner or keeper of any stallion, jack, or blooded or imported bull or boar shall have a lien upon the get thereof, for the service of such stallion, jack, or blooded or imported bull or boar, for the period of one year from the birth of such get, which lien shall be superior to all other liens, except the lien for taxes. The lien herein provided for shall not become operative unless the same be recorded in the office of the clerk of the superior court of the county wherein the owner of the mother resides, within six months after the performance of the service; and said clerk shall keep a book in which all such liens are to be recorded, and said clerk shall receive 25 cents each for recording such liens: Provided, said animals shall be kept by the owners thereof inclosed in their own pastures or otherwise.

Livery-stable keepers.—Livery-stable keepers shall have a lien for their charges on the stock placed in their care for keeping, which shall be superior to other liens, except liens for taxes, special liens of landlords for rent, liens of laborers, and all general liens of which they had actual notice before the property claimed to be subject to lien came into their control, to which excepted liens they shall be inferior.

Enforcement of livery-stable keepers' liens.—In addition to the manner in this Code provided, every livery-stable keeper may assert the lien on stock placed in his care for keeping, by reducing to writing a statement of the amount due him for the care of said stock, a description of the stock on which said lien is claimed, making affidavit thereto, and recording the same in the clerk's office of the superior court of the county where said service was rendered. When said lien is so recorded, it shall have the same dignity and effect as is now given by law to the lien of livery-stable keepers where they retain possession of the stock placed in their keeping, which lien shall be recorded while such property is in the possession of such livery-stable keeper, and as mortgages on personalty are required to be recorded; said liens may be foreclosed as mortgages on personalty are now foreclosed by law.

Special lien of bailee for hire of labor and service.—The bailee for hire of labor and service shall have a special lien upon the thing bailed for his labor and services until he parts with possession; and if he delivers up a part, the lien shall attach to the remainder in his possession for the entire claim under the same contract.

Hawaii

Trespass on fenced cultivated land. If any cattle, horse, mule, ass, swine, sheep, or goat, trespasses on any properly fenced cultivated ground, the owner thereof shall pay to the owner of the land the full amount of damage or loss occasioned by the estray to the land owner, and 50 cents for each animal trespassing, excepting for sheep and goats, for which he shall pay 10 cents each; provided, that if in any particular case this provision shall have an onerous or unjust bearing, owing to the large number of animals trespassing, the court may diminish the forfeiture.

On unfenced cultivated land. If any of the animals trespasses on any unfenced, cultivated ground, the owner thereof shall pay to the owner of the land 25 cents for each animal trespassing, excepting for sheep and goats, for which he shall pay 10 cents each. The owner of the land shall not be entitled to claim any damages for the trespass other than the sum of 25 cents; provided, that if in any particular case this provision shall have an onerous or unjust bearing, owing to the large number of animals trespassing, the court may diminish the forfeiture.

On uncultivated land. If any of the animals trespasses on any properly fenced uncultivated land, the owner of the animals shall pay to the owner of the land 25 cents for the trespass of each animal, except for sheep and goats, for which he shall pay 10 cents each, and if any damage is done by the animals, the owner thereof shall further pay to the land owner the full amount of the damage.

On public roads, lands. If any animal trespasses or strays on any of the government roads in and around the city of Honolulu, town and district of Hilo, towns of Wailuku and Lahaina, or upon any government road bounded on both sides by legal fence, or upon any government land, any police officer or such person as may be thereunto authorized in writing by the board of supervisors, or city council, may take up the animal and impound the same as the board or council shall provide. The owner of the animals so taken up or impounded shall pay to the police officer or such person as may be authorized not more than $1.50 for each animal so trespassing as expenses incurred in taking up, driving and impounding the animal, together with all pound fees as provided in any ordinance relating thereto. If any damage is done by the animals, the owner thereof shall further pay such amount as shall be fixed by the board or council. In case the charges and pound fees are not paid, the animals impounded shall be sold at public auction as provided by any ordinance relating thereto.

Misdemeanor to permit continued trespassing by animals. In case cattle, horses, mules, asses, or sheep trespass on any land, the owner of the animals, if known, shall be notified by the owner or occupier of the land trespassed upon, and if the owner of the animals does not remove them within twenty-four hours, if the animals are trespassing on a homesite, garden, or truck farm, or within forty-eight hours, if the animals are trespassing on any other type of land, he shall be fined not more than $100.

Stallions. Every person on whose land any stallion of twelve months old or upwards is found trespassing, may, without any notice, cause the stallion to be impounded, and the owner shall pay to the person upon whose land the trespass is committed $10 for every trespass, to be collected by the pound keeper as provided by any ordinance relating thereto.

Animals, lien for care of. Whoever pastures, feeds, or shelters animals by virtue of a contract with or by the consent of the owner of the animals for a compensation agreed upon, has a lien on the animals for pasturing, feeding, or sheltering to secure payment thereof with costs.

Enforcement by sale of animals. If the owner of the animals, after demand and notice in writing that the lien will be enforced has been served upon him, fails to pay the amount due for the pasturing, feeding, or sheltering within thirty days, the holder of the lien may cause the animals to be sold at public auction, upon notice of sale being given for fifteen days by publication in a newspaper of general circulation in the county where the animals are pastured, fed, or sheltered.

Excess returned to owner. Any excess over the amount due, and costs of sale, and advertising realized from the sale, shall be paid to the owner of the animals sold.

Brands to be recorded, etc. Every owner of livestock in the State shall have his brand or mark, in order to secure its validity and individuality, recorded in a separate book kept for that purpose by the department of agriculture to be known as the "Hawaii Brand Book." No brand or mark shall be recorded which may be similar or approximate in design to any brand or mark which has been previously recorded. The fee for each application for registration shall be $1. The application may be made directly to the department, through its duly authorized agents, or through any duly authorized police officer. The chief of police of the respective counties shall authorize police officers to receive applications for registration of brands under this section. All moneys so received shall be paid to the director of finance. A signed and dated receipt shall be issued for each paid application. All applications shall be promptly forwarded to the department. If it is determined that the application seeks the registration of a brand which either has not already been recorded by another person or is not similar in design to any other previously recorded brand which has not expired, then a certificate showing that such brand or mark has been duly recorded shall be issued forthwith to the applicant. No record shall be made of any ear mark, except only as supplemental identification of a brand. Numerals from 1 to 9 and 0, not used in combination or with symbols, as a brand, shall not be subject to preemptive use but shall be the common property of all persons.

Owners of unbranded animals. All cattle, horses, mules, donkeys, sheep, goats, and swine, over twelve months of age, not marked or branded, which may be running wild at any time on any lands in the State, shall belong to and be the property of the owners or lessees of the lands on which the animals are then running.

Idaho

Animal breaking inclosure—Recovery of damages.—If any animal before mentioned breaks into any inclosure or through any fence conforming to the requirements of chapter 1 of title 35, the owner of such animal must, for such trespass, pay to the party injured the full amount of damages he has sustained by reason of such trespass, to be recovered with costs in any court having jurisdiction.

Animal may be taken up.—The party injured may take up any animal breaking into such inclosure, and keep the same at the expense of the owner, and the said taker-up has a lien upon such animal for damages, costs and expenses; but the owner may at any time pay charges, costs and expenses and take such animal.

Stallions not permitted to run at large.—The owner of any stallion over the age of eighteen (18) months must not allow the same to run at large, unless it is of the market cash value of $250, or more, and is at such value assessed.

Stallions running at large—Penalty for violation.—If any stallion of less than $250 market cash and assessed value, ridgeling, or any unaltered male mule or jackass over the age of eighteen (18) months be found running at large, the owner must be fined for the first offense twenty dollars ($20.00), and for each subsequent offense not more than $100, nor less than forty dollars ($40.00), to be recovered before a justice of the peace in the name of any person who will prosecute the same, one half (½) to his own use and the other half to the use of the county school fund.

Stallion may be taken up.—Any person may take up and safely keep any such stallion, mule, ridgeling or jackass found running at large or in his inclosures; and, when so found, must give the owner thereof five (5) days' notice that such animal is in his possession; and if, at the expiration of the aforesaid time, the owner neglects to remove such animal and pay all reasonable charges for keeping the same, then the taker-up must notify the sheriff or any constable, whose duty it is to sell such animal at public auction, on the premises where taken up, after first giving five (5) days' notice of such sale; and the proceeds of such sale must be applied, first, to the fees of the officer making such sale, which are the same as on execution; second, to the payment of the charges of the taker-up of such animal; and the remainder, if there be any, must be paid to the owner of such animal.

Stallions taken up—Notice and sale.—If the owner or claimant of any stallion, ridgeling, unaltered male mule or jackass
be unknown, the taker-up must give ten (10) days' notice,
with the description of the animal or animals, its marks or
brands, by posting up at least three (3) written or printed
notices in at least three (3) conspicuous places in the county,
calling upon the owner to claim the property; and if, at the
expiration of the ten (10) days, the owner neglects to remove
such animal or animals and pay all costs, then the taker-up
shall call on the sheriff or any constable of the county to sell
such animal or animals; and after deducting the fees of the
officer making such sale and the reasonable charges of the
taker-up, the balance, if any there be, shall be paid into the
county treasury, to be applied to the county school fund.

Ranging stock in towns unlawful.—It shall be unlawful for
any person or persons owning livestock, or the agent or employee of such person or persons, to allow any cattle, horses,
sheep or hogs to range or graze within the platted limits of
any incorporated town or village of more than five hundred
(500) inhabitants, between the first day of September and
the first day of April, without a herder.

Brands

Definitions.—Every person, association or corporation who
owns any cattle, *horses,* mules, asses or sheep in this state, and
is engaged in the business of *breeding,* growing or raising the
same for *profit* or otherwise, is deemed a stock grower, and all
cattle, horses, mules, asses and sheep are deemed livestock.

Use of brands restricted.—Every stock grower in this state
must use a brand for cattle, and a *brand for horses,* mules and
asses, which brand must be placed in a conspicuous place on
the animal. It shall be unlawful for any person to use any
brand as herein provided, unless such brand be designated
in the application for the recording of the brand and the
brand be recorded with the state brand inspector. Each application for the recording of a brand shall include only one (1)

brand for cattle and one (1) brand for horses, mules and asses, but separate application may be filed for the recording of a brand for sheep, and separate applications may be filed by any stock grower to have any additional brand recorded.

Artificial insemination of domestic animals— License to practice

Scope of act.—The practice of artificial insemination of domestic animals in the state of Idaho is subject to the regulations prescribed in this act. Nothing herein shall be held to apply to, interfere with or prohibit the activities of duly licensed veterinarians, or to permit persons licensed under this act to use or prescribe medicine, including chemical drugs, perform surgical operations or practice obstetrics.

Definition.—Artificial insemination as used in this act shall for the purposes herein mean the fertilization of or the attempt to fertilize the female domestic animal by placing and implanting by artificial means in the vagina of the female domestic animal the seminal fluid obtained from the male animal.

License required.—It is unlawful for any person to practice artificial insemination of domestic animals unless he shall first obtain a license so to do as provided in this act. Provided, no license shall be required of or by any person to perform artificial insemination upon his own domestic animals.

Liens for services on or caring for property.—Every person who, while lawfully in possession of an article of personal property, renders any service to the owner thereof, by labor, or skill, employed for the protection, improvement, safe keeping, or carriage thereof, has a special lien thereon, dependent on possession, for the compensation, if any, which is due him from the owner, for such service. Livery or boarding or feed stable proprietors, and persons pasturing livestock of any kind, have a lien, dependent on possession, for their compensation in caring for, boarding, feeding or pasturing such livestock. If the liens as herein provided are not paid within sixty days after the work is done, service rendered, or feed or pasturing

supplied, the person in whose favor such special lien is created
may proceed to sell the property at public auction, after giving
ten days' notice of the sale by advertising in some newspaper
published in the county where such property is situated, or if
there be no newspaper published in the county then by posting
notices of the sale in three of the most public places in the
county, for ten days previous to such sale. The proceeds of
the sale must be applied to the discharge of the lien and costs;
the remainder, if any, must be paid over to the owner.

Illinois

Domestic animals running at large

Hereinafter, it shall be unlawful for any animal of the
species of horse, ass, mule, cattle, sheep, goat, swine or geese,
to run at large in the State of Illinois: Provided, that no
owner or keeper of such animals shall be liable for damages
in any civil suit for injury to the person or property of another
caused by the running at large thereof, without the knowledge
of such owner or keeper, when such owner or keeper can
establish that he used reasonable care in restraining such animals from so running at large.

Damages by animals entering fenced enclosure. If any horse,
mule or ass, or any neat cattle, hogs or sheep, or other domestic
animals, shall break into any person's inclosure, the fence
being good and sufficient, the owner of such animal or animals shall be liable, in a civil action, to make good all damages to the owner or occupier of the inclosure. This section
shall not be construed to require such fence, in order to
maintain an action for injuries done by animals running at
large contrary to law.

Stable keepers, etc. Stable keepers and any persons shall
have a lien upon the horses, carriages and harness kept by
them for the proper charges due for the keeping thereof and
expenses bestowed thereon at the request of the owner, or
the person having the possession thereof.

Agisters. Agisters and persons keeping, yarding, feeding or pasturing domestic animals, shall have a lien upon the animals agistered, kept, yarded or fed, for the proper charges due for the agisting, keeping, yarding or feeding thereof.

Marks and brands

Cattle, horses, etc.—Manner of marking and branding— Record. Every person in this state, who hath cattle, *horses,* hogs, sheep or goats, *may have* an ear mark and brand, and but one of each, which shall be different from the ear mark and brand of his neighbors; which ear mark and brand may be recorded by the county clerk of the county where such cattle, horses, hogs, sheep or goats shall be.

Record book as prima facie evidence. If any dispute shall arise about any ear mark or brand, it shall be decided by reference to the book of marks and brands kept by the county clerk, but such book shall be prima facie evidence only.

Purchaser—Re-branding—Certificate. Any person purchasing or acquiring horses, cattle, hogs, sheep or goats, when he brands or marks the same in his brand or mark, after the acquisition of the same, may do it in the presence of one or more of his neighbors, who are authorized to certify to the fact of the marking or branding being done, when done, and in what brand or mark the same were, previously, and in what brand or mark they were re-branded or remarked. Such certificate shall not be deemed evidence of property in the animal branded, but only prima facie evidence of the facts therein certified to.

Alteration of brands. Every person who shall mark or brand, alter or deface the mark or brand of any horse, mare, colt, jack, jennet, mule, or any one or more domestic fowl, or any one or more head of meat cattle or sheep, goat, hog, shoat or pig, the property of another, with intent thereby to steal the same, or to prevent identification thereof by the true owner, if the value thereof is $15 or more, shall be imprisoned in the penitentiary not less than one nor more than three years; if the value is less than $15, he shall be confined in the county jail not exceeding one year, or fined not exceeding $1,000, or both.

Service of stallions and jacks

Stallion or jack for public service to be registered. Every person, firm, company or corporation standing or offering any stallion or jack for public service in this State shall cause the name, description and age, and in the case of a pure-bred animal the pedigree, of such stallion or jack to be enrolled by the Department of Agriculture, and secure a license from said department as provided in section two (2) of this Act.

License certificate. In order to obtain the license certificate herein provided for, the owner or owners of each stallion or jack shall forward an application and the fee to the Department of Agriculture, together with an affidavit executed by said owner or owners individually or by a graduate veterinarian acceptable to the Department of Agriculture to the effect that such stallion or jack is free from hereditary, infectious or contagious disease or unsoundness, or in the event of said stallion or jack being unsound, the nature and extent of said unsoundness shall be specified in the application, a notation of which shall be embodied in the certificate of license issued, as follows: Amourosis [amaurosis], bog spavin, side bone, navicular disease, curb, chorea, string halt or roaring.

The owner of any pure-bred stallion or jack making application for license, shall furnish to the Department of Agriculture at the time the application for license is made, the stud book certificate of registry of said stallion or jack, and also all transfers, together with all other papers necessary to establish the breeding and ownership. Upon verification of pedigree, certificate of breeding, transfers of ownership and affidavit of soundness as provided for in this Act, a license certificate shall be issued to the owner making application for same. The refusal or failure to forward papers showing breeding and ownership as provided for in this section, shall be taken as evidence of their non-existence, and in all such cases, licenses as pure-bred animals shall be denied.

Lien for service fee—Precedence of lien. Every owner of

any licensed stallion or jack kept for public service, who, at
the request of the owner of any mare or jennet, or his authorized agent, shall cause such mare or jennet to be served by his
stallion or jack, shall have a lien on the mare or jennet served
and first lien upon the progeny of such mare or jennet for the
service fee of such stallion or jack and each lien conferred by
this Act shall take precedence of all other liens or claims
thereon not duly recorded prior to recording claim of lien as
hereinafter provided.

Claim for lien—Filing with recorder of deeds. Any owner
of a licensed stallion or jack desiring to secure the benefits of
this Act shall, within twenty-four (24) months after any mare
or jennet has been served by his stallion or jack, file with the
recorder of deeds in the county in which such mare or jennet
is, a claim for lien in writing and under oath, setting forth
therein his intention to claim a lien upon such mare or jennet
or progeny thereof, or both, for the service fee of his stallion
or jack.

Such claim for lien shall state the name and residence of
the person claiming the lien, the name of the owner or reputed
owner of the mare or jennet or progeny thereof, or both,
sought to be charged with the lien, and a description of such
animal or animals sufficient for identification upon which the
lien is claimed, and the amount due the claimant for the
service fee of his stallion or jack.

The claim for lien filed with the recorder of deeds shall
expire and become void and of no effect if suit is not brought
to foreclose the same within thirty (30) months after the date
of such service by such stallion or jack.

Duty of recorder. It shall be the duty of the recorder of
deeds, upon presentation to him of any such claim for lien,
together with the recording fee, to file the same in his office
in the same manner as provided by law for the filing and
recording of chattel mortgages.

Indiana

Trespassing animals.—If any domestic animal break into
an inclosure or wander upon the lands of another, the person

injured thereby shall recover the amount of damage done, provided, that in townships where, by order of the board of county commissioners, said domestic animals are permitted to run at large, it shall appear that the fence through which said animal broke was lawful; but where such animal is not permitted to graze upon the uninclosed commons, it shall not be necessary to allege or prove the existence of a lawful fence in order to recover for the damage done.

Tender or offer to confess.—If, before trial, the owner of such trespassing animal shall have tendered to the person injured any costs which may have accrued, and also an amount, in lieu of damage, which shall equal or exceed the amount of damages afterward awarded by the court or by a jury, or shall offer, in writing, to confess judgment for the same, and if, notwithstanding, the said injured person, refusing the said offer, cause the trial to proceed, he shall pay costs, and recover only the damages awarded.

Feeding stock—Liens of liverymen and others.—The keepers of livery stables and all others engaged in feeding horses, cattle, hogs and other livestock shall have a lien upon such property for the feed and care bestowed by them upon the same, and shall have the same rights and remedies as are provided for those persons heretofore having, by law, such lien in the act to which this is supplemental.

Marks and brands—Recording.—It shall be the duty of the recorder of each county to record, in a book provided by him for that purpose, the ear-marks of cattle, sheep, hogs, and the marks and brands of *horses,* mules and asses which any person may wish to have recorded in said book; but he shall not record the same marks or brands of two [2] different persons of the same township, and the marks and brands of each township shall be recorded separately in said book; and he shall deliver to the owner a certificate thereof.

Iowa

"All animals shall be restrained by the owners thereof from running at large."

Trespass on lawfully fenced land. Any animal trespassing

upon land, fenced as provided by law, may be distrained by
the owner of such land, and held for all damages done thereon
by it, unless it escaped from adjoining land in consequence of
the neglect of such landowner to maintain his part of a lawful partition fence.

Neglect to maintain partition fence. The owner of the
land from which such animal escaped shall also be liable
for such damages if it escaped therefrom in consequence of
his neglect to maintain his part of a lawful partition fence, or
if the trespassing animal was not lawfully upon his land, and
he had knowledge thereof.

Lien for Care of Stock

Nature of lien. Livery and feed stable keepers, herders,
feeders, keepers of stock and of places for the storage of motor
vehicles, boats and boat engines and boat motors shall have a
lien on all property coming into their hands, as such, for their
charges and the expense of keeping, but such lien shall be
subject to all prior liens of record.

Lien for Services of Animals

Nature of lien—forfeiture. The owner or keeper of any
stallion or jack kept for public service shall have a prior lien
on the progeny of such stallion or jack, to secure the amount
due such owner or keeper for the service resulting in such
progeny, but no such lien shall obtain where the owner or
keeper misrepresents his animal by a false or spurious pedigree,
or fails to substantially comply with the laws of Iowa relating
to such animals.

Period of lien—sale or removal. The lien herein provided
for shall attach at the birth of such progeny and shall remain
in force on such progeny for one year and shall not be lost
by reason of any sale, exchange, or removal from the county
of the animals subject to such lien.

Registration of Animals

Services of stallion. No person shall offer for public service
any stallion unless he shall have had said animal enrolled

with the department of agriculture as a registered animal, and shall have procured from the department a certificate of soundness.

Services of jack. No person shall offer for public service any jack unless he has procured from the department a certificate of soundness. Such certificate shall state whether the animal is registered or unregistered.

Registered animals. No person shall offer for sale, transfer, or exchange any stallion or jack over two years old as registered unless he shall have had said animal enrolled with the department as a registered animal, and shall have procured from the department a certificate of soundness.

Unregistered jacks. No person shall offer for sale, transfer, or exchange for public service any unregistered jack over two years old unless he shall have procured from the department a certificate of soundness.

Adoption of brand. Any person having cattle, sheep, *horses,* mules, or asses shall have the right to adopt a brand for the use of which he shall have the exclusive right in this state, after recording such brand as provided in sections

Must be recorded. No evidence of ownership by brand shall be permitted in any court in this state unless the brand shall be recorded. In no case shall cryo-brands be accepted as evidence of ownership.

Recording—fee. Any person desiring to adopt a brand shall forward to the secretary proper brand application forms of such desired brand, together with a recording fee of fifteen dollars. Upon receipt of such application and fee, the secretary shall file the same and unless such brand is of record as that of some other person or conflicts with or closely resembles the brand of another person, the secretary shall record the same. If the secretary determines that such brand is of record or conflicts with or closely resembles the brand of another person he shall not record it but shall return such facsimile and fee to the forwarding person. The power of examination, approval, acceptance, or rejection shall be vested in the secretary. It shall be the duty of the secretary to file all brands offered for record pending the examination provided for in this section. The secretary shall make such examination as promptly as possible. If the brand is accepted, the ownership thereof shall vest in the person recording it from the date of filing.

Effect of record. The recording shall secure the brand to the person and shall be considered personal property of said owner.

Kansas

Stock Running at Large

Damages. The owners of domestic animals so required to be confined in accordance with the provisions of section 1 of this act shall be liable to any person who shall suffer damage from the depredations of such animals during the period that such animals shall be required to be confined by the order above provided for, without regard to the condition of his or her fence; and the person so damaged shall have a lien upon said stock for the amount of damage done, and the costs of proceedings to recover the same.

Freighters and drovers liable for damages. All damages done by stock owned by freighters or drovers to crops adjacent to roads along which the trains or droves may be passing or herded shall be paid by the owners of the stock to the owners of the crops so damaged, without regard to fences.

Stallion or jack; penalty. If any stallion or jack over the age of two years be permitted to run at large, the owner shall be notified thereof; and if said owner fail or refuse to take such stallion or jack and confine the same, he shall be fined for the first offense five dollars, and for every subsequent offense ten dollars, in a criminal prosecution before any justice of the peace in the county.

Same; negligently permitting such escape; penalty; damage liability, when. If any stallion or jack, kept for the purpose of breeding, shall escape from the owner by his neglect, the owner thereof shall be liable for all damages sustained by any person and shall be fined for the first offense $5, and for every subsequent offense $10 as specified in the preceding section. It any stallion or jack shall escape from his owner by accident, the owner shall be liable for all damages, but shall not be liable to be fined as above provided.

Taking up stallion or jack; castration. If any stallion or jack not used for breeding, over the age of two years, shall be found running at large, and any person shall have taken up the same, he shall notify the owner in person, or if not to be found, by leaving a written notice at his place of residence; and if he fail or neglect to take such property and confine the same within three days after he has been notified, or if he or his residence is not known, then the taker-up of such animal may castrate the animal, using the ordinary precautions for the preservation of the life of the animal, and the animal to be retained possession of by the taker-up until all charges are paid.

Lien for feed and care of livestock; sale for charges and expenses. The keepers of livery stables, and all others engaged in feeding horses, cattle, hogs, or other livestock, shall have a lien upon such property for the feed and care bestowed by them upon the same, and if reasonable or stipulated charges for such feed and care be not paid within sixty days after the same becomes due, the property, or so much thereof as may be necessary to pay such charges and the expenses of publication and sale, may be sold as provided in this act.

Marks and Brands

Definitions. As used in this act, except where the context clearly indicates a different meaning:

(*a*) The term "person" means every natural person, firm, copartnership, association or corporation;

(*b*) the term "livestock" means cattle, sheep, horses, mules or asses.

Adoption of brands; facsimile recorded; fee; period of registration; renewal fee; delinquency status; abandonment, when.

Any person may adopt a brand for the purpose of branding livestock and shall have the exclusive right to use same in this state, after recording such brand with the livestock brand commissioner. Any person desiring to record a livestock brand shall forward to the commissioner a facsimile of such brand and shall accompany same with a fee of ten dollars ($10). Upon receipt of such facsimile and fee, the commissioner shall record same unless such brand or some such similar brand is already recorded as belonging to some other person, in which case the commissioner shall not record same, but shall return such facsimile and fee to the party sending same.

Each person making application for the recording of a brand which is available shall be issued a certificate of brand title for a period ending four years subsequent to the next April 1, following date of issuance: *Provided,* The expiration date on all current brand registrations is herewith extended to the first April 1, following date of expiration stated thereon. For the purpose of revising the brand records, it shall be the duty of the commissioner to collect a renewal fee of ten dollars ($10) on all brands upon which recording period expires, and any person submitting renewal fee of ten dollars ($10) shall be entitled to a renewal of registration of his brand for a five-year period from the date of expiration of registration of his brand as shown by his last certificate of brand title. The brand of any person who fails to pay such renewal fee within a grace period of six (6) months after expiration of the registration period shall be placed in a delinquency status.

The use of a delinquent brand shall be unlawful. If the owner of any delinquent registered brand shall fail to renew registration of such brand within one (1) year after such brand became delinquent such failure shall be and is hereby declared to constitute an abandonment of any and all claim to any property right in said brand. Upon the expiration of said one-year delinquency period without any request for renewal and required remittance from the last record owner of a brand, or his heirs, legatees, or assigns, and with the termination of property rights by abandonment, the commissioner is authorized to receive and accept an application for such brand to the same extent as if said brand had never been issued to any one as a recorded brand.

Kentucky

Horse, jack or bull running at large may be taken up; notice when owner known.

If any ungelded horse or jack over one year old, or any bull known to be mischievous and breachy, is permitted by its owner to run at large outside of his inclosure, it may be taken up and confined by any person. If the owner of the animal is known, notice in writing of the confinement shall be given him, and he shall forthwith take the animal into his possession, and pay two dollars to the taker-up. The owner shall be allowed one day for each twenty-five miles he may have to travel after notice has been served on him.

Animal taken up to be gelded.

If the animal taken up under KRS is not called for within the time allowed, the taker-up shall, at the expiration of such time, take it before a justice of the peace within the district where he resides. Upon proof of the facts, the justice of the peace shall order the animal to be gelded by someone skilled in the art. The fee for gelding shall be one dollar.

Owner of animal unknown; notice; gelding.

When the owner of an animal taken up under KRS is unknown to the taker-up, and the taker-up swears that the owner is unknown to him, he shall take the animal before a justice of the peace within his district, who shall cause it to be appraised and dealt with as a stray, except that a notice in writing of the description of the animal and residence of the taker-up shall be posted at the door of the court house and at one or more public places in the county. If the animal is not called for by the time and proved to be his property within two weeks the taker-up shall again take it before the justice of the peace who shall cause it to be gelded.

Lien of keeper of livery stable or agister for care of livestock.

Any owner or keeper of a livery stable, and a person feeding or grazing cattle for compensation, shall have a lien upon the cattle placed in the stable or put out to be fed or grazed by the owner, for his reasonable charges for keeping, caring for, feeding and grazing the cattle. The lien shall attach whether the cattle are merely temporarily lodged, fed, grazed and cared for, or are placed at the stable or other place or pasture for regular board. The lien shall be subject to the limitations and restrictions placed upon a landlord's lien for rent.

Enforcement of lien for care of livestock.

(1) Any person in whose favor a lien provided for in KRS exists may, before a justice of the peace or a judge of the quarterly court of the county where the cattle were fed or grazed, by himself or agent, make affidavit of the amount due him and in arrear for keeping and caring for the cattle, and describing as nearly as possible the cattle so kept by him. The justice or judge shall then issue a warrant, directed to the sheriff or any constable or town marshal of the county, authorizing him to levy upon and seize the cattle for the amount due, with interest and costs. If the cattle are removed with the consent and from the custody of the livery stable keeper or the person feeding or grazing them, the lien shall not continue longer than ten days from and after the removal, nor shall the lien in case of such removal be valid against a bona fide purchaser without notice at any time after the removal. The warrant may be issued to a county other than that in which the cattle were fed or grazed, and the lien may also be enforced by action as in the case of other liens.

(2) The proceedings under a warrant shall, in all respects, be the same as in the case of a distress warrant, and none of the cattle fed or grazed shall be exempt from seizure or sale.

Lien for service fee of stallion, jack or bull; enforcement of lien.

(1) Any licensed keeper of a stallion, jack or bull shall have a lien for the payment of the service fee upon the get of the stallion, jack or bull, for one year after the birth of the progeny.

(2) This lien may be enforced by action as in cases of other liens, or by warrant as permitted in the case of the enforcement of the lien of the keeper of a livery stable or an agister.

Giving false pedigree of stock to purchaser.

Any person who knowingly and willfully furnishes to any purchaser of stock any false pedigree of the stock, shall be fined not less than one hundred dollars nor more than one thousand dollars, or imprisoned for not less than three nor more than twelve months, or both.

Louisiana

Damage caused by animals

The owner of an animal is answerable for the damage he has caused; but if the animal had been lost, or had strayed more than a day, he may discharge himself from this responsibility, by abandoning him to the person who has sustained the injury; except where the master has turned loose a dangerous or noxious animal, for then he must pay for all the harm done, without being allowed to make the abandonment.

Enrollment of stallions and jacks

Every person, firm, company, or corporation using any stallion or jack for public service in this State shall cause the name, description, and pedigree of the stallion or jack to be enrolled by the Louisiana State Live Stock Sanitary Board, and shall procure a certificate of enrollment from the board. The enrollment certificate shall be recorded by the clerk of the court of the parish in which the stallion or jack is used for public service.

Lien or privilege on mare and produce for service fee; prescription

Any owner, or his duly authorized agent, of any stallion or jack standing for public service, with a license from the Louisiana State Live Stock Sanitary Board, shall have a lien and privilege on any mare and her produce for service fee to the stallion or jack, provided the owner or agent shall take a note or obligation of owner or agent of the mare for the service, stating dates of service, etc. The note or obligation shall be recorded with the clerk of court of the parish in which the owner or agent of the mare resides at the time of the service. The lien herein granted shall prescribe within six months from the date of birth of the produce, unless proceedings to enforce the lien shall have been commenced in a court of competent jurisdiction.

Right to adopt brand or mark

Any person or association of persons having cattle, sheep, horses, or mules may adopt a brand or mark, for the use of which the owner of the brand or mark shall have the exclusive right in this state after recording the brand or mark with the commission.

Filing certificate of soundness; diseases which will bar enrollment

In order to obtain the enrollment certificate, the owner of each stallion or jack shall file a certificate of soundness, signed by a duly qualified veterinarian, who shall be a graduate of a recognized veterinary college, stating that the stallion or jack is free from hereditary, contagious, or transmissible disease, or unsoundness, and shall forward this veterinarian's certificate, together with the stud-book certificate of registry of the pedigree of the stallion or jack, and other necessary papers relating to his breeding and ownership, to the Louisiana State Live Stock Sanitary Board.

The presence of any of the following named diseases or conditions may disqualify a stallion or jack for public service:

Cataract; Amaurosis; Recurrent Ophthalmia (moon blindness) ; Laryngeal Hemiplegia (roaring or whistling) ; Pulmonary Emphysema (heaves or broken wind) ; Chorea or St. Vitus' Dance (shivering) ; String Halt; Bone Spavin; Ring Bone; Side Bone; Navicular Disease; Bog Spavin; Curb, with curby formation of hock joint; Glanders; Maladie due Coit; Urethral Gleet; Mange; Melanosis.

The Louisiana State Live Stock Sanitary Board may refuse its certificate of enrollment to any stallion or jack affected with any one of the diseases or conditions hereby specified, and to revoke the previously issued enrollment certificate or license of any stallion or jack found on investigation by the board to be so affected.

Maine

Damages by animals; remedy; lien

Any person injured in his land by sheep, swine, horses, asses, mules, goats or neat cattle, in a common or general field, or in a close by itself, may recover his damages by taking up any of the beasts doing it, and giving the notice, or in a civil action against the person owning or having possession of the beasts at the time of the damage, and there shall be a lien on said beasts, and they may be attached in such action and held to respond to the judgment as in other cases, whether owned by the defendant or only in his possession. If the beasts were lawfully on the adjoining lands, and escaped therefrom in consequence of the neglect of the person suffering the damage to maintain his part of the partition fence, their owner shall not be liable therefor.

Sale of strays when no owner appears

If the owner does not appear and prove his title to the beasts within said 2 months, the finder may sell them at public auction, first giving notice of such sale at least 4 days before the time of sale in 2 public places in the town in which the beasts were taken up. The proceeds of the sale, after deducting all lawful charges, shall be deposited in the town treasury.

Recovery of strays without paying charges; penalty

Whoever takes away a beast held as a stray, without paying all lawful charges incurred in relation to the same, shall forfeit to the finder double the amount of said charges, not exceeding the value of the beast, and in addition thereto shall be liable for any trespass committed by him in so doing.

Service fee for colts

There shall be a lien on all colts foaled in the state to secure the payment of the service fee for the use of the stallion begetting the same. Such lien shall continue in force until the foal is 6 months old and may be enforced during that time by attachment of such foal.

Pasturage, food and shelter

Whoever pastures, feeds or shelters animals by virtue of a contract with or by consent of the owner has a lien thereon for the amount due for such pasturing, feeding or sheltering, and for necessary expenses incurred in the proper care of such animals and in payment of taxes assessed thereon to secure payment thereof with costs, to be enforced in the same manner as liens on goods in possession and choses in action. The court rendering judgment for such lien shall include therein a pro rata amount for such pasturage, feed and shelter provided by the lienor from the date of the commencement of proceedings to the date of said judgment.

False registration of domestic animals

Whoever by any false pretense obtains from any club, association, society or company for improving the breed of cattle, horses, sheep, swine or other domestic animals the registration of any animal in the herd register or other register of any such club, association, society or company, or a transfer of any such registration, and whoever knowingly exhibits, makes or gives a false pedigree of any animal shall be punished by a fine of not more than $300 or by imprisonment for not more than 90 days, or by both.

Disguising horses in premium shows

Whoever, for the purpose of competing for purses or premiums, knowingly and designedly enters or drives any horse that shall have been painted or disguised, or that represents any other or different horse from the one which is purported to be entered, or shall knowingly and designedly, for the purpose of competing for premiums or purses, enter or drive a horse in a class to which it does not properly belong shall be punished by a fine of not more than $500 or by imprisonment for not more than 6 months, and such horse, after such notice to the owner as the court may order and a hearing thereon, may be forfeited in the discretion of the court and sold; ½ of the net proceeds of such sale shall go to the informant and the other ½ to the county in which the offense is committed. The pecuniary penalty shall be enforced by indictment and the forfeiture by a libel filed by the informant and proceedings in the manner provided in Title 33, chapter 21.

Maryland

Trespassing animals.

If the owner or occupant of any enclosure who may find any horse, sheep, hog, cow or other domestic animal trespassing upon the said enclosed premises, the owner of which is known, he may impound the same and have the damages valued on oath by two disinterested citizens of the county, and after so doing shall give notice to the owner thereof of his having impounded the same and the amount of damages ascertained, and unless the said damages and a reasonable compensation for feeding the property impounded are paid or tendered him, may after giving ten days' notice, exclusive of the days of sale and the day of impounding, describing the property and stating the time and place of sale to be posted at three or more public places in the neighborhood, sell the same at public auction to the highest bidder for cash, and after deducting from the proceeds of sale the amount of damages valued to him and a reasonable compensation for keeping the said property while impounded, he shall pay over the residue when demanded to the owner thereof.

Sale of estrays.

If no person claims an estray within thirty days after the same shall be so advertised as aforesaid, then the person taking up the same shall apply to a justice of the peace of the county, who upon being satisfied that the notices heretofore directed have been given, shall order him to sell the same at public auction on ten days' notice to be set up at three of the most public places of the neighborhood, and after deducting from the proceeds of sale all expenses incident to taking up, keeping, advertising and selling the same, the residue shall be retained by the person selling the same, unless the owner of such estray shall within twelve months from time of sale claim such residue and prove before some justice of the peace that he is entitled thereto.

Lien on livestock for board, etc., due.

(a) *Creation of lien.*—The owner or operator of every livery stable or other establishment giving care or custody to any horse or other livestock shall have a lien thereon for any reasonable charge for board and custody, training fees, veterinarians' and blacksmiths' charges, and for other proper maintenance expenses.

(b) *When sale may be made.*—Any person, association or corporation having a lien under the provisions of this section may sell the horse or other livestock at public auction sale, if the account is due and unpaid for a period of thirty days after any such fee, charge or other expense shall have accrued and if the lienor still retains possession of the same.

(c) *Notice to owner prerequisite to sale.*—The lienor must give at least one month's notice to the owner of the horse or other livestock, by registered mail addressed to the owner's last known address, before he may proceed with any such sale. If the whereabouts of the owner be unknown, such notice may be given by written or printed notice set up at the courthouse door of the county wherein the animal is located, or City of Baltimore, as the case may be.

(d) *Procedure following notice.*—Following such notice, if the account still remains due and unpaid, the lienor may proceed to sell the horse or other livestock at public auction sale to satisfy the said account. Such sale shall not be held unless advertised in the public press at least twice, seven days apart. The proceeds of such sale shall be applied to the expenses thereof and then to the liquidation of such indebtedness and the balance, if any, shall be paid over to the debtor.

Lien for veterinarian.

Any duly qualified veterinarian as defined in Article 43 of the Annotated Code of Maryland, 1951, title "Health," subtitle "State Board of Veterinary Examiners," giving care or custody, or performing medical services, or any services necessary or incidental to his profession to any animal in his care or custody, may after said animal is ready for delivery to the owner thereof notify the owner or the person by whom said animal was delivered to said veterinarian that the animal is ready for delivery in person or by giving 30 days' notice by registered letter mailed to the given address, of such owner or person, or the last known address, or if said address is unknown such notice shall be rendered by posting at the courthouse door of the city or county wherein the animal is located for a period of 30 days. After the expiration of said 30 days' notice, either by registered letter or by posting at the courthouse door of the city or county wherein the animal is located, if the animal is not claimed, it shall be considered that title of the owner to the animal is forfeited and the veterinarian shall have the right to:

(a) Sell the animal at public sale, except for purposes of experimentation or vivisection, provided such sale is advertised in a local newspaper on at least two occasions seven days apart. Proceeds of such sale shall be applied, first, to the expenses thereof, second, to the liquidation of such indebtedness, and the balance, if any, shall be held for the benefit of the owner or client for a period of 30 days, after which time the veterinarian shall turn the same over to the local board of education; or

(b) Turn the animal over to an animal welfare agency located within the county where said animal is located or if no such agency is located in that county then to the nearest such agency.

The exercise of any of the rights hereinabove given shall not prevent subsequent action at law for the collection of any moneys remaining due and unpaid to the veterinarian.

Obtaining registration by false representations.

Every person who, by any false pretense, shall obtain from any club, association, society or company, for improving the breed of cattle, horses, sheep, swine or other domestic animals, the registration of any animal in the herd register, or other register of any such club, association, society or company, or a transfer of any such registration; and every person who shall knowingly give a false pedigree of any animal, upon conviction thereof, shall be punished by imprisonment in a county jail for a term not exceeding one year, or by a fine not exceeding one thousand dollars, or by both such fine and imprisonment.

Massachusetts

Beasts at Large without Keeper to Be Taken Up. Every field driver shall take up horses, mules, asses, neat cattle, sheep, goats or swine going at large in the public ways, or on common and unimproved land within his town and not under the care of a keeper; and any other inhabitant of the town may take up such cattle or beasts so going at large on Sunday, and for taking up such beasts on said day the field driver or such other inhabitant of the town may in tort recover for each beast the same fees which the field driver is entitled to receive for taking up like beasts. This section has two objects in view—*to secure all persons against direct injury, either to their persons or property; and also to enable owners to regain possession of their stray beasts.*

Distraint of Beasts Doing Damage. If a person is injured in his land by horses, mules, asses, neat cattle, sheep, goats or swine, he may recover his damages in an action against the owner of the beasts or by distraining the beasts doing the damage and proceeding therewith as hereinafter directed.

Stallions

Registration; Fees; Penalty. The owner or keeper of a stallion for breeding purposes shall, before advertising the service thereof, file a certificate of the name, color, age, size and pedigree, as fully as obtainable, of said stallion, and of the name of the person by whom he was bred, with the clerk of the city or town where said stallion is owned or kept, who shall, upon payment of the fee provided by clause (72) of section thirty-four of chapter two hundred and sixty-two, record the same in a book to be kept for that purpose. Whoever neglects to make and file such certificate shall recover no compensation for the services of his stallion, and whoever knowingly and wilfully makes a false certificate shall be punished by a fine of one hundred dollars.

Lien for Pasturing, Boarding and Keeping Domestic Animals. Persons having proper charges due them for pasturing, boarding or keeping horses or other domestic animals which are brought to their premises or placed in their care by or with the consent of the owners thereof shall have a lien on such animals for such charges.

Michigan

Recovery for damages caused by beasts. When any person is injured in his land, by sheep, swine, horses, asses, mules, goats or neat cattle, he may recover his damages in an action of trespass, or trespass on the case, against the owner of the beasts, or against the person having the care and control of such beasts, or by distraining the beasts doing the damage, and proceeding therewith as hereinafter directed; but if the beasts shall have been lawfully on the adjoining lands, and shall have escaped therefrom in consequence of the neglect of the person who has suffered the damage, to maintain his part of the division fences, the owner or person having the control of the beasts shall not be liable for such damage.

Lien of mechanic, artisan or tradesman; for manufacture of goods or keeping of animals. Wherever any person shall deliver to any mechanic, artisan, or tradesman, any materials or articles for the purpose of constructing in whole or in part, or completing any furniture, jewelry, implement, utensil, clothing or other article of value, or shall deliver to any person any horse, mule, neat cattle, sheep, or swine to be kept or cared for, such mechanic, artisan, tradesman, or other person shall have a lien thereon for the just value of the labor and skill applied thereto by him, and for any materials which he may have furnished in the construction or completion thereof, and for the keeping and care of such animals, and may retain possession of the same until such charges are paid.

Stallions, enrollment, certificate; words construed. Every person, firm, association or company offering for use for public service any stallion in this state shall cause the name, description, pedigree and physical condition of such stallion to be enrolled by the commissioner of agriculture and shall procure a certificate of such enrollment from said commissioner. The word "stallion" whenever used in this act shall be construed to include "jack." The word "mare" whenever used in this act shall be construed to include "jenny."

Enrollment certificate, procedure to obtain. In order to obtain the enrollment certificate hereinafter provided for, the owner of each stallion shall forward to the commissioner of agriculture the stud book, certificate of registration, and any other document that may be necessary to define and describe such stallion, his breeding and ownership. The commissioner of agriculture shall examine and pass upon the merits of such pedigree and shall use as his standard of action the stud books and signatures of the duly authorized officers of the various pedigree registration associations, societies or companies recognized by him.

Upon verification of the pedigree or certificate of breeding the commissioner of agriculture shall notify the owner of such stallion to this effect and shall proceed to examine such stallion at the owner's premises to determine the condition of soundness of such stallion. The commissioner of agriculture shall authorize the state veterinarian or his regularly appointed representative, to proceed at the time and place designated in said notice to said owner to make an examination of such stallion and shall certify to the best of his knowledge and belief the physical condition of such stallion, specifying the nature and extent of unsoundness, if any, of such stallion, and shall immediately forward such certificate to the office of said commissioner of agriculture.

Advertising stallions. Every bill or poster issued by the owner of any stallion licensed under the provisions of this act, or used by him or his agent for the purpose of advertising such stallion, shall contain a copy of the certificate of enrollment of such stallion, and said bills or posters shall not contain illustrations, reference to pedigree or other statements that are untruthful or misleading. Reference to such stallions in newspapers, stock papers and other advertising mediums shall contain the name of such stallion, number of certificate of enrollment, and shall designate in letters not smaller than pica the true breeding of such stallion as given in said certificate of enrollment.

Enrollment certificate, issuance, contents; refusal to issue; posting. The commissioner of agriculture shall issue enrollment certificates. Such enrollment certificate shall have a dis-

tinctive number and be such as to show the true breeding and
physical condition of the stallion enrolled. The commissioner
of agriculture may refuse to issue an enrollment certificate for
any stallion in which stallion the presence of any 1 of the
following named diseases in a transmissible, hereditary or contagious form shall be shown so as to render such stallion unsuitable to improve the horse stock of the state: Cataract;
amaurosis (glass eye) ; periodic ophthalmia (moon blindness) ;
laryngeal hemiplegia (roaring or whistling) ; pulmonary emphysema (heaves, broken wind) ; chorea (St. Vitus' dance,
crampiness, shivering, string halt) ; bone spavin; ringbone;
side bone; navicular disease; bog spavin; curb, with curby
formation of hock; glanders, farcy; maladie du coit; urethral
gleet; mange; melanosis; or any contagious or infectious disease. [The commissioner of agriculture may refuse to issue an
enrollment certificate for any stallion deemed unfit to improve
the horse stock of the state.] The owner of any stallion to
whom an enrollment certificate shall be issued shall post and
keep affixed copies of such enrollment certificate in a conspicuous place both within and upon the outside of every
building where such stallion is kept for public service.

*Enrollment fees; expiration of certificate, renewal; transfer
of ownership, fee; death; disposition of fees.* A fee of five [5]
dollars shall be paid, by the owner of each stallion offered for
enrollment, to the commissioner of agriculture at the time of
the first application for a certificate of enrollment. The fee so
paid shall be in full for the examination and enrollment of
such pedigree, the physical examination of such stallion, and
the issuance of a certificate of enrollment. Enrollment certificate shall expire December thirty-first [31st] of the year immediately following the year in which issued. The owner of any
stallion whose certificate of enrollment has expired may make
application for a new certificate of enrollment by filing with
the commissioner of agriculture the last issued certificate of
enrollment and paying a fee of three [3] dollars on or before
March fifteenth [15th], in the year following such expiration,
and a new certificate of enrollment shall be issued by the commissioner of agriculture to the owner of such stallion. Such

certificate of enrollment shall expire December thirty-first [31st] of the year immediately following the year in which issued. Upon transfer of ownership of any stallion enrolled under the provisions of this act, the certificate of enrollment must be transferred to the new owner by the commissioner of agriculture upon submittal of satisfactory proof of such transfer of ownership and upon the payment of a fee by the owner of such stallion of one [1] dollar. In case of death or change of ownership of any stallion enrolled under the provisions of this act, the owner of the same shall immediately inform the state commissioner of agriculture. All fees received by the commissioner of agriculture under the provisions of this act shall be paid into the state treasury to be credited to the general fund.

Powers of commissioner. The commissioner of agriculture is hereby authorized to provide for official examination of pedigrees and certificates of breeding and ownership, to issue license certificates for stallions enrolled under this act, to compile and publish statistics relative to horse breeding in Michigan and other information of value to the horse breeders of this state, and to incur such other reasonable expenses as may be necessary to carry out and enforce the provisions of this act.

Complaint; revocation of certificate; use of unenrolled stallion prohibited. The commissioner of agriculture shall have the right at any time to take cognizance of any complaint reporting unsoundness of any stallion enrolled under the provisions of this act, and to examine such stallion if deemed necessary. In case any such stallion upon such examination shall be found to be unsound [or] not suitable to improve the horse stock of this state, the commissioner of agriculture shall revoke the certificate of enrollment issued to the owner of such stallion. No person, firm, company or association shall offer for use for public service, in this state any stallion which is not enrolled under the provisions of this act. The breeding of any mare with any stallion or jack shall be construed as offering said stallion or jack for public service: Provided, That nothing in this act shall be construed to prevent the individual owner of any unlicensed stallion or jack from breeding any mares kept on his own premises and of which mares he is the bona fide and sole owner.

Stallions imported; examination, certification, fee. Every stallion brought into this state from another state or from a foreign country to be offered for sale or for public service shall, before any such sale or use is made, be examined by the state veterinarian, or his official representative, and certified by said state veterinarian, or his representative, that said stallion is free from hereditary, contagious or transmissible unsoundness or disease and is of good formation and breed type and suitable to improve the horse stock of this state. A fee of five [5] dollars shall be paid therefor before such examination is conducted: Provided, If application is made for enrollment before such examination is made said five [5] dollars will also cover fee for enrollment.

Penalty. Any person, firm, company or association violating any of the provisions of this act shall be deemed guilty of a misdemeanor, and shall upon conviction thereof be punished by a fine of not less than twenty-five [25] dollars nor more than one hundred [100] dollars, or by imprisonment in the county jail not more than thirty [30] days, or by both such fine and imprisonment in the discretion of the court.

Lien for service of stallion; statement, filing; sale of mare or foal; enforcement of lien. Having complied with the provisions of this act, the owner of any stallion shall have a lien for the sum stipulated to be paid for the service thereof, upon the mare served by any such stallion in breeding, thereof, and upon the offspring of such stallion by filing at any time within 18 months after the date of service, a statement of the account thereof, together with a description as to color, and white markings of the female served, and the name of the owner at the date of service, in the office of the [register of deeds of the county] wherein the owner of said female resided at the time of service. Such lien shall exist for a period of 1 year from the date of foaling of said colt, or if credit is given, from the expiration of the credit, and shall have priority over all other liens and encumbrances upon the offspring. Neither the mare nor the foal shall be sold within 18 months after the date of service, unless the service fee shall be paid, unless such sale shall be agreed to and approved in writing by the owner of the stallion at the time of the sale or transfer of the mare or foal. At any time after the offspring shall have been foaled, any person having such lien may enforce the same by the same proceedings and in the same manner as is provided by sections of the Compiled Laws of 1929: Provided, however, That the owner of any such stallion may institute suit to collect the lien in the county in which the mare is served.

Branding Live Stock

Ear mark or brand; recording, dissimilarity. SECTION 1. *The People of the State of Michigan enact,* That every person who has cattle, *horses,* hogs, sheep, goats, or any other domestice animals, may adopt an ear mark or brand, which ear mark or brand may be recorded in the office of the county clerk of the county where such cattle, horses, hogs, sheep, goats, or other domestic animals shall be: Provided, That the mark or brand so adopted and recorded shall be different from all other marks or brands, adopted and recorded in such county.

Record book of county clerk; recording fee. SEC. 2. It shall be the duty of the county clerks of the several counties of this state, to keep a book in which they shall record the mark or brand adopted by each person who may apply to them for that purpose, for which they shall be entitled to demand and receive twenty-five [25] cents.

Minnesota

Animals at Large

Running at large; defined; prohibited; treble damages. The herding of any animal of the species of cattle, horse, ass, mule, sheep, swine, or goat upon any land over the protest and against the will of the owner shall be deemed a running at large.

It shall be unlawful for any owner or any person having the control of any such animal to permit the same to run at large in the state.

Any person who shall knowingly permit the running at large of any such domestic animal shall be liable to the person aggrieved for treble damages sustained by him, to be recovered in a civil action brought for that purpose.

Animals Doing Damage

Distraint of animals doing damage. The owner or occupant of lands may distrain any beast doing damage thereon, either while upon the premises or upon immediate pursuit of such beast escaping therefrom, and before returning to the enclosure or immediate care of the owner or keeper, and keep such beast upon his premises, or in some public ground in his town, until his damages shall be appraised, as hereinafter provided.

Animals doing damage.

Subdivision 1. Notice, appraisers. The person distraining shall give notice to the owner of such beast, if known to him, within 24 hours if he resides in the same town, and within 48 hours if he resides in another town in the same county, Sundays excepted; specifying in the notice the time when and the place where distrained, the number of beasts, and the place of their detention, and that at a time and place stated therein, which shall not be less than 12 hours after the service of the notice, nor more than three days after such distress, he will apply to a designated justice of the peace of the county for the appointment of appraisers to appraise the damages. If the owner be unknown, or does not reside in the county, the distraining person shall apply for the appointment of such appraisers within 24 hours after such distress without notice. Upon such application the justice shall appoint in writing three disinterested freeholders of such town to appraise the damages, for which the justice shall receive a fee of 50 cents.

Subd. 2. Owners right to appraisal. If the distraining person fails to apply for appointment of appraisers within the time designated in subdivision 1, the owner of the beasts distrained may in the same manner apply for appointment of appraisers.

Poundmaster; custody; sale; time; notice. The poundmaster shall receive and keep in the public pound any beasts so delivered to him; and, unless seized or discharged according to law within six days, shall sell the same or as many as shall be necessary to pay such damages, fees, and costs, at public auction, giving three days posted notice thereof, and posting one such notice on the pound.

Liens

For keeping, repairing. Whoever, at the request of the owner or legal possessor of any personal property, shall store or care for or contribute in any of the modes pentioned in following section to its preservation, care, or to the enhancement of its value, shall have a lien upon such property for the price or value of such storage, care, or contribution, and for any legal charges against the same paid by such person to any other person, and the right to retain the property in his possession until such lien is lawfully discharged; but a voluntary surrender of possession shall extinguish the lien herein given.

For what given. Such lien and right of detainer shall exist for:

(1) Transporting property from one place to another as a common carrier or otherwise;

(2) Keeping or storing property as a warehouseman or other bailee;

(3) Keeping, feeding, pasturing, or otherwise caring for domestic animals or other beasts, including medical or surgical treatment thereof and shoeing the same;

(4) Making, altering or repairing any article, or expending any labor, skill or material thereon.

Such liens shall embrace all lawful charges against such property paid to any other person by the person claiming such lien, and the price or value of such care, storage or contribution and all reasonable disbursements occasioned by the detention or sale of the property.

Certain male animals or breachy cattle.

Subdivision 1.   Running at large; penalty. The owner of any stallion over the age of one year, bull over the age of nine months, boar or ram over the age of three months, or of any breachy cattle, who shall suffer the same to run at large in any town, shall forfeit to such town $5 for each day any such animal shall be so at large. "Run at large" means any animal which is not picketed, confined in a corral or otherwise restricted by a properly constructed and maintained legal fence as defined by Minnesota Statutes 1945.

Subd. 2.   Owner notified; proceeding; sale. Upon notice that any such animal is running at large, the chairman of the town board shall forthwith notify its owner, and, if he does not immediately confine such animal, the chairman shall cause suit to be brought against him, in the name of the town, to recover the forfeiture, and the animal may be sold under execution in such action to pay the forfeiture and costs.

Subd. 3.   Disposal of proceeds. After deducting the costs and expenses of suit, all such forfeitures collected shall be paid into the town treasury for the use of the road and bridge fund.

Subd. 4.   When owner not found. If unable to find the owner of any such animal, the chairman shall cause it to be confined in the public pound, if there be one, and, if not, in some other enclosure, for three days; and, if not then claimed, he shall cause it to be sold, at public auction, upon five days' posted notice. From the proceeds of the sale he shall deduct the amount of the forfeiture and expenses, and deposit the balance with the town treasurer, which shall be paid to the owner of the animal if applied for within one year. If not so applied for, the same shall be paid into the town treasury for the use of the town.

Subd. 5.   Castration; limitation of liability in case of rams. If, after being notified, the owner of any such stallion, bull, boar, or ram shall permit the same to continue or again to run at large, such chairman shall forthwith cause the same to be taken up and castrated in the usual manner, and shall have a lien on such animals for the expenses of so doing, and may also recover the amount of such expenses from the owner of the animal in a civil action brought in the name of the town; provided, that any such ram running at large may be castrated without liability for damages by any person among whose sheep he shall be found. Any chairman who shall refuse or neglect to perform any of the duties required by this section shall be guilty of a misdemeanor.

Marks and brands; definitions.

Subdivision 1. Unless the context clearly indicates otherwise the terms defined in this section have the meanings given them.

Subd. 2. "Board" means the state livestock sanitary board.

Subd. 3. "Brand," except as otherwise provided in this section, means a permanent identification mark of which the letters, numbers, and figures used are each four inches or more in length or diameter and are burned into the hide of a live animal with a hot iron, and is to be considered in relation to its location on such animal; and such term relates to both the mark burned into the hide and the location of this mark. In the case of sheep, the term includes, but is not limited to, a painted mark which is renewed after each shearing.

Subd. 4. "Mark" means a permanent identification cut from the ear or ears of a live animal.

Subd. 5. The term "animal" means any cattle, horse, sheep, or mule.

Registration of marks or brands with livestock sanitary board. The board shall approve marks or brands for registration, issue certificates of approval, and administer the provisions of sections of this chapter. The board shall publish a state brand book which shall contain a facsimile of each and every mark or brand that is registered with it, showing the owner's name and address together with the pertinent laws, rules, and regulations pertaining to brand registrations and re-registrations.

County records of marks and brands. After April 30, 1965, but before July 1, 1965, the register of deeds of each county shall submit to the board such information as the board may require relating to marks or brands recorded in the county pursuant to Minnesota Statutes, including but not limited to a description of each mark or brand so recorded and the name and address of the person who recorded the mark or brand. After July 1, 1965, it shall be unlawful for a register of deeds to record a mark or brand.

Notice to mark and brand holders; application for registration; penalties, duplicate brands. Immediately upon receipt of the information required by the above section, the board shall notify each holder of a mark or brand that marks or brands are registered pursuant to said sections and that the board will, on or before January 1, 1966, and every ten years thereafter, cause to be published a state brand book showing all marks or brands recorded with the board prior to September 1, 1965, and every ten years thereafter. The board shall prepare a standard form which shall be mailed to all holders of registered county marks or brands. The board also shall supply these forms to county auditors for distribution to those who desire to apply for a brand. The application shall show a left and right side view of the animals upon which a mark or brand will be eligible for registry. The mark or brand location shall be designated to the following body regions: Head, bregma, and right and left jaw, neck, shoulder, rib, hip, and breech. The applicant shall select not less than three distinct marks or brands and list them in preferred order and he shall likewise select three locations on the animal and list them in preferred order. The application shall be properly signed and notarized and accompanied by a fee of $10. The mark or brand, if approved and accepted by the board, shall be of good standing during the ten year period in which it is recorded. Any person who knowingly places upon any animal a mark or brand which has not been registered with the board and which is in duplication of a mark or brand that is registered with the board is guilty of a felony. "Duplication" constitutes the use of a similar mark or brand, used in any position on the animal designated for the use of a registered mark or brand, such as the head, bregma, jaw, neck, shoulder, rib, hip, or breech. Any person who alters or defaces a brand or mark on any animal to prevent its identification by its owner, is guilty of a felony.

Mississippi

Owner liable for damages.

Every owner of such live stock shall be liable for damages for all injuries and trespasses committed by such animals by breaking and entering into or upon the lands, grounds, or premises of another person; and the person injured shall have a lien upon the animal, or animals, trespassing for all such damage. The damages for such trespass shall not be less than fifty cents for each horse, cow or hog, and 25 cents for each of the other kinds of stock; and for every succeeding offense, after the owner has been notified of the first trespass or injury, double damages shall be recovered with costs. For breaking or entering into a pasture or waste ground, however, double damage shall not be recoverable, and the damages in such cases may be assessed as low as 40 cents for each horse, cow or hog and 20 cents for each of the other kinds of live stock.

Stable keepers.

The owner of every livery stable, sale stable, feed stable or public pasture shall have a lien on every horse, mule, cow, or other animal for the price of feeding, grooming, training, grazing, or keeping the same, at the instance of the owner of the animal, and shall have the right to retain possession of the animal until such price be paid. If the price be not paid in ten days after it is due, the person to whom it is owing may commence suit therefor before a justice of the peace where the principal of the amount does not exceed two hundred dollars, and in the circuit court where it exceeds that sum, setting forth the amount of the debt, how it accrued, and a description of the animal; and, upon proof of the debt that it is due for feeding, grooming, training,

grazing or keeping the animal, he shall be entitled to judgment against the owner for the amount due and sued for
and the price of feeding, grooming, training, grazing and
keeping the animal since the institution of the suit if the
whole amount do not exceed the jurisdiction of the court,
with costs as in other cases, and to a special order and execution for the sale of the property upon which the lien exists
for the payment of such judgment and costs, and to an
execution, as in other cases, for the residue of what remains
unpaid after sale of the property. The lien created by this
section shall be subordinate to any prior encumbrance on
such animal of which the owner of the stable had notice,
actual or constructive, unless the animal were fed, groomed,
trained, grazed or kept by the consent of the encumbrancer.

Not lawful for drover to drive animals from range.

It shall not be lawful for a drover or other person to drive
any horse, mule, cattle, hog, or sheep of another from the
lands to which the same may belong, whether the same be
an estray or not; but it shall be his duty, if any other such
stock shall join his, immediately to halt at the nearest convenient place and separate such stock as does not belong to
him or to the person for whom he may be employed; and if
any person shall violate the provisions of this section, he shall
forfeit twenty dollars for every offense, with costs, recoverable
before a justice of the peace, by and for the use of any person
who will sue for the same, and shall also be liable in damages
to the party injured; and when any person employed in
driving stock shall violate the provisions of this section, he
and his employer shall be liable to the like penalties; but
the recovery of such penalty shall not be a bar to indictment
for larceny.

Stallion suffered to run at large may be gelded.

If any person shall suffer any stallion above the age of
two years to run at large, out of an inclosure, it shall be
lawful for any person to confine and geld such stallion, at the

risk of the owner; but this section shall not apply to such stallions as are usually kept up, and happen to get out by accident.

Owner of stallion, jackass, or bull.

The owner of a stallion, jackass or bull shall have a lien on each foal begotten by his stallion or jackass, and on each calf begotten by his bull, for the price agreed to be paid therefor, and such lien shall be prior to all other encumbrances on such foal or calf and shall bind the same even in the hands of subsequent purchasers and encumbrances for a valuable consideration without notice; but the said lien shall expire twelve months after the birth of said foal or calf unless within that time judicial proceedings have been begun to enforce the lien; provided, that if the owner shall have falsely represented the breeding, registration, or pedigree of his stallion, jackass or bull, by advertisement or otherwise, he shall not have a lien on the foal begotten by such stallion or jackass, or on the calf of such bull, as against any person who acted under the belief that such representation was true; and, in such case, the owner of the animal shall not have any claim for the service of the stallion, jackass, or bull.

False pretenses and cheats—frauds in obtaining registration of animals and giving false pedigree.

If any person shall, by any false pretense whatever, obtain from any person, club, association, society, or company for improving the breed of cattle, horses, sheep, swine, or goats, or other domestic animal, the registration of any animal in the herd register, or other register of such person, club, association, society, or company, or a transfer of any such registration, and every person who shall knowingly publish or give to any person, club, association, society, or company a false pedigree of any animal, shall be guilty of a misdemeanor, and, on conviction, shall be fined not exceeding five hundred dollars, or imprisoned in the county jail not exceeding six months, or both.

Missouri

Domestic animals restrained from running at large

It shall be unlawful for the owner of any animal or animals of the species of horse, mule, ass, cattle, swine, sheep or goat, in this state, to permit the same to run at large outside the enclosure of the owner of such stock, and if any of the species of domestic animals aforesaid be found running at large, outside the enclosure of the owner, it shall be lawful for any person, and it is hereby made the duty of the sheriff or other officer having police powers, on his own view, or when notified by any other person that any of such stock is so running at large, to restrain the same forthwith, and such person or officer shall, within three days, give notice thereof to the owner, if known, in writing, stating therein the amount of compensation for feeding and keeping such animal or animals and damages claimed, and thereupon the owner shall pay the person, or officer, taking up such animal or animals a reasonable compensation for the taking up, keeping and feeding such animal, or animals, and shall also pay all persons damaged by reason of such animals running at large, the actual damages sustained by him or them; provided, that said owner shall not be responsible for any accident on a public road or highway if he establishes the fact that the said animal or animals were outside the enclosure through no fault or negligence of the owner. If the owner of such stock be not known, or if notified and fails to make compensation for the taking up, feeding and keeping of animals taken up under the provisions of this chapter, the same shall be deemed strays, and shall be dealt with in the same manner as required by law with respect to such property as strays, under the stray law. Any failure or refusal on the part of such officer to discharge the duties required of him by this section shall render him liable on his bond to any person damaged by such failure or refusal, which damages may be sued for and recovered in any court of competent jurisdiction.

Lien for keeping or training horses and other animals

Every person who shall keep, board or train any horse, mule or other animal, shall, for the amount due therefor, have a lien on such animal, and on any vehicle, harness or equipment coming into his possession therewith, and no owner or claimant shall have the right to take any such property out of the custody of the person having such lien, except with his consent or on the payment of such debt; and such lien shall be valid against said property in the possession of any person receiving or purchasing it with notice of such claim.

Giving false pedigree forfeits claim

If any keeper of such stallion, jack or bull shall offer and advertise to let the service of any such animal, and shall give a false or fictitious pedigree, knowing the same to be false, or shall falsely represent said animal to be recorded or eligible to record in any of the various books of record kept for recording animals of that breed, he shall forfeit all claim to the value of the services rendered by any such animal, and shall not be entitled to the benefits of any provision of this chapter.

Stallions, mules and jackasses not to run at large, when—penalty

If any stallion or any unaltered male mule or jackass, over the age of two years, be found running at large, the owner shall be fined, for the first offense three dollars, and for every subsequent offense not exceeding ten dollars, to be recovered by civil action before a magistrate, in the name of any person who will prosecute for the same, one-half to his own use and the other half to the use of the county.

Such animal may be castrated, when

Any person may take up any such horse, mule or jackass, found running at large, and if not claimed within five days, castrate him in the usual manner, and so as to endanger his life as little as possible, for which he shall recover three dollars from the owner by civil action before a magistrate.

May be killed, when

If any such horse, mule or jackass be running at large, and cannot be taken up, he may be killed, if notice be first put up at the courthouse door and at three other public places in the county, for ten days, describing the color, marks and brands, as near as practicable, of the animal, and that he will be killed unless taken away and secured.

Montana

Liability of owners of stock for trespass. If any cattle, horse, mule, ass, hog, sheep, or other domestic animal break into any inclosure, the fence being legal, as hereinbefore provided, the owner of such animal is liable for all damages to the owner or occupant of the inclosure which may be sustained thereby. This section must not be construed so as to require a legal fence in order to maintain an action for injury done by animals running at large contrary to law.

Stock trespassing may be retained. (1) If any such animal breaks into an inclosure surrounded by a legal fence, or is wrongfully upon the premises of another, the owner or occupant of the inclosure or premises may take into his possession the animal trespassing, and keep the same until all damages, together with reasonable charges for keeping and feeding are paid. The person taking any such animal into his possession shall, within seventy-two hours thereafter, give written notice to the owner or person in charge of the animal, stating that he has taken up such animal; said notice shall also give the date of such taking, the description of the animal or animals taken up, including marks and brands, if any, the amount of damages claimed and the charge per head per day for caring for and feeding the same, and shall describe, either by legal subdivisions or other general description, the location of the premises upon which said animals are held. In all cases a copy of said notice shall likewise be posted at a point where said stock was taken up.

(2) Such notice shall be given to the owner or person in charge only when said owner or person in charge of the animal or animals is known to the person taking up the same and resides within twenty-five miles of the premises upon which such animals have been taken up. In case the owner or person in charge of such animals resides more than twenty-five miles from the place of such taking, notice as aforesaid shall be mailed to him, and in such case, and also in case the owner be unknown, a like notice shall be mailed to the Montana livestock commission and the sheriff of the county in which such animals have been taken up. Upon receipt of such notice, the sheriff shall post a copy thereof at the court-house and shall send by registered mail a copy thereof to the owner of the stock, if known to him; if unknown to him, the sheriff shall send a copy of such notice to the nearest state livestock inspector.

(3) In case the parties do not within five days thereafter agree as to the amount of damages, the lien claimant must within ten days thereafter institute a civil action to foreclose his lien in any court of competent jurisdiction, pending the outcome of which suit, the person taking up said stock may, at the expense of the owner, retain a sufficient amount of such stock to cover the amount of damages claimed by him; provided, however, that the defendant may, after the institution of an action as aforesaid, upon filing in said cause a bond executed by two or more sureties and approved by the court, in double the sum sued for, conditioned for the payment to the plaintiff of all sums, including costs that may be recovered by said plaintiff, have the return to him of all livestock held as aforesaid, and said person shall be liable to such owner for any loss or injury to said stock occurring through his fault or neglect. If the person taking up said stock shall fail to recover in said action a sum equal to that offered him by the owner of the stock, the former shall bear the expense of keeping and feeding same while in his possession.

(4) Any person taking or rescuing any such animal from the possession of the person taking the same, without his consent, is guilty of a misdemeanor, and upon conviction thereof shall be punishable by a fine of not less than one hundred dollars nor more than five hundred dollars.

Agisters' liens and liens for service—priority. Every person who, while lawfully in possession of an article of personal property renders any service to the owner or lawful claimant thereof by labor or skill employed for the making, repairing, protection, improvement, safekeeping, or carriage thereof, has a special lien thereon, dependent on possession, for the compensation, if any, which is due to him from the owner or lawful claimant for such service and for material, if any, furnished in connection therewith. A ranchman, farmer, agister, herder, hotel-keeper, livery, boarding, or feed stable-keeper, to whom any horses, mules, cattle, sheep, hogs, or other stock are entrusted, and there is a contract, express or implied, for their keeping, feeding, herding, pasturing, or ranching, has a lien upon such stock for the amount due for keeping, feeding, herding, pasturing, or ranching the same, and is authorized to retain possession thereof until the sum due is paid. The lien hereby created shall not take precedence over perfected security interests under the Uniform Commercial Code—Secured Transactions, or other recorded liens on the property involved, unless within ten days from the time of receiving the property, the person desiring to assert a lien thereon shall give notice in writing to said secured party or other lien holder, stating his intention to assert a lien on said property, under the terms of this act, and stating the nature and approximate amount of the work, or feed, performed or furnished or intended to be performed or furnished therefor.

Such service may be made either by personal service or by mailing by registered mail a copy of said notice to the secured party or other lien holder at his last known post-office address. Said service shall be deemed complete upon the deposit of the notice in the post office.

Secured party may take possession of property. Within ten days after the date of such mailing, or five days after such personal service, the secured party or other lien holder, or his representative, shall have the right to take possession of said property upon payment of the amount of the lien then accrued. A failure on the part of such secured party or other lien holder so to do shall constitute a waiver of the priority of such security interest or other lien over the lien created by this act.

Male equine animals not to run on open range—definition of "open range." It shall be unlawful for any owner, person, firm, corporation or association having the management or control, of any stallion, ridgeling, unaltered male mule, or jackass, over the age of one year, to permit or suffer such animal to run at large on the open range. The term "open range" means all lands in the state of Montana not inclosed by a fence of not less than two wires in good repair; the term "open range" includes all highways outside of private inclosures and used by the public whether or not the same have been formally dedicated to the public.

Declaration of animals running at large as nuisance—abatement. Any such animal so running at large shall be, and it is hereby declared to be, a public nuisance, which, in addition to the means and proceedings prescribed by this act for its abatement and removal, may be abated and removed by the means and proceedings now, or hereafter to be, provided by law for the abatement or removal of public nuisances.

Castration of animals running at large—notice to owner—expense and charges. Any person may take up and secure any such animal found running at large on the open range. After taking it up he shall, without unnecessary delay, post at the United States post office or as near as may be to the place where the animal was taken up, a notice truly dated and subscribed by him, or his agent, to the effect that the animal, describing it by marks and brands (if any), color, and sex, was taken up on the day named while it was running at large on the open range in the county (naming the county) and that unless claimed and removed within five days next after the date of the posting the animal will be castrated at the expense of the owner thereof. Should the owner, person, firm, corporation or association having management or control, of such animal be known to the person who took the animal up, personal service of such notice upon the owner, person, firm, corporation or association having management or control of the animal shall be the equivalent to the posting, provided, the notice if personally served may state that unless the animal is claimed and removed within two days next after the date of the notice served personally, the animal will be castrated at the expense of the owner thereof.

If such animal so taken up be not claimed and removed within said five days or said two days, as the case may be, it may lawfully be castrated in the usual manner and doing no more harm than is necessary. The expense of castration shall be paid by the owner. If such animal be claimed within the time herein prescribed, the claimant shall pay to the person who took the animal up, the reasonable expense of the keeping and feed thereof since it was taken up, and also the sum of five dollars for the taking up and giving of the notice aforementioned; upon making such payments the claimant shall immediately remove and take away said animal.

Killing of animal running at large—notice—posting and service. If any such animal so running at large cannot, by reasonable effort, be captured, taken up, or corralled, it may lawfully be killed unless the owner, or person having the management or control of it shall take the animal off the open range and restrain it from running at large thereon within ten days next after the giving of notice as hereinafter provided. The notice shall be signed by one or more taxpayers of the vicinity of the range whereon such animal be at large, and be substantially as follows:

"To whom it may concern:

Take notice, that a certain (stallion, ridgeling, unaltered male mule, or jackass, as the case may be) is running at large on the open range (identify the range by general description) in _____ county, Montana. Unless said animal be removed therefrom and restrained from running at large on open range, within ten days next after the date of this notice, it will be killed.

(Date)   (Signature or signatures) ."

The notice shall be posted at the post office nearest the

place where the animal was last seen on the range, and like notices in two other of the most public places in the vicinity of said range, and like notice shall at once be mailed to the owner or person having management or control of the animal, if his name and address be known.

Killing animal to prevent injury not prohibited. This act is not intended, and it shall not be interpreted or understood, to limit or deny the right now existing to destroy or kill any such animal to prevent injury by it to any person or property.

Penalty for violations. Any owner, person, firm, corporation or association violating any provisions of this act shall be guilty of a misdemeanor, and upon conviction thereof shall be fined not less than ten dollars ($10.00) or more than twenty-five dollars ($25.00).

Recording brands

Recorder of marks and brands. The secretary of the livestock commission is the general recorder of marks and brands.

Recording of brands required. It shall be unlawful for any person, firm, or corporation to artificially brand or mark, or cause to be artificially branded or marked, any domestic animal or livestock, running at large, or upon the public domain, or open range, or which may run or stray at large or upon the public domain or open range, unless such artificial brand or mark has been recorded or re-recorded as provided by law, in the office of the general recorder of marks and brands, in the name of such person, firm, or corporation, within the period of ten years immediately preceding such branding or marking.

Application for recording—record of brands. Any person, firm, or corporation desiring to have recorded an artificial mark or brand for use in distinguishing or identifying the ownership of any domestic animal or livestock, shall make application therefor to the secretary of the livestock commission, who is in this act designated the general recorder of marks and brands. Such application must be in writing, and must contain the name, residence and post-office address of the applicant, and the species of the animals on which the mark or brand is to be used. The said recorder shall thereupon designate for the applicant's use some practical form of mark or brand, distinguishable with reasonable certainty from all other marks and brands recorded, or re-recorded, within the period of ten years immediately preceding the time of filing the application, as in this act provided, in the name of some person, firm, or corporation other than the applicant, and he shall designate the position on the animals upon which the mark or brand shall be placed, and the species of animals on which the mark or brand may be used. The general recorder of marks and brands shall keep a record in a book kept by him for that purpose, of the particular mark or brand, the position on the animal where the same is to be used, the species of animals on which the same is to be used, and the date of recording. Such record shall be a public record and shall be prima-facie evidence of the facts therein recorded.

Nebraska

Estrays and trespassing animals

Estrays, trespassing animals; damages; liability. The owners of cattle, horses, mules, swine and sheep in this state, shall hereafter be liable for all damages done by such stock upon the cultivated lands in this state.

Trespassing animals; damages; lien. All damages to property so committed by such stock running at large shall be paid by the owners of such stock; and the person, whose property is so damaged thereby, may have a lien upon such trespassing animals for the full amount of damages and costs, and may enforce the collection of the same by the proper civil action.

Trespassing animals; distraint; notice. When any such stock shall be found upon the cultivated lands of another, it shall be lawful for the owner or person in possession of such lands, to impound such stock, and if the owner of the stock can be found, and is known to the distrainor, it shall be the duty of the distrainor to notify the owner by leaving a written notice at his usual place of residence with some member of his family over the age of fourteen, or in the absence of such person, by posting on the door of such residence a copy of the notice of the distraint of the stock, describing it, and stating the amount of damages claimed and the name of the arbitrator, and requiring the owner within forty-eight hours after receiving such notice to take the stock away, after making full payment of all damages and costs to the satisfaction of the distrainor of trespassing animals. The notice may be in the following form:

Mr. _____:

You are hereby notified that on this _____ day of _____, 19_____, your stock, of which I now have in my possession _____ (here describe the animal or animals) did trespass upon my land, and damage the same to the amount of _____. You are required to pay the above charges within forty-eight hours from the delivery of this notice.

Livestock; agister's lien; foreclosure. When any person shall procure, contract with, or hire any other person to feed and take care of any kind of livestock, the person so procured, contracted with, or hired, shall have a first, paramount and prior lien upon such property for the feed and care bestowed by him upon the same for the contract price therefor, and in case no price has been agreed upon, then for the reasonable value of such feed and care, provided the holders of any prior liens shall have agreed in writing to the contract for the feed and care of the livestock involved. The person entitled to a lien under the provisions of this section, may foreclose the same in the manner provided by law for the foreclosing of chattel mortgages; *Provided,* at least thirty days before the sale of the property for the satisfaction of such lien, the person entitled thereto shall file in the office of the county clerk in the county in which said livestock may be fed and kept, an affidavit describing said livestock, and setting forth the amount justly due for the feeding and keeping of the same.

Stallion, jack or bull; lien for service. Every owner, lessee,

agent or manager of any stallion, jack or bull shall have a
lien upon any mare and her colt or upon any cow and her
calf served by such stallion, jack or bull for the full amount
of the reasonable or agreed value or price of such service.
Every such owner, lessee, agent or manager of such stallion,
jack or bull desiring to perfect a lien upon any mare and
her colt, or upon any cow and her calf, shall at any time
after breeding any such animal to any such male, file with
the county clerk of the county a verified notice of lien describing such animal with reasonable certainty, giving the
name of the owner and his place of residence if known, and
the name and residence of the person having the possession
of such animal, the location of such animal, the terms of
payment for such service, the amount thereof, the name of
the male, the date of service, and the time or event when the
same shall become due and payable and such other matters
as to make the same more certain. Thereafter such lienor shall
have a first lien upon such animal or animals described
therein, and their offspring as soon as the same may be born,
subject, however, to the lien of record of any prior mortgage
in good faith.

Driving off another's livestock; penalty. Any cattle drover,
or his employee, who shall drive off any neat cattle, horses,
mules, or sheep belonging to another person, intentionally or
through neglect, shall upon conviction thereof be fined in
any sum not more than one hundred dollars for each and
every head of cattle, horses, mules or sheep so driven off.

Herd laws; actions; proof of ownership. In any indictment
or complaint the description of any kind or class of neat cattle
shall be deemed sufficient if described as cattle; and the proof
of brand shall be deemed to be prima facie evidence of ownership of such stock.

Male animal running at large; liability of owner. The owner
of any stallion, jack, bull, buck, or boar shall restrain the
same, and any person may take possession of any such animal
running at large in the county in which such person resides,
or in which he occupies or uses real estate. He shall give notice
thereof to the sheriff or any constable in the county in which

such animal is taken, who shall give notice to the owner of such animal, if known to him, by delivering a written notice to said owner, or leaving the same at his usual place of abode, giving a description of the animal so taken. If such owner does not appear within ten days after such notice to claim his property and pay costs and damages if any, then the sheriff or constable shall sell the animal so taken, at public auction to the highest bidder for cash, having given twenty days' notice of the time and place of sale, with a description of the property, by publishing the same in a newspaper of general circulation in the county, or if there is no such paper, by posting such notice in three public places in the township or precinct in which such animal was found at large. Out of the proceeds of such sale he shall pay all costs and any damages done by such animal, to be ascertained and determined by him, and the sheriff or constable shall pay the remainder, if any, into the county treasury for the use of the county. If legal proof is made to the county board by the owner of such animal of a right thereto at any time within one year of the sale, the county board shall order the proper amount to be paid to the owner by its warrant drawn for that purpose. If the owner, or any person for him, on or before the day of sale shall pay the costs thus far made and all damages, to be determined by the sheriff or constable if the parties cannot agree, and make satisfactory proof of his ownership, the sheriff or constable shall release the animal to him; *Provided,* this remedy shall not be construed as a bar to any suit for damages sustained and not covered by the proceeds of the sale as hereinbefore provided.

Cattle drover; trespassing animals; duty to prevent. Any person owning or having charge of any drove of cattle, horses or sheep, numbering one head or more, who shall drive the same into or through any county of Nebraska of which the owner is not a resident, or landowner, or stock grower, and when the land in said county is occupied, it shall be the duty of such owner or person in charge of such horses, cattle or sheep to prevent the same from mixing with the cattle, horses or sheep belonging to the occupiers. The owner shall also prevent the drove from trespassing on such land as may be the property of the actual occupier, or may be held by him under a preemption, or a leasehold right, and used by him for the grazing of animals, growing hay or timber, or other agricultural purposes, or doing injury to the ditches made for irrigation of crops.

Cattle drover; trespassing; penalty; liability for damages. If any owner or person in charge of any drove of cattle, horses or sheep shall willfully, carelessly or negligently injure any resident within the state by driving such drove from the public highways and herding the same on the lands occupied and improved by persons in possession of the same, he shall be deemed guilty of a misdemeanor, and shall be punished by a fine of not less than twenty dollars and not more than one hundred dollars, and shall be liable for such damages as may be done to the property.

Brands and marks

Brand, defined. For the purpose of these sections a brand is defined as an identification mark that is burned into the hide of a live animal by a hot iron on either side in any one of three locations, the shoulder, ribs, or hip.

Brand; use of hot iron required; violation; penalty. After January 1, 1962, it shall be unlawful to brand any live animal except by the use of a hot iron. Any person, association, firm, or corporation violating the provisions of this section shall, upon conviction thereof, be fined in a sum not less than fifty dollars nor more than five hundred dollars.

Brands and marks; adoption and use. Any person or persons, association, firm, or corporation having cattle, sheep, horses, mules or asses, shall have the right to adopt a brand or mark, for the use of which he shall have the exclusive right in this state, after recording such brand or mark.

Nevada

Damages for trespass

Damages for livestock trespass; liability of landowners for injury to trespassing livestock; trespassing livestock treated as estrays.

1. If any livestock shall break into any grounds enclosed by a lawful fence, the owner or manager of such livestock shall be liable to the owner of such enclosed premises for all damages sustained by such trespass. If the trespass is repeated by neglect of the owner or manager of such livestock, he shall, for the second and every subsequent offense or trespass, be subject to double the damages of such trespass to the owner of the premises.

2. If any owner or occupier of any grounds or crops trespassed upon by livestock entering upon or breaking into his grounds, whether enclosed by a lawful fence or not, shall kill, maim or materially injure the livestock so trespassing, he shall be liable to the owner of such livestock for all damages, and for the costs accruing from a suit for such damages, when necessarily resorted to for their recovery.

3. The owner or occupier of such grounds or crops so damaged and trespassed upon may take up and safely keep, at the expense of the owner or owners thereof, after due notice to the owners, if known, such livestock, or so many of them as may be necessary to cover the damages he may have sustained, for 10 days, and if not applied for by the proper owner or owners before the expiration of 10 days, the same may be posted under the estray laws of the state, and before restitution shall be had by the owner or owners of such livestock, all damages done by them, as well also as the expense of posting and keeping them, shall be paid. Any justice of the peace in the township shall have jurisdiction of all such reclamation of livestock, together with the damages, and expense of keeping and posting the same, when the amount claimed does not exceed $100.

4. When two or more persons shall cultivate lands under one enclosure, neither of them shall place or cause to be placed any livestock on his ground, to the injury or damage of the other or others, but shall be liable for all damages thus sustained by the other or others. If repeated, after due notice

is given, and for every subsequent repetition, double damages shall be recoverable in any court having jurisdiction.

Trespass of livestock on cultivated lands; damages not to be awarded if land not enclosed by legal fence; "legal fence" defined.

1. No person, firm or corporation shall be entitled to collect damages, and no court in this state shall award damages, for any trespass of livestock on cultivated land in this state if such land, at the time of such trespass, shall not have been enclosed by a legal fence as defined in subsection 2.

2. A legal fence is defined for the purposes of this section as a fence with not less than four horizontal barriers, consisting of wires, boards, poles or other fence material in common use in the neighborhood, with posts set not more than 20 feet apart. The lower barrier shall be not more than 12 inches from the ground and the space between any two barriers shall be not more than 12 inches and the height of top barrier must be at least 48 inches above the ground. Every post shall be so set as to withstand a horizontal strain of 250 pounds at a point 4 feet from the ground, and each barrier shall be capable of withstanding a horizontal strain of 250 pounds at any point midway between the posts.

Owner may adopt brand, mark; must be legally recorded; unlawful earmarks.

1. Every owner of animals in this state may design and adopt a brand or brands, or brand and mark, or brands and marks, with which to brand or brand and mark his animals.

2. It shall be unlawful for any owner of such animals to brand or brand and mark, or cause to be branded or branded and marked, his animals with a brand or brand and mark not at the time of legal record as provided in NRS.

3. It shall be unlawful for any owner of such animals to use an earmark which involves the removal of more than one-half of the ear, measuring from the extreme tip of the ear to the head, or which brings the ear to a point by removing both edges of the ear.

Powers, duties of executive director of state department of agriculture. The executive director is empowered and authorized to carry out the terms and provisions of NRS and, for that purpose, to make such rules and regulations not inconsistent therewith, and to appoint such agents, under his direction, as he deems necessary therefor. All expense in connection therewith shall be met from the livestock inspection fund, except as provided in NRS.

Application for recording of brand, marks; Contents.

1. Any owner of animals in this state desiring to adopt and use thereupon any brand, or brand and mark, or marks, as provided for in NRS shall, before doing so, forward to the department an application, on a form approved and provided by the department for that purpose, for the recording of such brand, or brand and mark or marks, and receive a certificate of recordation as provided in NRS.

2. The application shall:

(a) Include a drawing, exact except as to size, of the brand, together with any earmarks or other marks desired or intended to be used therewith, and the location upon the animal or animals concerned where such brand and earmarks or other marks are desired or intended to be used;

New Hampshire

Trespassing Stock. If any person having the charge or custody of any sheep, goats, cattle, horses, or swine shall willfully or negligently suffer or permit the same to enter upon, pass over, or remain upon any improved or enclosed land of another without written permission of the owner, occupant, or his agent, and thereby injure his crops, or property, he shall be fined not more than ten dollars and he shall be liable for all damages done.

Deceit in Live Stock Registration. If any person by any false pretense shall obtain the registration of any animal in the herd register or other register of any club, association, society, or company for improving the breed of horses, cattle, sheep, swine, or other domestic animals, or a transfer of any such registration, or shall give a false pedigree of any animal, he shall be fined not more than two hundred dollars.

Certificate. Every person who offers for hire the service of a stallion for breeding purposes shall make a certificate stating the name, color, age, size and pedigree, so far as known, of the stallion, and the name and residence of the person by whom he was bred, and shall cause the certificate to be recorded by the commissioner of agriculture. He shall also insert a copy of the certificate in all posters and notices advertising the stallion, and shall give a copy of it to the keeper of each mare served by the stallion for hire.

Record. It shall be the duty of the commissioner to record all such certificates offered for record in a book to be kept in his office for that purpose, upon tender of lawful fees therefor.

Liens for board, lodging; agistment, service of stallion

Pasturage, etc. A person to whom horses, cattle, sheep or other domestic animals shall be intrusted to be pastured or boarded shall have a lien thereon for all proper charges due for such pasturing or board until the same shall be paid or tendered.

Service Fee. Colts foaled in this state shall be subject to a lien to secure the payment of the service fee for the stallion, which shall continue in force until the colt is eight months old, and may be enforced by an attachment of such colt at any time after it is four months old; said lien shall take precedence of any other claim.

Limitation. Such lien shall not be enforced unless the owner or manager of such stallion shall have complied with the requirements of this chapter.

New Jersey

Damages by and to animals

Damages by animals breaking through lawful fences. When horses, cattle or sheep shall get over, creep through or break down any fence declared lawful by this chapter, the owner of the animals shall pay to the person injured all damages occasioned thereby, to be appraised and certified in writing by two substantial and indifferent men of the neighborhood mutually chosen by the parties, which men, unless otherwise agreed upon by the parties, shall be owners of a class of property similar to that damaged. If the owner of the animals shall neglect or refuse to choose one of the appraisers then the injured party may choose both such appraisers himself. When the appraisers cannot agree upon the damages they may choose a freeholder of the neighborhood to join them, whereupon the appraisement by any two of them, made and certified in writing, shall be binding and conclusive upon the parties.

Impounding and sale of such animals. The person injured as provided in sections of this title may take and impound the animals found trespassing or doing damage, as therein provided, in his field or other inclosure for twenty-four hours and shall give notice thereof to the owner of the animals, if known and easily to be found.

If the animals are not redeemed within the twenty-four hours by payment of or satisfaction for the damages certified as provided in said section, the person damaged shall take them to the public pound of the township, where the poundkeeper shall receive and keep them until the damages so certified and the charges of conveying and pounding are paid.

The person damaged shall have twenty-five cents per head for horses and cattle and fifteen cents for sheep, for taking the animals to the pound, and the poundkeeper shall have the same fees for letting in and out of the pound, and forty cents per head for horses and cattle and twenty-five cents for sheep for every twenty-four hours they shall remain in the pound.

If the owner of the impounded animals does not pay the damages and charges of impounding within four days after the animals are impounded, or replevy them, the pound-keeper shall set up advertisements in at least three of the most public places in the township to which the pound belongs, and in one or more of the most public places in the two next adjoining townships, particularly describing the animals and giving at least thirty days' notice of an intended day and place of sale, and stating that if the owner does not appear and redeem the animals before the time so notified, they will be sold at public sale.

If the owner, or another for him, does not appear and redeem the animals at the time and place of the sale, the pound-keeper shall sell them accordingly, and out of the money arising therefrom shall pay the damages and charges of conveying to the pound, retain his fees for pounding, keeping and feeding the animals and the further sum of one dollar for each animal for setting up the advertisements and notice of sale and selling such animal, and return the surplus to the owner.

If the owner does not appear and claim the surplus within twelve calendar months after the sale, it shall be paid to the clerk of the township where the animals were impounded, for the use of the township.

Livery stables, and boarding and exchange stable keepers.

Right of lien; retention of property when amount due unpaid. Every keeper of a livery stable or boarding and exchange stable, shall have a lien on all animals left with him in livery, for board, sale or exchange and upon all carriages, wagons, sleighs and harness left with him for storage, sale or exchange for the amount due such proprietor for the board and keep of such animal and also for such storage, and shall have the right, without process of law, to retain the same until the amount of such indebtedness is discharged.

Sale of retained property; disposition of proceeds. Property retained by the proprietor under this article shall be sold at public auction, after the expiration of 30 days from the date of such retention.

Permitting stallion to run at large; penalty. A person who shall willfully or negligently suffer a stallion of the age of eighteen months or over, of which he is the owner or keeper, to run at large out of the inclosed ground of the owner or keeper, after having been notified thereof and been admonished to confine such stallion, shall forfeit and pay the sum of ten dollars ($10.00), to be recovered, with costs, by any person who shall sue for it, in a civil action, in any court of competent jurisdiction.

False statements as to pedigree of animals. Any person who, by any false statement or pretense as to the pedigree or breeding of a domestic animal, obtains registration or transfer of registration of the animal in the herd register or other register of any club, association, society or company for improving the breed of cattle, horses, sheep, swine or other domestic animals, or who knowingly or designedly, with intent to defraud, gives a false pedigree of any animal, is guilty of a misdemeanor.

New Mexico

Estrays

Definition of "estray."—Any bovine animal, horse, mule or ass, found running at large upon public or private lands, either fenced or unfenced, in the state of New Mexico, whose owner is unknown in the section where found, or which shall be fifty [50] miles or more from the limits of its usual range or pasture, or that is branded with a brand which is not on record in the office of the cattle sanitary board of New Mexico, shall be known as an "estray," and it shall be unlawful for any person, persons, corporation or any company, or their or either of their employees or agents to take up any such estray and retain possession of same, except as provided in this article.

Taking up of estray animals.—No person shall take up an estray animal except in the county where he resides and is a householder, nor unless the same be found in the vicinity of his residence. When any person shall take up an estray, he or she shall within five (5) days thereafter make out a written description of such animal or animals, as the case may be, setting forth all marks or brands appearing upon such animal, and other marks of identity, such as color, age, size, sex, and forward the same by mail to the secretary of the cattle sani-

tary board; Provided, that any person having knowledge of
any estray animal or animals upon any public or private
range, fenced or unfenced, may notify the cattle sanitary
board's secretary or any authorized brand inspector of said
board, giving description of said estray or estrays, and upon
instructions from said board, or from an authorized inspector
of said board, said estrays may be driven to a railroad shipping
point and there turned over to a duly authorized inspector
of said board for disposition as the said board may direct
according to law; Provided further that it shall be lawful
for any person having knowledge of any estray horse, mule or
ass grazing on the public domain, public highways or other
lands used for grazing purposes in conjunction with the public
domain, and who shall have the prior approval of or be acting
in co-operation with an authorized agent of the New Mexico
cattle sanitary board to impound and detain such estray animal or animals in an inclosure or roundup for a period not to
exceed seventy-two (72) hours for the purpose of ascertaining
ownership by brand and trespass statutes of said estray animal.
The owner or owners of such estray animal found to be in
trespass shall be allowed forty-eight (48) hours from receipt
of notice of impoundment within which to claim said animal
or animals and make settlement for trespass damage. If said
owner or owners shall fail to claim such animal or animals
and effect a settlement for trespass damages within the time
allowed, the estray animals detained shall be turned over to
a duly authorized inspector or agent of the cattle sanitary
board for disposition in the same manner as provided for other
estray animals under this section.

   Liens for board, feed, shelter or pasture—Priority.—A.   Innkeepers, livery stable keepers, lessors, and agistors, and those
who board others for pay, or furnish feed, shelter or pasture
for the property and stock of others, shall have a lien on the
property and stock of such guest or guests and lessees, or of
those to whom feed or shelter has been furnished until the
same is paid, and shall have the right to take and retain
possession of such property and stock until the indebtedness
is paid.

   B. It shall be unlawful for a lessee or owner to remove livestock from the leased premises, feedlot or pasture without the consent of the lessor, feedlot operator or agistor unless the amount due for pasturage or feed be paid.

C. The liens provided for in this section shall not take precedence over prior filed or recorded chattel mortgages, duly filed or recorded as provided by law, unless the holder of such mortgage shall expressly so consent in writing; Provided, that the giving of such written consent shall not affect the rights or priority under a prior mortgage as against a subsequent mortgage but the rights, liens and priorities of all such mortgages shall be and remain the same as if no such written consent had been given.

Brands of horses, mules, asses or neat cattle—Recording—Evidence of ownership.—No brands except such as are recorded under the provisions of this article shall be recognized in law as evidence of ownership of the horses, mules, asses or neat cattle upon which such brand may be used.

Shall have lien.—Owners of stallions and jacks for which license certificates are issued under the provisions of this act and owners of bulls, boars and rams which have been registered in accordance with the provisions of this act, shall have a lien upon the animal or animals bred by contract to such stallion, jack, bull, ram or boar and upon the progeny of such stallion, jack, bull, ram or boar, shall file in the office of the county clerk of the county in which such service is had, a description of such animal or animals served and such progeny, with approximate date of birth of such progeny, within six [6] months after the birth of such progeny. Said lien may be foreclosed as chattel mortgages in this state at any time after filing such description.

When unlawful to remove animals.—It shall be unlawful for the owner of any mare, jennet, cow, sow or ewe served by any stallion, jack, bull, ram or boar as mentioned in section 23 to sell such animal or animals or remove same from the county in which service was had before satisfaction of the lien created in said section, without first having obtained the written consent of the owner of said stallion, jack, bull, ram or boar, and such sale or removal shall constitute a misdemeanor and upon conviction thereof, shall be punished by

confinement in county jail not less than thirty [30] days nor
more than sixty [60] days, or by fine not to exceed fifty dollars
[$50.00].

Transfer of properties.—The secretary of the New Mexico
registration board is hereby authorized to transfer any and
all funds, records and properties of the said stallion registration board to the New Mexico sire registration board, and the
New Mexico stallion board is hereby abolished.

License certificate required for stallions and jacks.—Every
owner or keeper of any stallion or jack kept or offered for
sale, transfer, exchange or public service, who represents such
stallion or jack to be fit for service, shall procure a license
certificate and keep the same, or an exact copy thereof, posted
in a conspicuous place on or immediately adjacent to every
barn, shed or building in which such stallion or jack is kept
for service and shall mention the same in all advertisements,
as herein provided. Such license certificate shall be procured
from the New Mexico sire registration board.

How to obtain license certificate.—In order to obtain such
license certificate there shall be presented to said sire registration board an affidavit, signed by a qualified veterinarian, who
is not interested in the buying or selling of horses, mules or
jacks, and who has been appointed by said board (said veterinarian may be disqualified for cause), to the effect that he
has personally examined such stallion or jack and that to the
best of his knowledge and belief such stallion or jack is free
from such hereditary, infectious, contagious or transmissible
diseases or defects as: urethal [sic] gleet, melanosis, periodic
ophthalmia (moon blindness), laryngeal hemiplegia (roaring), dourine, glanders, farcy or serious defect in general conformation, and if the stallion or jack is purebred there shall
be presented to the veterinarian inspector for his examination
and comparison also a certificate of registration of such stallion or jack issued by one of the clubs, associations, societies
or companies recognized by the sire registration board.

Soundness required after four years.—Four [4] years after
this act becomes a law, the affidavit of the authorized veterinarian inspector shall be to the effect that he has personally
examined such stallion or jack, and that to the best of his

knowledge and belief such stallion or jack is free from such hereditary, infectious, contagious or transmissible diseases as: urethal gleet, melanosis, periodic ophthalmia (moon blindness), laryngeal hemiplegia (roaring), dourine, glanders, farcy, cataract, amaurosis, chorea (St. Vitus dance), string halt, bone spavin, bog spavin, ring bone, side bone, curb, curby formation of hock or any serious defects in general conformation.

Three forms of certificate.—The certificate for stallions shall be of three [3] forms as follows:

A. "Purebred" for animals correctly recorded in the stud book of any club, association, society, or company recognized by the sire registration board; for the purposes of this act a "standard bred" stallion registered in the stud book of the club, association, society, or company recognized by the sire registration board, shall be considered a purebred animal, and the words "purebred" wherever used in this act shall be construed to include "standard bred" stallions; the words "standard bred" may be used in lieu of the words "pure bred" in affidavits, license certificates, and advertisements relative to such stallions.

B. "Grade" for animals of which either the sire or dam was a pure-bred animal as evidenced by an affidavit of two [2] persons, not the owner or keeper of the animal, presented to the inspecting veterinarian.

C. "Scrub" for animals of which neither the sire nor dam was a purebred animal or which has not been registered in any stud book of any club, association, society or company recognized by the sire registration board.

The words "purebred," "grade" or "scrub" shall be set forth in conspicuous type at least once, near the top of each license certificate issued. Each license certificate shall state the name of the stallion or jack and if purebred the register name and number of the stud books in which such stallion or jack is registered. Each license certificate shall bear the name of the importer or breeder, the name of the present owner, a description of the color, the year foaled and the inspector's statement as to whether said stallion or jack is sound or unsound. If unsound, the license certificate shall contain the names of the diseases or defects of hereditary unsoundness with which the

animal is affected, the location of which shall be indicated by
means of a small diagram of a stallion properly marked by
the veterinarian inspector, by plainly writing or printing the
name or description of the hereditary defect or unsoundness
on the diagram with an arrow pointing to and plainly indicating on such diagram the location of the hereditary defect
or unsoundness. Each certificate shall bear the signatures of
the inspector and the secretary of the sire registration board
and shall have attached thereto the official seal of said board.

Qualifications.—No stallion or jack which may come into
the state of New Mexico, after this act shall take effect, shall
be given a license certificate if such stallion or jack is affected
with one [1] or more of the following diseases or defects,
namely: urethal gleet, melanosis, periodic ophthalmia (moon
blindness), laryngeal hemiplegia, (roaring) [sic] cataract,
amaurosis, chorea (St. Vitus dance), string halt, bone spavin,
bag, [sic] spavin, ring bone, side bone, curb, with curby formation of hock, or is seriously defective in conformation, or
vicious disposition of [or] habits.

New York

Damages for insufficient fence

Whenever the electors of any town shall have made any rule
or regulation prescribing what shall be deemed a sufficient
division fence in such town, any person who shall thereafter
neglect to keep a fence according to such rule or regulation
shall be precluded from recovering compensation for damages
done by any beast lawfully kept upon the adjoining lands that
may enter therefrom on any lands of such person, not fenced
in conformity to the said rule or regulation, through any such
defective fence. When the sufficiency of a fence shall come in
question in any action, it shall be presumed to have been
sufficient until the contrary be established.

When the owners of adjoining lands shall choose to let them
lie open, as provided in section three hundred, neither of such
owners shall be liable to the other in any action or proceeding
for any damages done by animals lawfully upon the other's

premises going upon the lands so lying open or upon any other lands of the owner thereof through such lands so lying open. Either owner of any lands so lying open and adjoining may, unless the agreement is for a specified period, and after such agreement has expired may then have the same inclosed, by giving written notice to that effect to the owners or occupants of the adjoining lands, whereupon it shall be the duty of both parties to build and maintain their several proportions of a division fence.

Lien of bailee of animals

Any veterinarian, duly licensed to practice under the laws of this state, who in connection with such practice renders professional services in the treatment of any dog, cat, or other domestic animal or boards any such animal on his premises, or a person keeping a *livery stable,* or boarding stable for animals, or pasturing or boarding one or more animals, or who in connection therewith keeps or stores any wagon, truck, cart, carriage, vehicle or harness, has a lien dependent upon the possession upon each dog, cat or other animal kept, pastured or boarded by him, and upon any wagon, truck, cart, carriage, vehicle or harness, of any kind or description, stored or kept provided an express or implied agreement is made with the owners thereof, whether such owner be a mortgagor remaining in possession or otherwise, for the sum due him for the professional service rendered, care, keeping, boarding or pasturing of the animal, or for the keeping or storing of any wagon, truck, cart, carriage, vehicle and harness, under the agreement, and may detain the dog, cat or other animal or wagon, truck, cart, carriage, vehicle and harness accordingly, until such sum is paid.

Protecting the breeding of pure bred stock

It shall be unlawful for any person or persons owning or in the possession of any bull of the age of more than six months, any stallion of the age of more than eighteen months, or buck or boar over five months of age, to suffer or permit such animal or animals to go, or range, or run at large on any lands or premises without the consent of the person entitled to the possession of such land or premises.

No right of action shall accrue under this section to any person who, being liable to contribute to the erection or repair of a division fence as required by the town law, shall neglect or refuse to make and maintain his proportion of such fence, or shall permit the same to be out of repair, for damages done by any animal described in this section coming, by reason of such defective fence, from adjoining lands where such animal was lawfully kept.

Enrollment of stallions required

No person, firm or corporation shall use or offer for use for service in this state any stallion, unless and until he shall have caused the name, description, breeding and pedigree of such stallion to be enrolled, and such stallion has been inspected in accordance with the provisions of this article and a certificate, showing such enrollment and inspection, has been issued as hereinafter provided. Use or offer for use for service in this state of any stallion shall mean the mating of any stallion, by any person, firm or corporation, to mares other than his, their, or its own.

False pedigree of animals

Every person who by any false pretense shall obtain from any club, association, society or company for improving the breed of cattle, horses, sheep, swine or other domestic animals the registration of any animal in the herd register or other register of any such club, association, society or company or a transfer of any such registration, and every person who shall knowingly give a false pedigree of any animal, shall be deemed guilty of a misdemeanor.

North Carolina

Allowing stock at large in stock-law territory forbidden.—If any person shall allow his livestock to run at large within the

limits of any county, township or district in which a stock law
prevails or shall prevail pursuant to law, he shall be guilty of
a misdemeanor, and fined not exceeding fifty dollars or imprisoned not exceeding thirty days.

Impounding stock at large in territory.—Any person may
take up any livestock running at large within any township or
district wherein the stock law shall be in force and impound
the same; and such impounder may demand one dollar for
each animal so taken up, and fifty cents for each animal for
every day such stock is kept impounded, and may retain the
same, with the right to use under proper care, until all legal
charges for impounding said stock and for damages caused by
the same are paid, the damages to be ascertained by two disinterested freeholders, to be selected by the owner and the impounder, the freeholders to select an umpire, if they cannot
agree, and their decision to be final.

Persons entitled to lien on personal property.—Any person
engaged in the business of boarding animals has a lien on the
animals boarded for reasonable charges for such boarding
which are contracted for with an owner or legal possessor of
the animal and which become due and payable within 90
days preceding the mailing of notice of sale. This lien shall
have priority over perfected and unperfected security interests.

Owners of stock to register brand or marks.—Every person
who has any horses, cattle, hogs or sheep may have an earmark
or brand different from the earmark or brand of all other
persons, which he shall record with the clerk of the board of
commissioners of the county where his horses, cattle, hogs or
sheep are; and he may brand all horses eighteen months old
and upwards with the said brand, and earmark all his hogs
and sheep six months old and upwards with the said earmark;
and earmark or brand all his cattle twelve months old and
upwards; and if any dispute shall arise about any earmark or
brand, the same shall be decided by the record thereof.

*Obtaining property by false representation of pedigree of
animals.*—If any person shall, with intent to defraud or cheat,
knowingly represent any animal for breeding purposes as being
of greater degree of any particular strain of blood than such
animal actually possesses, and by such representation obtain

from any other person money or other thing of value, he shall be guilty of a misdemeanor, and upon conviction thereof shall for each offense be punished by a fine of not less than sixty dollars nor more than three hundred dollars, or by imprisonment for a term not exceeding six months.

Obtaining certificate of registration of animals by false representation.—If any person shall, by any false representation or pretense, with intent to defraud or cheat, obtain from any club, association, society or company for the improvement of the breed of cattle, horses, sheep, swine, fowls or other domestic animals or birds, a certificate of registration of any animal in the herd register of any such association, society or company, or a transfer of any such registration, upon conviction thereof he shall be punished by imprisonment for a term not exceeding three months or a fine not exceeding one hundred dollars, or by both such fine and imprisonment.

North Dakota

Certain animals not to be permitted to run at large at any time—Penalty.—The owner or person in charge of any stallion, jack, boar, ram, bull, or any animal known to be vicious who permits such animal to run at large shall be liable in a civil action to any person who is injured, either directly or indirectly, by such violation for all damages resulting therefrom and shall be guilty of a misdemeanor and shall be punished by a fine of not less than ten dollars nor more than fifty dollars. The provisions of this section, however, shall not prevent the keeping of any stallion, jack, bull, or ram with any herd or flock which is attended by a herder if such stallion, jack, bull, or ram is kept with such herd or flock by the herder.

Trespass and injury to property—Liability of owner of trespassing horses, mules, and cattle.—The owner or possessor of any horse, mule, or head of cattle which shall inflict any damage to the crops or other property of another or which shall trespass upon the lands of another, whether such lands are fenced or unfenced, shall be liable to the persons sustaining the injuries or to the owner of the lands for all damages suffered by him, together with the statutory costs of the action to recover such damages, and a reasonable attorney's fee therein to be allowed by the court.

Agister's lien authorized.—Any person to whom any horses, mules, cattle, or sheep shall be entrusted by the owner thereof for the purpose of feeding, herding, pasturing, or ranching shall have a lien upon the horses, mules, cattle, or sheep for the amount that may be due for feeding, herding, pasturing, or ranching, and shall be authorized to retain possession of the horses, mules, cattle, or sheep until the amount is paid. These provisions shall not be construed to apply to stolen stock.

Priority of agister's lien—Notice to holders of prior liens.—An agister's lien shall have priority over all other liens on the property for ten days after the receipt thereof, and thereafter shall have priority over all other liens on the property if the person to whom the property is entrusted as provided in this chapter, within such ten days, shall serve written notice upon the holders of prior liens that the property has been entrusted for one or more of the purposes mentioned in above section, specify which purpose, and the name of the person entrusting the property therefor. If the residence of the holder of the lien is unknown, or if he is not a resident of this state, the notice may be served by publication thereof in one issue of a newspaper published in the county in which the property is being kept.

Office for recording brands.—A general office for recording marks and brands shall be maintained in the office of the commissioner of agriculture and labor.

Application for exclusive use of brand or mark—Recording of brands and marks.—Any person desiring the exclusive use of any mark or brand shall file with the commissioner of agriculture and labor an application:

1. Setting forth a description of the mark or brand of which he desires the exclusive use and a facsimile thereof;

2. Stating the kind or kinds of livestock upon which the mark or brand is to be used; and

3. Indicating clearly the place or position upon each kind of livestock where such brand is to be placed, except that the hips of any cattle shall not be used for registered

numerical brands, but shall be used exclusively for numbers used for the individual identification of each animal.

The commissioner shall record the mark or brand described in the application if the same has not been recorded previously in favor of another person, and shall show in his record the place or position such mark or brand will occupy on each kind of livestock. The mark or brand for which an applicant applies shall be given to him whenever it is possible to do so without conflicting or interfering with any previously recorded mark or brand, and if the mark or brand applied for has been recorded previously, the commissioner shall notify the applicant of this fact and permit such applicant to apply for another and different mark or brand.

Exclusive use of brand or mark on poultry—How obtained. —The exclusive use of any mark or brand upon poultry may be obtained in the manner provided in this chapter. The fee for recording poultry brands or marks, including stenciling, tattooing, and indelible marking, shall be the same as is provided in this chapter for the recording of a livestock mark or brand. Poultry may be branded or marked upon either wing.

Record of brands kept—Inspection of record—Certificate of ownership of brand—Fee.—The commissioner of agriculture and labor shall keep a record of all marks and brands showing the names and residences of the persons owning the same, a description and facsimile of each mark or brand, and in the case of livestock, the range occupied by such stock, as nearly as the same may be determined. Such record shall be open to the inspection of any person interested therein. The commissioner shall deliver to the owner of each mark or brand a certificate thereof, and such certificate shall be evidence of ownership of the mark or brand described therein. The fee for such certificate shall be five dollars.

Regulations governing fraudulent registration of purebred livestock—Penalty.—Any person who shall:

1. Fraudulently represent any animal to be purebred;
2. Post or publish, or cause to be posted or published, any false pedigree or certificate;
3. Procure by fraud, false pretense, or misrepresentation

the registration of any animal which is to be used for service, sale, or exchange in this state for the purpose of deception as to the pedigree thereof;

4. Sell or otherwise dispose of any animal as a purebred when he knows or has reason to believe that the animal is not the offspring of a regularly registered purebred sire and dam; or

5. Sell or otherwise dispose of any animal as a registered purebred by the use of a false pedigree or certificate of registration,

shall be guilty of a misdemeanor and shall be punished by a fine of not less than twenty-five dollars nor more than one thousand dollars, or by imprisonment in the county jail for not less than thirty days nor more than six months, or by both such fine and imprisonment.

Abuse of animals prohibited—Penalty.—Any person who shall willfully:

1. Overdrive any animal;

2. Overload any animal;

3. Drive any animal when the same is overloaded;

4. Overwork any animal;

5. Torture any animal;

6. Torment any animal;

7. Deprive any animal of necessary food or water;

8. Cruelly beat any animal;

9. Work any animal which is unfit for work;

10. Expose any animal to heat or cold or leave the same hitched and uncovered in cold or stormy weather; or

11. Cause or procure any of the things enumerated in this section to be done,

shall be guilty of a misdemeanor and shall be punished by imprisonment in the county jail for not less than ten days nor more than thirty days, or by a fine of not less than five dollars nor more than one hundred dollars, or by both such fine and imprisonment.

Ohio

Damage by trespassing animals.

If a horse, mule, ass, hog, sheep, goat, or any neat cattle, injures or trespasses upon land or an enclosure bounded by a partition fence, in consequence of the failure or neglect of a person to keep up and maintain in good repair his share of such fence, such person failing or neglecting shall pay to the person injured the damages sustained thereby, to be assessed, under oath, by three judicious, disinterested men, residents of the county, appointed by a judge of a municipal court having jurisdiction of the township in which the premises are situated. If such damages are not paid after demand therefor, the amount thereof may be recovered in an action with cost of suit.

Liability of owner of trespassing animal.

If a horse, mule, ass, hog, sheep, goat, or any neat cattle, running at large, breaks into or enters an enclosure, other than enclosures of railroads, the *owner of such* animal is liable to the owner or occupant of such enclosure for all damages occasioned thereby. An animal, so breaking into or entering, is not exempt from execution on a judgment rendered in a court, or before an officer having jurisdiction, for damages occasioned by such trespass.

Lien for care of animals.

As used in sections of the Revised Code "animal" means any animal other than man and includes fowl, birds, fish, and reptiles, and "owner" means and includes the person who holds legal title to an animal, or any other person, having lawful custody of an animal, who contracts for food, board, or professional services for such animal.

Any person who feeds or boards an animal under contract with the owner shall have a lien on such animal to secure payment for food and board furnished.

Sale of animal to satisfy claim.

If the owner of an animal, upon written demand by the lienholder, fails to satisfy a lien acquired under section of the Revised Code the lienholder may sell the animal at public sale to satisfy such lien, provided that before the animal is offered for sale the lienholder shall give ten days' notice of the time and place of sale in a newspaper of general circulation in the county where food or board was furnished. The lienholder, on the day following publication, shall mail a copy of the public notice to the owner by registered mail at the last known address of such owner. If the animal is sold for a price which exceeds the amount of the lien, plus costs incurred by the lienholder, the remaining balance shall be paid by the lienholder to the owner or to such other person as may be legally entitled to receive same. If the lienholder sells or otherwise disposes of any animal without first giving the notice required by this section he shall not pursue any deficiency upon such obligation.

Lien upon get for service.

The keeper of any stallion, jack, or registered pure-bred bull, has a lien upon its get for the period of twelve months after birth thereof, for the payment of the service of such stallion, jack, or bull.

Enforcement of lien.

A keeper or owner of any stallion, jack, or registered pure-bred bull may enforce his lien for service by replevin of the property before any justice of the peace of the township, or judge or magistrate of the municipal corporation, where it is found. Upon gaining possession thereof, on first giving ten days' notice to the reputed owner of his intention to do so, he may sell it at public sale after two weeks' notice of the time and place of sale by notices posted in five conspicuous and public places in the township or municipal corporation where proceedings in replevin are had.

Out of the proceeds of sale such keeper or owner may retain

the amount due him for such service, with the costs by him incurred in the replevin suit. He must account to the owner of the get for any surplus realized by the sale. When payment is made to him, or his agent, for any such get, the owner of any such stallion, jack, or bull shall deliver to the payee a receipt in full for the amount thereof, and stating for what paid.

Furnishing false pedigree.

No person shall willfully furnish the purchaser of an animal with a false pedigree or false certificate of sale, or willfully use a false pedigree or false certificate of sale for deceiving, whether furnished, given, or procured in this state or elsewhere.

Whoever violates this section shall be fined not less than twenty-five nor more than five hundred dollars or imprisoned not more than six months, or both.

Unlawfully obtaining registry or transfer in herd registry.

No person shall, by a false pretense, obtain from any club, association, society, or company for improving the breed of cattle, horses, sheep, swine, or other domestic animals, the registration, or a certificate thereof, of any animal in the herd register, or any other register of such club, association, society, or company, or a transfer of such registration, or make, exhibit, or give a false pedigree in writing of any animal.

Whoever violates this section shall be fined not less than fifty nor more than one thousand dollars or imprisoned not more than two years, or both.

Oklahoma

Restraint of all domestic animals—Damages for trespass

All domestic animals shall be restrained by the owner thereof at all times and seasons of the year from running at large in the State of Oklahoma. Damages sustained by reason of such domestic animals trespassing upon lands of another shall be recovered in a manner provided by law. For the purpose of this act, domestic animals shall include cattle, horses, swine, sheep, goats, and all other animals not considered wild but shall not include domestic house pets.

Liability for damages by animals unlawfully at large—Action—Distraint—When animals not considered running at large. The owner of any stock or domestic animal prohibited by law, from running at large or prohibited by police regulation adopted by vote of any stock district from running at large within the district at any times shall be liable for all damages done thereby while wrongfully remaining at large upon the public highway or upon the lands of another; which damages may be recovered by action at law; or the party injured may at his option distrain the trespassing animals and retain the same in some safe place, at the expense of the owner, until damages are paid, as provided in this Article, said damages to be assessed pro rata per head, and each owner, if more than one owner, shall be liable for the pro rata amount, and each owner shall have the right to discharge his stock from distraint by paying the said pro rata amount to the person damaged, together with his pro rata share of the costs of such distraint: Provided, However, that no stock or domestic animal prohibited from running at large by virtue of such police regulation shall be considered as running at large so long as the same is upon unimproved and uncultivated lands of the owner of said stock and under the immediate care and control of the owner or upon the public highway under such control; but if permitted while under such care and control to stray upon the lands of another, it shall be held to be at large.

Letting male animals to service—Advertisement of terms—Publication or posting—Acceptance. The owner or keeper of any stallion, jack or bull may advertise the terms upon which he will let such animal to service by publication thereof in some newspaper in the county where such animal is kept for a period of sixty days during the season of each year, or by printed handbills conspicuously posted during such period, in four or more public places in said county, including the place where such animal is kept; and the publication or posting as aforesaid of the terms of such service shall impart notice thereof to the owner of any female animal served by such stallion, jack, or bull, during such season; and in all actions and controversies in respect to the foal or other product of such service, the owner of such female animal so served shall be deemed to have accepted and assented to said terms, when so advertised or posted as provided herein.

Filing of certificate of service—Lien on offspring—Notice to third parties—Lien without certificate. When the said terms of such service by any such animal, published or posted as provided in the next preceding section, shall provide that the foal or other product of such service will be held for the money due for the service of such stallion, jack or bull, then and in that event the owner or keeper of any such animal may file with the register of deeds of the county in which such animal is kept for service, a certificate signed by the owner of the female bred, or his representative, also by the owner or keeper of the male animal rendering the service, stating the terms of such service, a description of the female served, also a description of the male rendering the service, the date of service and acceptance of terms by owner of female; and such certificate, if filed within three months after the rendering of such service, shall become and continue a lien on the offspring for the period of six months after the birth thereof, and the filing of such certificate shall be constructive notice to any third party of the existence of the lien: Provided, that as between the owner of any stallion, jack or bull, as provided in the preceding section, and the owner of any female served, a lien shall exist notwithstanding no certificate as herein provided.

False or fictitious pedigree—False representation of recording or eligibility for record—Forfeiture of rights. If any keeper of such stallion, jack or bull, shall offer and advertise to let the service of such animal, and shall give a false or fictitious pedigree, knowing the same to be false, or shall falsely represent such animal to be recorded or eligible to be recorded in any of the various books of record kept for recording animals of that breed, he shall forfeit all claim to the value of the services rendered by such animal, and shall not be entitled to the benefits of any provision of this article.

Lien for feeding, grazing and herding. Any person employed in feeding, grazing or herding any domestic animals, whether in pasture or otherwise, shall have a lien on said animals for the amount due for such feeding, grazing or herding.

Lien for furnishing feed. Any person, partnership, firm or corporation in this State, or in any border county of the adjacent States, furnishing or providing to the owner of such domestic animals any corn, feed, forage or hay, for the sustenance of such domestic animals, shall have a lien on said animals for the amount due for such corn, forage, feed and hay.

Lien for keeping, boarding or training animal—Scope. Every person who shall keep, board or train any animal, shall, for the amount due therefor, have a lien on such animal, and on any vehicle, harness or equipment coming into his possession therewith, and no owner or claimant shall have the right to take any such property out of the custody of the person having such lien, except with his consent, or on the payment of such charge; and such lien shall be valid against said property in the possession of any person receiving or purchasing it with notice of such claim.

Stallions and Jacks, Licenses and Liens

Necessity of license certificate—Members of Live Stock Registry Board. Every person, persons, firm, corporation, company or association that shall stand, travel, advertise or offer for public service in any manner any stallion or jack in the State of Oklahoma, before being entitled to the benefit of the lien hereinafter provided for the services of such animals, shall secure a license certificate for such stallion or jack, from the Oklahoma Live Stock Registry Board, as hereinafter provided. Said Board shall consist of the dean of the division of Agriculture, head of the animal husbandry department, and the head of the veterinary department of the Oklahoma State Agricultural College.

Requirements to obtain license certificates—Registry certificates and other papers—Breeding affidavits—Statements—Fees. To obtain a license certificate as herein provided, the owner of such stallion or jack shall comply with the following requirements:

First. The owner of a pure bred stallion or jack shall forward to the Oklahoma State Live Stock Registry Board of Inspection, the registry certificate, or a certified copy of the registry certificate of such stallion or jack, also other necessary papers or documents, relating to the breeding and ownership of such stallion or jack.

Second. Owners of cross-bred or grade stallions or jacks shall forward to the Oklahoma State Live Stock Registry Board affidavit showing the breeding of such stallion or jack.

Third. Owners of scrub stallions or jacks shall forward to the Oklahoma Live Stock Registry Board a statement of the age, color and size of such stallion or jack.

Livestock Brands

Livestock Brand. Except as otherwise provided herein and except as may be directed by the State Board of Agriculture, the powers, duties and functions vested by this Article in the State Board of Agriculture shall be exercised and performed through a division of the State Department of Agriculture to be known as the Livestock Brand Division of the State Department of Agriculture, which is hereby established. Such Division shall be under the immediate supervision of a Director, who shall be appointed by the Board and whose compensation and duties, other than those specified in this Article, shall be fixed by the Board.

Definitions. For the purposes of this Article and as used therein:

(a) A "brand" shall mean a permanent identification mark of which the letters, numbers and figures used are each three (3) inches or more in length or diameter and are burned into the hide of a live animal with a hot iron, and is to be considered in relation to its location on such animal, and such term relates to both the mark and location;

(b) A "mark" shall mean a permanent identification cut from the ear or ears of a live animal;

(c) The term "animal" shall mean any cattle, *horse* or mule;

(d) The term "livestock" shall mean any cattle, horse or mule;

(e) The term "Board" shall mean the State Board of Agriculture;

(f) The term "Division" shall mean the Brand Division of the State Department of Agriculture.

Oregon

Male stock running at large on open range

Male stock running at large on open range. (1) No person shall turn upon, or allow to run upon, the open range, any bull other than a purebred bull of a recognized beef breed. The department shall by regulation define "purebred bull of a recognized beef breed." No person shall turn upon, or allow to run upon, the open range, any female breeding cattle unless he turns with such female breeding cattle one purebred bull of a recognized beef breed for every 25 females or fraction thereof of 10 or over.

(2) No owner of any stallion or jackass, of the age of 18 months or more, shall permit it to run upon the open range during the period April 1 to October 31 of each year. No owner of any ram shall permit it to run at large upon the open range during the period July 1 to October 31 of each year.

Taking up and selling animals; estrays; interfering with animals

Definitions. As used in ORS: "estray" means livestock of any unknown owner which is unlawfully being permitted to run at large or which is found to be trespassing on land inclosed by an adequate fence. Where an animal has broken through a fence on the open range and a determination is necessary as to the adequacy of the fence in order to enable the department to determine if the animal is an estray, the determination shall be made by the department.

Owner of lessee of property taking up livestock unlawfully permitted to run at large; notice to owner and department.

(1) A person who finds livestock unlawfully being permitted to run at large upon his premises, or premises of which he has lawful possession or control, may take up the livestock if the owner thereof is known to him.

(2) A person taking up livestock shall within five days give notice of the taking up by certified or registered mail addressed to the owner or person having control of the livestock. The notice shall:

(a) Contain a concise description of the livestock, including marks and brands, if any.

(b) State that the livestock will be released to and sold by the department as an estray unless redeemed before such sale.

(c) Designate the time and place of sale, as approved by the department. The sale shall be held not less than 30 days nor more than 45 days from the date of the taking up.

(3) A person taking up livestock shall within five days of giving the notice provided in subsection (2) of this section forward a copy of the notice to the department or give a copy of the notice to a brand inspector or other agent of the department.

Delivery of livestock to department or owner; payment of costs to person taking up livestock. (1) If the owner of the livestock does not appear in response to the notice given under subsection (2) of ORS, the livestock shall be delivered to the department at least 48 hours in advance of the date of sale and shall be sold by the department as an estray. If the department is satisfied that adequate notice has been given to the owner, the department need not publish notice as required by subsection (2) of ORS.

(2) If the owner of the livestock does appear, the livestock shall be delivered to him or his agent if he pays to the person taking up the livestock, before the date of sale:

(a) The cost of taking up the livestock;

(b) The cost of giving notice;

(c) The cost of keeping the livestock; and

(d) The cost of repairing any damage done by the livestock to the property of the person taking it up.

The person taking up the livestock, upon delivery thereof to the owner, shall notify the department that such action has been taken.

(3) If the owner is unable to agree with the person taking up the livestock as to the amount of the costs, the owner and the person taking up the livestock shall each name one arbitrator and the two arbitrators so named shall choose a third. The arbitrators may hear witnesses, take testimony, inspect the livestock and the premises and decide the amount to be allowed. Their decision shall be final, except as provided in subsection (2) of ORS.

(4) If the owner refuses to arbitrate or to be bound by the award thereof, the livestock shall be delivered to the department and sold by it as an estray. If the person taking up the livestock refuses to arbitrate or to be bound by the award thereof, the livestock shall not be sold; and the owner shall be entitled to the possession thereof.

Alternative procedure for person taking up livestock. A person taking up livestock, in lieu of following the procedure established by ORS, may, within five days after the taking up, deliver the livestock to the department. The person shall have no claim, right or title to the livestock or the proceeds from the sale thereof. The livestock shall be disposed of by the department as an estray.

Taking up estray prohibited without giving notice. No person shall knowingly take up or retain possession, custody or control of an estray without giving the notice required by ORS.

Notice to department of taking up estray. A person taking up an estray shall notify the department of such fact in writing within five days of the taking. The notice shall be sent to the department at its Salem office.

Investigation by department upon receipt of notice. (1) The department, when it receives a notice of taking, shall undertake to determine the animal's true owner from the recorded brand, marks and other identifying characteristics and other relevant information tending to establish ownership.

(2) A record of such information, together with the findings of the department supporting its determination of ownership, shall be made and preserved for three years.

Sale of estray if owner not found; notice of sale. (1) If the department does not determine who is the true owner of the estray, it shall, not sooner than 30 days nor more than 45 days after receiving the notice of taking, cause the estray to be sold at public sale.

(2) The department shall cause a notice of taking up to be published in a newspaper of general circulation through the area in which the estray was taken up, once a week for two successive weeks or two publications in all prior to the sale. The notice shall state, among other things, that the estray will be sold at a stated time and place if not claimed by the true owner prior to the date of sale.

Claim by owner prior to sale. If the owner of an estray appears and claims it prior to sale, he shall pay all costs.

Stablekeeper's lien

Stablekeeper's lien. Stablekeepers shall have a lien on animals, carriages, wagons, sleighs and harness left with them for board, storage, sale or exchange for the amount of the bill due the stablekeeper for the board and storage, and may, without process of law, retain the same until such indebtedness is discharged.

Foreclosure. All property retained by any stablekeeper pursuant to ORS may, after the expiration of 30 days from the date of such retention, be sold at public auction, by first giving notice of such sale for a period of two weeks in some newspaper of general circulation published in the city in which such stable is situated, and also by five days' notice posted in five of the most public places in the city or place where the sale is to be had; provided, if no newspaper is published in such city, the notice shall be given in some newspaper of general circulation published within the county. The proceeds of the sale shall be applied, first, to the payment of the lien and the expense of the sale, and the balance, if any, to the owner of the property or his authorized representative.

Lien for stud or artificial insemination services

Lien for stud or artificial insemination services. The owner of any stallion or jack which is kept and licensed for the breeding of mares not owned by the owner of the stallion or jack, and any person who artificially inseminates any female domestic animal, shall have a lien upon any female animal to which such male is let or which has been artificially inseminated, and her offspring, for the sum contracted therefor, which lien shall attach at the time of service of the male or of artificial insemination, and shall not be lost by reason of any sale, exchange or removal from the county, or other disposition of the female animal or her offspring without consent of the person holding the lien.

Foreclosure. At any time within 20 months after his right of action accrues, the holder of the lien described in ORS may file with any justice of the peace in the county, a written statement, duly verified, setting forth the amount of his claim, his cause of action, and a description of the animal upon which he has a lien, and the justice shall thereupon issue summons as in other cases and embody therein a description of the animal and an order to the constable to take the animal and her offspring, if any, and hold them subject to the order of the court. If upon trial, judgment is rendered for the plaintiff, the court shall order a sale of the animals as on execution, to pay the judgment.

"Brand" defined. (1) "Brand" as used in this chapter, ORS and other laws relating to animals, means a distinctive design, mark or identification, made or applied to the hide, skins or wool in places on animals by the use of a hot iron or by any other method or process approved by the department.

After one or more public hearings and under the provisions of ORS chapter 183, the department may promulgate rules relating to:

The brands, and the animals to which such brands may be applied, which in addition to a hot iron brand shall be legal in Oregon and which shall be subject to and covered by this chapter and other laws prescribed in this section.

The designation of places and the limitation of the places on animals to which a brand shall only be used or applied thereon.

The process, method or the means of making, applying and using a brand which shall include but not be limited to the use of a hot iron brand on an animal in Oregon.

"Livestock" means all cattle, horses, mules and asses, or other animals designated by the department.

"Department" means the State Department of Agriculture.

"Director" means the Director of Agriculture.

Recording brands with department; furnishing copies of brands. (1) The department shall record livestock brands.

(2) The department, upon request, shall furnish to the county sheriffs of the respective counties a copy of all brands used by stock growers and stock owners within such county.

Pennsylvania

Distraint of trespassing horses and cattle

If any horse, mare, colt, cattle or sheep, after the publication of this act, shall trespass, by breaking into the inclosure of any person or persons within this province, the same being made according to the act, entitled, "An act for erecting pounds in each township of this province," every such person, being injured by such trespass, may seize and distrain such horse, mare, colt, cattle or sheep, and the same, so seized and distrained, may retain, until he shall recover and receive the damages sustained by such trespass, together with the costs of advertising, and reasonable charges for keeping such distress, in manner hereinafter directed.

Certain animals not permitted to run at large

From and after the passage of this act, no stallion, bull, boar, ram, or jack, shall be permitted to run at large on the public highways of this commonwealth.

Pedigree to be filed in quarter sessions

Every owner or agent who may have the custody or control of any stallion, who shall charge a fee for the services of such stallion, shall, before advertising or offering such services to the public for any fee, reward or compensation, file with the clerk of the court of quarter sessions of the county in which such owner or owners, agent or agents reside, or in which such stallion shall be kept for service, a written statement giving the name, age, pedigree and record, if known, and if not known, then that the same is unknown, the description, terms and condition[s] upon which such stallion will serve. Upon filing such statement, the clerk of the court of quarter sessions for the county shall issue a certificate or license to the owner or owners, agent or agents having the custody and control of such stallion, that such a statement has been filed in his office. The clerk of the court of quarter sessions to receive one dollar for each and every certificate so issued, and the county commissioners are hereby authorized and required to furnish registration books and blanks for such purposes. The owners, agent or agents of the owners of such stallion shall then post a written or printed copy of the statement, so filed with such clerk of the court of quarter sessions, in a conspicuous place in each locality in which said stallion shall be kept for service.

Penalty for false pedigree or for non-compliance

Every owner or agent who shall file, proclaim or publish a false or fraudulent pedigree or record or statement of any kind regarding any stallion, or who shall neglect or refuse to comply with the provisions of section one of this act, shall forfeit all fees for the services of such stallion, and the person or persons who may be deceived or defrauded by such false or fraudulent pedigree or record or statement may sue and recover, in any court of competent jurisdiction.

Lien on horses

From and after the passing of this act, all livery stable keepers and innkeepers within this commonwealth shall have a lien upon any and every horse delivered to them to be kept in their stables, for the expense of the keeping; and in case the owner of the said horse or horses, or the person who delivered them for keeping to the keeper of the livery stable or innkeepers, shall not pay and discharge the said expense, provided it amount to thirty dollars, within fifteen days after demand made of him personally, or in case of his removal from the place where such livery stable or inn is kept, within ten days after notice of the amount due, and demand of payment in writing left at his last place of abode, the livery stable keeper or innkeeper may cause the horse or horses aforesaid, to be sold at public sale according to law, and after deducting from the amount of sales the costs of sale and the expense of keeping, shall deliver the residue upon demand to the person or the agent of the person who delivered the horse or horses to him for keeping: Provided always, That nothing in this act contained shall be construed to impair any right of action which the said livery stable keepers or innkeepers may have against any person or persons, for the keeping his or their horse or horses.

Rhode Island

Damage by animals

Male animals at large—Absolute liability for damages.—No stallion over one (1) year old, nor bull over six (6) months old, nor boar, nor ram, nor billy goat over four (4) months old shall run at large; and if the owner or keeper shall, for any reason, suffer any such animal so to do he shall forfeit five dollars ($5.00) to the person taking it up and be liable in addition for all damages done by such animal while so at large, although he escapes without the fault of such owner or keeper; and the construction of any lawful fence shall not relieve such owner or keeper from liability for any damage committed by an animal of the enumerated class upon the enclosed premises of an adjoining owner.

Animals breaking into enclosure—Action for damages—Impoundment.—If any neat-cattle, horses, sheep or hogs shall break through a lawful fence into the enclosure of any person, the person aggrieved thereby may recover his damages either by action against the owner of the trespassing beasts or by impounding such beasts.

Appraisal of damages for recovery by impoundment.—The party aggrieved, in order to be entitled to recover damages by impounding, shall, within two (2) days after such beasts break into his enclosure, get two (2) qualified electors of the town wherein the trespass is committed, to appraise the damage and give a statement thereof in writing, under their hands, and shall lodge the same with the poundkeeper.

Notice to owner of impoundment.—Whenever beasts are impounded, the poundkeeper shall, within forty-eight (48) hours thereafter, give notice thereof in writing to the owner, if the owner shall be known to him and resides within six (6) miles from the pound; which notice shall be delivered to the owner or left at his place of abode, and shall contain a description of the beasts and a statement of the time and cause of impounding; and in case the owner shall not be so known, or resides more than six (6) miles from the pound, the person impounding shall post up such notice in three (3) public places in the town in which the beasts are impounded.

Sale of impounded animals.—If the owner of such beasts impounded as aforesaid shall not, within ten (10) days after the impounding thereof, pay and satisfy the damages appraised as aforesaid and the charges of impounding and feeding said beasts, or shall not replevy the same, the poundkeeper shall cause them to be sold by public auction in the town where they are impounded.

Estrays

Taking up on private land.—If any person shall find any horse, neat-beast, sheep or hog on his land doing damage, not knowing to whom the same belongs, he may take up such animal as an estray, and within two (2) days thereafter he shall repair to the town clerk of the town in which the same was taken up and give notice thereof.

Notice and publication of estrays.—The town clerk shall thereupon cause to be made three (3) notifications, attested under his hand, setting forth the natural and artificial marks of such animal, one of which notifications he shall cause to be set up in some public place in the said town and the other two in some public places in the several adjoining towns in the state, and shall also cause such notifications to be published in one of the newspapers published in the several adjoining towns to that in which such estray shall be taken up.

Retention of estrays by taker.—Every animal so strayed and taken up shall be kept by the person who took it up thirty (30) days, and, if it be a horse, shall have a withe kept about his neck the whole of said time.

Reclaimer of estrays by owner.—Any person laying just claim to such animal may, at any time within the thirty (30) days, have the same again upon paying the just and reasonable charges of keeping and notifying as aforesaid over and above the actual benefit derived from the use of the same.

Settlement of disputes as to maintenance charges.—In case any difference shall arise between the said parties about the charge of keeping such animal, the same may be referred to the district court having jurisdiction in said town, which shall hear and determine the same and tax costs as in other cases.

False animal registrations and pedigrees.—Every person who by any false pretense shall obtain from any club, association, society or company for improving the breed of cattle, horses, sheep, swine or other domestic animals, the registration of any animal in the herd register or other register of any such club, association, society or company, or who knowingly shall obtain a transfer of any such registration, and every person who shall knowingly give a false pedigree of any animal, upon conviction thereof shall be punished by imprisonment for a term not exceeding one (1) year, or by a fine not exceeding five hundred dollars ($500), or by both such fine and imprisonment.

Fraudulent stock certificates.—Every president, secretary, cashier, treasurer or other officer or agent of any incorporated company or institution, who shall fraudulently issue any stock or certificate of stock of any such company or institution, shall be fined not less than one thousand dollars ($1,000) and shall be imprisoned not exceeding ten (10) years, nor less than one (1) year.

South Carolina

Liability of owners of stock trespassing.—Whenever any domestic animals shall be found upon the lands of any other person than the owner or manager of such animals, the owner of such trespassing stock shall be liable for all damages sustained and for the expenses of seizure and maintenance. Such damages and expenses shall be recovered, when necessary, by action in any court of competent jurisdiction. And the trespassing stock shall be held liable for such damages and expenses, in preference to all other liens, claims or encumbrances upon it.

Stock trespassing may be seized.—Any freeholder or tenant of land, his agent or representative, may seize and hold possession of any domestic animal which may be trespassing upon his premises and as compensation for such seizure may demand of the owner of every such horse, mule, ass, jennet, bull, ox, cow, calf or swine the sum of fifty cents, and of every such sheep, goat or other animal not herein named the sum of twenty-five cents, together with just damages for injuries sustained. Such claim shall, when possible, be laid before the owner of the trespassing stock within forty-eight hours after seizure of the stock.

Liability of owner for maintenance; bond; recovery of pos-

session.—In case the claim shall not be amicably or legally adjusted and the trespassing animals recovered by the owner within twelve hours after the receipt of such notification, the owner shall further become liable in a sum sufficient to cover the maintenance and care of his stock up to the time of its removal. But the owner shall be entitled to recover immediate possession of his stock on due execution of such bond to cover expenses and claimed damages as any magistrate shall decide to be good and sufficient.

Rescuing trespassing stock a misdemeanor.—Whenever any animal shall be taken up under the provisions of this article, it shall be unlawful for any person to rescue it or deliver it from the custody of the person impounding it; and whoever shall violate this provision shall be guilty of a misdemeanor and be punished by a fine of not less than five nor more than thirty dollars or by imprisonment in the county jail not less than five nor more than thirty days.

Lien of stable or kennel keeper on horse or dog.—A stable or kennel keeper shall have a lien upon any horse or dog which is left with him for upkeep, rest and training until the cost of the upkeep, rest and training has been paid by the owner of the horse or dog. The owner of the horse or dog shall also be responsible for payment of the cost of upkeep, rest and training of the horse or dog after notice of the lien. If the owner of the horse or dog has not paid the cost of upkeep, rest and training of the horse or dog after actual notice of the lien within sixty days of such notice, the stable or kennel keeper may sell the horse or dog after having advertised the time and place of the sale in a newspaper having general circulation in the county wherein the stable or kennel is located at least fifteen days before the sale is to be held. After the sale of the horse or dog the stable or kennel keeper may deduct the cost of the upkeep, rest and training of the horse or dog before and after date of the notice of the lien, plus all expenses incurred from the advertising and sale provided in this section, and shall submit the balance of the proceeds of the sale to the previous owner of the horse or dog.

Definitions.—The following words and phrases, as used in

this article, shall have the following meanings, unless the context otherwise requires:

(1) *"Livestock"* includes neat cattle, *horses,* mules, asses, hogs, sheep and goats; and

(2) *"Owner"* and *"stock owner"* mean any person who owns livestock.

Branding lawful.—It is lawful to brand livestock with the owner's brand in accordance with the provisions of this article.

Earmarking.—In addition to, or as an alternative to, a brand, any person may have an earmark for marking livestock. All provisions of this article relating to brands shall apply to earmarks.

One brand per person.—No person shall have or use more than one brand.

Wife or minor may have own brand.—A wife who owns livestock separate from her huband or a minor who owns livestock separate from his father or guardian may have a brand. The father or guardian of any minor who has a brand shall be responsible for the proper use thereof.

Application for adoption of brand; fee.—Any person desiring to adopt any brand for branding livestock, which brand is not then the recorded brand of another, shall forward to the Secretary of State a facsimile of the desired brand together with a written application to adopt the brand. The application shall state where the brand will appear on the livestock. A fee of three dollars shall be enclosed with the application.

Issuance of certificate.—Upon receipt of the application and the fee, the Secretary of State shall register the brand and issue to the applicant a certificate showing that his brand has been registered, unless the brand is already registered as the brand of another or unless the brand would probably be mistaken for a brand already registered.

Lien of owners of stock, etc., on issue.—The owner of any stock horse, jack, bull, boar or ram, kept by him for the purpose of raising from, having a claim by contract against the owner of any mare or cow or other stock for service shall have a prior lien on the issue of such mare, cow or other stock for the amount of such claim, provided an action shall be instituted to enforce such claim by suit before a magistrate or other officer having jurisdiction within twelve months from the time such claim shall have accrued.

South Dakota

Permitting adult male animal to run at large as misdemeanor—Penalty.—It shall be unlawful for the owner or person in charge of any stallion over the age of eighteen months, or any bull over the age of ten months, or any ram or boar over the age of eight months to permit the same to run at large in this state. Any person violating the provisions of this section shall be guilty of a misdemeanor and upon conviction, shall be punished by a fine of not less than ten dollars nor more than fifty dollars.

Castration lawful for adult male animal running at large—Liability for unauthorized castration.—It shall be lawful for any person to castrate or cause to be castrated any animal described above found running at large; but if any person shall castrate any stallion, bull, ram, or boar, and it shall be proved that such animal was not of a class of stock prohibited from running at large, such person shall be liable for damages to the amount of the value of such animal so castrated.

Running at large defined.—For the purpose of this chapter the term "running at large" shall mean intentionally left outside of the inclosure of a legal fence, and off of the lands owned or controlled by the owner of such animal.

Owner or person in charge of livestock liable for damage from trespass on lands of another.—Except as in this chapter otherwise provided, any person owning or having in his charge or possession any horses, mules, cattle, goats, sheep, or swine, which such animals shall trespass upon the land, either fenced or unfenced, owned by or in possession of any person, or being cropped by any person injured by such trespass, shall be liable to any such person injured for all damages sustained by reason of such trespassing.

Trespass liability not applicable to unfenced lands within national forests.—No person shall be liable for damages caused by horses, cattle, mules, goats, or sheep owned by him, which trespass upon lands within the exterior boundaries of the Black Hills and Harney national forests, which lands were not at the time of the trespass inclosed by a legal fence.

Notice to livestock owner of injury from trespass.—The person claiming injury from trespass of livestock, before commencing action thereon shall notify the owner or person having in charge such livestock, of the injury and probable amount of the damages, provided he knows to whom such livestock belongs.

Retention of trespassing livestock until damages paid.—Any person suffering injury from trespass of livestock may retain and keep in custody such offending animal or animals until the damages and costs are paid, or until good and sufficient security be given for the same.

Notice to owner of seizure of trespassing animals.—Whenever any animal or animals are restrained, the person restraining the same shall forthwith notify the owner or person in whose custody the same were at the time the trespass was committed, of the seizure thereof, providing the owner or person who had the same in charge is known to the person making said seizure.

Agister's lien for service and supplies—Entitled to retain possession.—Any person to whom any domesticated animal shall be entrusted by the owner thereof or pursuant to his authority for the purpose of feeding, herding, pasturing, or ranging shall have a lien thereon for the amount that may be due for such service and supplies. Such lien shall entitle the person to retain possession of such domesticated animals until the amount due is paid.

Transportation of animal into state without certificate unlawful.—It shall be unlawful for any railroad, express, or other transportation company to transport into this state any stallion or jack unless it be accompanied by a state or federal veterinary certificate.

Exclusive right to use brand after registration.—Any person having cattle, swine, sheep, horses, mules, or asses shall have the right to adopt a brand, to the use of which he shall have exclusive right in this state, after registering such brand and renewing the same as provided in this chapter.

*Filing of application for brand—*Facsimile and description *included.—*Any person desiring to use any brand shall make and sign a witnessed or notarized application setting forth a facsimile and description of the brand which he desires to use, and file the same for registration in the office of the state brand board, and shall thereafter renew the same.

*Certificate of enrollment required for stallion or jack offered for public service—Recording with register of deeds—Contents of certificate.—*Every person standing or traveling any stallion or jack for public service in the state shall cause the name, description, and pedigree of such stallion or jack to be enrolled by the state livestock sanitary board, and shall procure a certificate of such enrollment from such board, which shall thereupon be recorded in the office of the register of deeds of the county or counties in which such stallion or jack is used for public service. Certificates of enrollment shall be signed by the president, attested by the secretary, with the seal of the board attached, and shall be in such form as the board may prescribe. Each certificate shall show the owner, name, age, color, and breeding of the animal to which it relates.

*Diseases disqualifying stallion or jack for public service—Refusal or revocation of certificate.—*Any one or more of the following diseases shall disqualify a stallion or jack for public service: specific ophthalmia, including moon-blindness, laryngeal hemiphlegia ("roaring" or "whistling"), bone spavin, ringbone, glanders, farcy, dourine (maladie du coit), urethral gleet, mange, bog-spavin, or a curb when accompanied by faulty conformation. The livestock sanitary board shall refuse a certificate of enrollment of any stallion or jack affected with any such disease, and revoke any certificate previously issued when the animal shall be found upon examination to be so affected.

Certificate and affidavit of veterinarian required for en-

rollment—Veterinarian's charges.—In order to secure the certificate of enrollment provided for in this chapter, the owner of each stallion or jack shall present to the livestock sanitary board a certificate and affidavit from a licensed veterinarian, to the effect that he has personally examined such stallion or jack and to the best of his knowledge and belief such animal is free from contagious, infectious, or transmissible disease. No veterinarian shall charge for making such examination and issuing such certificate and affidavit more than five dollars and necessary expenses for each animal examined.

Traveling veterinarian for isolated locations—Notice to owners—Maximum fee.—Whenever by reason of there being no licensed veterinarian located within a reasonable distance, owners in any part of the state cannot secure certificates of examination without unreasonable cost, the livestock sanitary board shall appoint a veterinarian to make examinations, under its orders, in such locality. Such veterinarian, having selected a centrally located place, shall notify all owners within a reasonable distance of the time when such examinations will be made. The veterinarian shall not charge for his services more than five dollars for each animal examined.

Re-examination by veterinarian not required unless demanded by customers.—After a stallion or jack has been properly examined by a licensed veterinarian and legally licensed, it need not be again examined unless an examination shall be deemed necessary for the best interests of the public and be demanded by three or more patrons of such animal.

Pedigree papers submitted to board—Issuance of certificate of enrollment.—Each owner of a stallion or jack shall furnish to the livestock sanitary board the stud book registry certificate of pedigree of the stallion or jack and all other necessary papers relating to its breeding and ownership. Upon verification of such pedigree and certificate of breeding in case of a purebred animal, and upon receipt of the veterinary certificate and affidavit a certificate of enrollment shall be issued to the owner.

Fees payable for enrollment and renewal.—A fee not exceeding two dollars shall be paid to the state livestock sanitary board for the examination and enrollment of each pedigree and the issuance of an enrollment certificate, as provided in this chapter; and a fee not exceeding two dollars shall be paid annually to such board for the renewal of any such certificate.

Transfer of certificate on transfer of ownership—Fee.—Upon the transfer of the ownership of any enrolled stallion or jack, its certificate of enrollment may be transferred by the secretary of the livestock sanitary board to the transferee, upon satisfactory proof of such transfer of ownership and upon payment of fifty cents.

Posting of certificate where animal stands for service—Contents—Grades defined.—The owner of any stallion or jack standing for public service in this state shall keep posted during the entire breeding season copies of the certificate of enrollment of such animal, in a conspicuous place upon the main door leading into every stable or building where such animal stands for public service. Such copies shall be printed in boldfaced type, not smaller than pica, especially the words "purebred," "grade," or "no-grade." For the purposes of this chapter a "purebred" shall be construed to mean an animal whose pedigree is registered in a stud book recognized by the United States department of agriculture or in any American stud book registry association that recognizes and records stallions and jacks that have five pure topcrosses, and whose sire and dam are of pure breeding; a "grade"

Stud service lien on female and offspring.—All owners or any person in charge of a stallion, jack, bull, or other sire shall have a lien for the service fees of the same upon the female served and upon the offspring of such service.

Statement filed with register of deeds for stud service lien—Contents.—Every owner of a sire charging a service fee, in order to have a lien for said service, shall file with the register of deeds of the county where the service is to be rendered, a statement, verified by oath or affirmation, to the best of his knowledge and belief, giving the name, age, description, and pedigree, if any, or if none, stating none, as well as the terms and conditions upon which such sire is advertised for service.

Certificate of stud service lien issued by register of deeds—

Filing and posting—Contents.—The register of deeds, upon receipt of the statement duly verified by affidavit, shall issue a certificate to the owner of said sire, a copy of which certificate shall be filed with the clerk of courts in the county where said sire is stationed or located, and other copies furnished the applicant shall be posted by the owner in conspicuous places where said sire may be stationed for service, which certificate shall state the name, age, description, pedigree, or if none, stating none, and ownership of said sire, the terms and conditions upon which the sire is advertised for service, and that the provisions of this chapter so far as relates to the filing of the statement have been complied with.

Stud service lien on particular female filed with register of deeds—Notice to purchasers and encumbrancers.—If the owner or person in charge of the sire desires to retain the lien provided for its service fee, he shall within twenty-four months after such service file with the register of deeds of the county where the female is situated, a description of said female, including the name, age, color, date of service, and amount of service fee on forms to be provided by the secretary of agriculture, and when so filed, the same shall operate as notice to all subsequent purchasers and encumbrancers during the life of such lien.

Stud service fee due on removal of female from county.—In case the female covered by a lien is sold or removed from the county where the service was rendered, and from the county of the residence of the owner, during the life of such lien, the fee for such service shall be due and payable at once.

Duration of stud service lien on female and offspring—Priority over other claims.—The owner of any sire, by complying with the statutes relating to such lien, shall obtain and have a lien upon the female and upon the get of such sire for a period of eighteen months from the date of birth of such get, and such lien shall have priority over all other purchases and encumbrances upon the get, and over all purchases and encumbrances on the female except those taken and filed in good faith and for value prior to filing notice of lien for service fees of said sire.

False advertising unlawful—Certificate included in advertisement.—It shall be unlawful for the owner of any stallion or jack enrolled under this chapter to issue or use any bill, poster, or advertisement, for the purpose of advertising such animal, which does not contain a copy of his enrollment certificate or which contains any registration pedigree or other matter that is untruthful or misleading.

Penalty for violation of chapter.—Violation of any of the provisions of this chapter shall be punished by a fine of not less than twenty-five dollars nor more than one hundred dollars for each and every offense.

Veterinarian's permit revoked for violations.—In addition to the penalty the livestock sanitary board may revoke the permit of any veterinary to examine stallions or jacks under the provisions of this chapter after the second violation of any of the provisions of this chapter by such veterinary.

Certificate of health required for importation of stallion or jack.—It shall be unlawful for any person to import into this state any stallion or jack for sale or breeding purposes without first having secured a certificate from a recognized state or federal veterinary officer, certifying that such animal is free from any of the following diseases or unsoundnesses: cataract, amaurosis, laryngeal hemiphlegia (roaring or whistling), stringhalt, glanders, sidebone, farcy, maladie du coit, urethral gleet, mange, bone spavin, ringbone, and curb when accompanied by curby hock; a copy of which certificate must be mailed to the secretary of the state livestock sanitary board at least five days before the importation of such animal into the state.

Tennessee

Damages for trespass—Determination—Recovery.—When any trespass shall have been committed by horses, cattle, hogs, goats, sheep, or other stock upon the cleared and cultivated ground of any person having the same fenced, he may complain to a justice of the peace of the county, who shall cause two (2) discreet and impartial freeholders to be summoned, and with them shall view and examine, on oath of the free-holders to do justice, whether the complainant's fence be a lawful fence, and what damage, if any, he has sustained by said trespass, and certify the result of such view and examination under the hands and seals of the justice and freeholders, which certificate the justice shall deliver to the complainant, and said certificate shall be prima facie evidence of the plaintiff's demand; and the owner of the stock shall be entitled to a hearing, but if not successful, shall make full satisfaction for the trespass and damages to the party injured, to be recovered as such damages and costs, subject to the right of appeal of either party. To secure the payment of any judgment, execution may be levied upon the stock committing the trespass; and after ten (10) days' notice such stock may be sold to satisfy the judgment so recovered.

Horses, cattle, and mules sufficiently fenced.—The following shall be sufficient and be deemed a lawful fence only as to horses, cattle, and mules: Any inclosure made by stretching not less than five (5) strands of barbed wire tightly between posts firmly set in the ground, or between growing trees and posts firmly set in the ground, not more than twenty (20) feet apart; the topmost wire not less than four and a half (4½) feet from the ground, the bottom wire not less than six (6) inches, and the next to the bottom wire not less than fifteen (15) inches from the ground.

Pasturage lien.—When any horse or other animal is received to pasture for a consideration, the farmer shall have a lien upon the animal for his proper charges, the same as the innkeeper's lien at common law; and in addition he shall have a statutory lien for six (6) months.

Lien on female for service of male.—Where the lien for pasturage shall occur, the charges shall include also those for the service of any jack, bull, ram, or boar; provided, that the charge for the service of such animal to the female shall have been agreed upon between the parties.

Livery stable keeper's lien.—Livery stable keepers shall be entitled to the same lien provided for section 1 on all stock received by them for board and feed, or vehicle kept and/or conditioned, until all reasonable charges are paid.

Lien on offspring for service of male.—Any person keeping a jack, bull, ram, or boar, for public use, shall have a lien on the offspring of the same for the season charge to be paid.

Duration of lien on offspring.—The lien provided above, so far as it affects the offspring of jacks and bulls shall exist for two (2) years from the birth of such offspring and so far as it affects rams and boars shall continue for twelve (12) months from the birth of such offspring.

Lien on female for service of male.—Where the lien for pasturage shall occur, the charges shall include also those for the service of any jack, bull, ram, or boar; provided, that the charge for the service of such animal to the female shall have been agreed upon between the parties. The provisions of this section shall likewise include the service of any stud or stallion.

Lien on offspring for service of male.—Any person keeping a jack, bull, ram, or boar, for public use, shall have a lien on the offspring of the same for the season charge to be paid. The provisions of this section shall likewise include the service of any stud or stallion.

Pedigreed jacks or bulls for breeding to be registered—Clerk's fee.—The pedigree of any jack or bull, claimed to be pedigreed livestock and used for public breeding, shall be filed and registered with the county court clerk, under oath that the same is genuine, and the clerk of the county court shall record said pedigree in a well-bound book to be kept in his office for that purpose, and he shall be allowed the sum of fifty cents (50¢) as fee for filing, recording, and making three (3) certified copies of said pedigree aforesaid.

Pedigrees to be posted.—The owner of such pedigreed stock shall, during breeding seasons, have posted conspicuously in three (3) different places in the county in which he lives, or in which the animal is being used for breeding purposes, a certified copy of said pedigree recorded as provided above.

Hiring of horse or vehicle—Distance and time of use to be stated.—Whenever any person shall hire any horse, buggy, or other animal or vehicle from any livery stable keeper or other person engaged in the business of keeping them for hire, he shall first state to the said owner or keeper, if asked by owner or keeper, the distance or the time in which he proposes to keep or travel with said horse, or other animal, or vehicle; and no person shall willfully and maliciously, and with a fraudulent intent to deceive such owner or keeper, exceed the limit of time or distance for which said horse, buggy, or other animal or vehicle has been engaged.

Hiring horse or vehicle under fictitious name or name of another without authority prohibited.—No person shall hire any horse, buggy, or other animal, or vehicle, under a fictitious name; nor shall any person hire any horse, buggy, or other animal, or vehicle, for any other person, unless it shall be shown to the satisfaction of the said owner or keeper that it is with the knowledge or consent of said other person.

Penalty for improper hiring of horse or vehicle—Prosecutor. —Any person violating the above provisions shall be guilty of a misdemeanor, and shall be subject to indictment or presentment, and upon conviction shall be fined not less than five dollars ($5.00) nor more than fifty dollars ($50.00), and be imprisoned in the county jail for not more than three (3) months, imprisonment only in the discretion of the court; provided, that no one shall become prosecutor except the owner of the animal or vehicle.

Obtaining or giving false pedigree—Selling animal under false representation of pedigree—Penalty.—Any person who, by any false pretense, shall willfully obtain from any club, association, or society or company for improving the breed of cattle, horses, sheep, swine, or any other domestic animals, a certicate of registration of any animal in the herd register or other register of any such club, association, society, or company, or a transfer of any such registration; and any person who shall knowingly give a false pedigree of any animal, or who shall sell any animal, falsely representing the same to be a registered animal, or entitled to registration in any such club, association, society, or company, shall, upon conviction, be punished by imprisonment in the penitentiary for a term not exceeding three (3) years nor less than one (1) year, or in the county jail for a term not exceeding one (1) year, or by a fine not exceeding one thousand dollars ($1,000), or by both such fine and imprisonment, in the discretion of the jury.

Marks and brands of animals running at large.—All persons

owning any cattle, hogs, sheep or goats, horses or other animals, running at large, shall have an earmark or brand different from those of his neighbors.

Horses to be branded.—The owner shall brand all horses,
from eighteen (18) months old and upwards, with the same
brand, and earmark and brand all his cattle from twelve (12)
months old and upwards with the same mark or brand.

Texas

Stock running at large

If any stock forbidden to run at large shall enter the inclosed
lands, or shall, without being herded, roam about the residence, lots or cultivated lands of any person other than the
owner of such stock without his consent, in any county or
subdivision in which the provisions of this chapter have become operative in the manner provided in this chapter, the
owner, lessee, or person in lawful possession of such lands
may impound such stock and detain the same until his fees
and all damages occasioned by said stock are paid to him;
provided that no animals shall be impounded except as provided in the preceding article, unless they have entered upon
the inclosed lands or be found roaming about the residence,
lots or cultivated land of another, and, whenever any stock is
impounded, notice thereof shall be given to the owner, if
known, and such owner shall be entitled to their possession
upon payment of fees and damages.

Stock not to be injured. If any person whose fence is insufficient under this law shall, with guns, dogs or otherwise
maim, wound or kill any cattle, or any horse, mule, jack or
jennet, or procure the same to be done, such person or persons
so offending shall give full satisfaction to the party injured
for all damages by such person or persons sustained, to be
recovered as in other suits for damages; provided, that this
article shall not be so construed as to authorize any person
in any event to maim, kill or wound any horse, mule, jack,
jennet or cattle belonging to another. When a trespass has
been committed by any cattle or horses on the cleared or culti-

vated land of any person who has complied with the provisions of this chapter, in the erection of a lawful fence, such
person may complain thereof to the justice of the peace of
the precinct in which such trespass shall have been committed;
and such justice is hereby authorized and required to cause
two disinterested and impartial freeholders to be summoned,
who shall on oath view and examine whether such complaint
be sufficient or not, and what damages have been sustained
by said trespass, and certify the same in writing; and, if it
shall so appear that said fence be sufficient, then the *owner of*
such cattle or horses *shall make just satisfaction for the trespass to the party injured,* to be recovered before any tribunal
having proper jurisdiction. In case of a second trespass by the
same cattle or horses, the owner or lessee of the premises upon
which the trespass is committed may, if he deem it necessary
for the protection and preservation of his premises or growing
crops thereon, cause said stock to be penned and turned over
to the sheriff or constable, and held responsible to the person
damaged for all damages caused by said stock and all costs
thereof. It shall be lawful for the owner or lessee of such inclosures as are contemplated in this law to charge twenty-five
cents per day per head for impounding such stock as referred
to in this law. Id.

Marks and brands

County brands. Each county shall have a brand for horses
and cattle, said brand to be known and designated as the
"county brand."

Stock breeder's lien. The owner or keeper of any stallion,
jack, bull or boar, who keeps the same confined for the purpose of standing him for profit, shall have a preference lien
upon the progeny of such stallion, jack, bull or boar to secure
the payment for the amount due such owner or keeper for
the services of such stallion, jack, bull or boar, and such lien
shall exist by reason of the force and effect of the provisions
hereof, and it shall never be necessary in order to secure and
fix said lien to secure, file or register any contract or statement
thereof with any officer, nor shall it be necessary that the
owner of such progeny execute any contract whatever, but

such preference lien may be foreclosed in the same manner as the statutory landlord's lien is by law enforced; provided, that where parties misrepresent their stock by false pedigree, no lien shall obtain. Said lien shall remain in force for a period of ten months from the birth of said progeny, but shall not be enforced until five months shall have elapsed after such birth.

Livery stables, etc. Proprietors of livery or public stables shall have a special lien on all animals placed with them for feed, care and attention, as also upon such carriages, buggies or other vehicles as may have been placed in their care, for the amount of the charges against the same; and this article shall apply to and include owners or lessees of pastures, who shall have a similar lien on all animals placed with them for pasturage.

Driving live stock from range. Whoever shall wilfully kill, destroy, drive, or remove any live stock not his own from its accustomed range, without the consent of the owner, under such circumstances as not to constitute theft, shall be fined not exceeding one thousand dollars. In any prosecution under this article, after proof of the act of killing, destroying, driving, using or removing from the range of any stock not belonging to or under the control of the accused, it shall devolve upon the accused to show any fact under which he can justify or mitigate his act.

Use of false pedigree or certificate of sale. Whoever shall wilfully furnish or give to a purchaser of any animal any false pedigree or false certificate of sale of such animal, or shall wilfully use, for the purpose of deceiving, any false pedigree or false certificate of sale of any animal, whether such false pedigree or false certificate was furnished, given or procured in this State or elsewhere, shall be fined not less than twenty-five nor more than five hundred dollars, or be imprisoned in jail not exceeding six months, or both.

Utah

Trespassing animals—Damages for.—If any neat cattle, horses, asses, mules, sheep, goats or swine shall trespass or do damage upon the premises of any person, except in cases where such premises are not inclosed by a lawful fence in counties where a fence is required by law, the party aggrieved, whether he is the owner or the occupant of such premises, may recover damages by a civil action against the owner of the trespassing animals or by distraining and impounding such animals in the manner provided herein; *provided,* that in cases where an action is brought for the recovery of such damages none of the animals trespassing shall be exempt from execution, and the fees in such cases shall be but one-half the fees in other civil actions.

Commingling animals—Trespass—Damages—Misdemeanor.—Every person having charge of, or engaged in driving, any drove of cattle, horses, mules or sheep shall use due diligence to prevent the same from mixing with the cattle, horses, mules or sheep belonging to actual settlers; and shall also prevent such drove from trespassing on the land of an actual settler used by him for grazing animals or growing hay, grain or timber, and from doing injury to irrigating ditches. If any person in charge of, or engaged in driving, any herd injures any resident in the state by driving or herding the same on lands or ditches owned or leased by settlers, the owner or lessee of such herd shall be liable to such owners or lessees for all damages done; and, if such injury is willfully committed, the person driving such animals is guilty of a misdemeanor, and may be fined in any sum not exceeding $100.

Running at large—Misdemeanor—Local option.—Every person owning or having in charge a stallion, jack or ridgeling over eighteen months old, or a ram over three months old, who permits the same to run at large within the limits of or on the summer range of any town or settlement is guilty of a misdemeanor, and may be fined in any sum not exceeding $25 for each offense; *provided,* that if two-thirds of the voters of any county or isolated part of a county shall desire and the board of county commissioners shall so decide, then the provisions of this section shall be inoperative in such county or part of the county during such time as the board may determine.

Board to pass on qualifications.—The state board of agriculture shall:

(1) Examine and pass upon all stallions and jacks and pass upon all documents as provided for in this article.

(2) Examine as to the merits of pedigrees.

(3) Issue certificates as specified in this chapter.

(4) Employ one or more licensed veterinarians or other accredited inspectors to make examinations of such stallions and jacks as are referred to herein.

(5) Make all rules and regulations necessary to carry out the provisions of this chapter.

Enrollment of animals.—Every person standing, traveling or offering for sale for breeding purposes any stallion or jack in this state shall cause the name, description and pedigree of such animal to be enrolled by the said board, and procure a certificate of such enrollment from said board.

Certificate for mongrel.—A certificate for a mongrel stallion or jack shall be in the following form:

State Board of Agriculture

Certificate of grade or mongrel. No. _____. The pedigree of the stallion or jack _____ (Name) _____. Owned by _____. Described as follows: Color _____. Foaled in the year _____ has been examined by the state board of agriculture of Utah, and it is found that the stallion or jack is not of pure breeding, and is therefore not eligible for registration in any studbook recognized by the United States Department of Agriculture.

(Signature) _____
Commissioner of Agriculture.

Advertisement to contain copy of certificate.—Every bill, poster or advertisement issued or used by the owner of any stallion or jack for advertising such stallion or jack shall contain a copy of its certificate of enrollment.

Fees for certificate and renewal.—A fee of $10 shall be paid the inspector for making an examination, which he shall forward to the state board of agriculture within five days, and the certificate which he issues shall be made in triplicate, describing the animal fully, and containing a receipt for the fee. One of the triplicates shall be given to the owner, one forwarded at once to the state board of agriculture and one retained in the book. A fee of $2 shall be paid annually to the commissioner of agriculture for the renewal of this certificate on or before March 1st of each year following its issuance, and failure to pay this fee forfeits the certificate.

Death or sale of animal—Lost or destroyed certificate.—All owners of stallions and jacks registered under this chapter on the death of any stallion or jack must report such death to the commissioner of agriculture, and return the certificate of said animal for concellation. Upon transfer of the ownership of any animal certificated under the provisions of this chapter the certificate shall be transferred by the commissioner to the buyer on proof of such transfer and upon payment of a fee of $2. In case a certificate is lost or destroyed and satisfactory proof of the same is furnished, a new one shall be issued by the commissioner on payment of a fee of $1.

Lien on mare and foal.—Every person in this state complying with the provisions of this chapter and having obtained the certificate for a pure-bred stallion or jack registered in a government-approved studbook shall have a lien on the mare served and a first lien upon the offspring resulting from such service to the agreed amount for a period of eighteen months after service, and it shall not be necessary in order to secure and fix said lien to secure, file or register any contract or statement thereof with any officer; nor shall it be necessary that the owner of such mare or foal execute any contract whatever. Such liens may be foreclosed in the same manner that a mortgage upon personal property is foreclosed.

Lien on livestock—For feed and care.—Every ranchman, farmer, agistor, herder of cattle, tavern keeper or livery stable keeper to whom any domestic animals shall be entrusted for the purpose of feeding, herding or pasturing shall have a lien upon such animals for the amount that may be due him for such feeding, herding or pasturing, and is authorized to retain possession of such animals until such amount is paid.

Artificial insemination of domestic animals

1. *"Livestock"* consists of cattle, *horses,* mules, asses, sheep, goats, hogs, and poultry.

2. "Board" means Utah state board of agriculture.

3. "Commissioner" means commissioner of agriculture.

4. "Person" means individual, firm, corporation, company, or association.

5. "Sell" includes offer for sale, expose for sale, have in possession for sale, exchange, barter or trade.

6. "Bona fide producer of livestock" means a person having livestock assessed in his name.

7. "Slaughterhouse" means any building, plant or establishment where meat food animals are killed or dressed, the meat or meat products of which are to be offered for sale for human consumption.

8. "Hides" includes hides and wool removed from any cattle, horses or mules, sheep or goats.

9. "Brands" means any recorded identification mark applied to any position on hide of animal by means of heat, acid, or chemicals.

10. "Mark" means cutting and shaping of ears of animals.

11. "Inspector" means all inspectors appointed by state board of agriculture to carry out the provisions of this act.

12. "Livestock sales ring" means a place or establishment conducted or operated for compensation or profit as a public market consisting of pens or other enclosures and their appurtenances in which live cattle, sheep, swine, horses, mules or goats are received, held or kept for sale and where any such livestock is sold or offered for sale at either public auction or private sale; except, that the provisions of this act shall not apply to:

Any place used solely for a dispersal sale of the livestock of a farmer, dairyman, livestock breeder or feeder who is discontinuing said business.

(a) The premises of any butcher, packer or processor who

receives animals exclusively for immediate slaughter.

(b) Any place where an association of breeders of livestock of any class assembles and offers for sale and sells under its own management registered livestock or breeding sires; provided, said association assumes all responsibility of such sale and guarantees title of said livestock and arranges with the board for the proper inspection of all animals sold.

Brands—Recording.—Every livestock owner who allows his livestock over six months of age to range upon the open range or without an enclosure, shall have and adopt a brand and shall brand his livestock with such brand, which brand must be recorded in the office of the state board of agriculture.

Vermont

Cattle, horses, sheep or swine

Person who knowingly permits cattle, horses, sheep or swine to run at large in a public highway, or yard belonging to a public building, without the consent of the selectmen, shall be fined not more than $10.00 nor less than $3.00.

Land or premises of another

A person who knowingly permits his cattle, horses, sheep, swine or domestic fowls to go upon the lands or premises of another, after the latter has given the owner notice thereof, shall be fined not more than $10.00 nor less than $2.00. Such person shall also be *liable for the damages suffered* which may be recovered in an action of tort on this statute.

Burial ground

A person who knowingly turns cattle, horses, sheep or swine into a burial ground, or who knowingly permits the same to run therein, if it is properly enclosed, shall be fined $25.00.

Stallions

(a) An owner or keeper of a stallion, more than one year

old, who wilfully or negligently permits such stallion to run at large out of the enclosure of such owner or keeper, shall be fined not more than $40.00 nor less than $10.00 and shall also be liable to a party injured for the damage done by such stallion while running at large.

(b) A person who owns or keeps a stallion over one year of age, between April 1 and December 1, in a private enclosure in such a manner as to disturb and annoy the owner or occupant of adjoining premises shall be fined $5.00 for each week he so keeps such stallion after he has received three days' notice from an adjoining owner or occupant to remove such stallion.

False registration of livestock

A person who, by false or fraudulent representations, obtains from a club, association, society or company for improving the breed of cattle, horses, sheep, swine or other domestic animals, a certificate of registration of an animal in the herd register, or other register of such club, association, society or company, or a transfer of such registration, shall be fined not more than $300.00.

Painting or disguising horses

A person who knowingly and designedly for the purpose of competing for a purse or premium offered by an agricultural society, corporation or association within the state, enters or drives a horse or horse kind painted or disguised, or who for such purpose falsely and fraudulently represents a horse to be another from what it really is, or who for such purpose knowingly or designedly enters or drives a horse or horse kind in a class in which it is not entitled to be entered under the rules of such society, corporation or association, shall be imprisoned not more than six months or fined not more than $500.00.

Misrepresenting livestock

(a) A person shall not make false or fraudulent representations for the purpose of obtaining a certificate of registration of an animal in a herd register or other register of a club, association, society, company or corporation.

(b) A person shall not make false or fraudulent representations for the purpose of transfer of such certificate of registration.

(c) A person shall not fraudulently represent that an animal is a registered animal, or has been registered, with the intent that such representation shall be relied upon by another.

(d) (1) A "person" under this section is a person as defined in section 128 of Title 1.

(2) A "registered animal" is an animal duly registered as a purebred in the official herd book or similar register of any recognized purebred registry association organized for the purpose of registering a particular breed of animals whose lineage has been established by registry records.

(3) An animal has been "registered" when it qualifies as a registered animal as defined in subdivision (2) .

(e) A person who violates a provision of subsections (a) , (b) or (c) shall be fined not more than $300.00 and shall be liable civilly for damages.

Liens for service of stallions

Colts foaled in this state and the mare producing the same shall be subject to a lien to secure the payment of the service fee of the stallion. Such lien shall continue in force until the colt is eight months old and may be enforced by attachment of such colt or mare at any time after the colt is four months old. Such lien shall take precedence of any other claim upon such colt, subject to the conditions of sections of this title.

Filing of statement claiming lien

On or before April 1, or within thirty days after such stallion is brought into such town, the owner or manager of the stallion shall annually file in the office of the clerk of the town where such stallion is kept a declaration of an intention to claim such lien and a statement containing the name and age of such stallion, his pedigree for two generations, if known, and the terms of service. A copy of such statement shall be furnished the owner of each mare served and all bills or posters advertising such stallion shall contain a copy of such statement.

False statements in claim of lien

If the owner or manager in such statement makes a false representation regarding the pedigree of such stallion, the lien for such service shall be discharged and the service fee thereon secured shall be forfeited.

Penalty for fraudulent sale of mare

When the owner or manager of a stallion has complied with the requirements of sections of this title, if the owner or person, in whose name a mare has been mated with such stallion for breeding purposes, disposes of such mare by sale or otherwise before foaling time without first settling with the owner or manager for the service of the stallion, or within ten days after the disposal of the mare, he shall be subject to the same penalties that he would be for disposing of a colt encumbered by a lien. If such mare is returned for trial to the stallion after three weeks from the date of the last service and found not to have become pregnant and is not again served during that breeding season, the provisions of this section shall not apply to the disposal of such mare.

Lien for keeping or pasturing animals

A person to whom charges are due for pasturing, boarding or keeping domestic animals placed with the consent of the owner thereof in his care, if the charges become due while such animals remain in his possession, may retain the same until such charges are paid. After thirty days from the time the charges become due, he may sell such animals in the manner provided for the sale of property under a lien for repairs, if such charges remain unpaid.

Virginia

Damages for trespass by animals.—If any horse, mule, cattle, hogs, sheep or goats shall enter into any grounds enclosed by a lawful fence, or by a river or stream or any part thereof which is by law a lawful fence, or into any ground in counties or magisterial districts, or selected portions thereof, wherein the boundary lines of lots or tracts of land have been constituted lawful fences, the owner or manager of any such animal shall be liable for the actual damages sustained, if the amount of such damage shall be one dollar or more, and such damage shall be assessed for each such entry and not for each such animal, except as hereinafter provided, and shall in no case be estimated and assessed at less than one dollar. And in case of such entry within that part of Henrico county, within three miles of the corporate limits of the city of Richmond, the minimum amount of damage assessed in any case shall be two dollars for each animal.

Punitive damages.—When punitive damages are awarded, the same shall not exceed twenty dollars in any case.

Double damages for succeeding trespasses.—For every succeeding trespass the owner or manager of such animal shall be liable for double damages, both actual and punitive, in no case to be less than two dollars.

Lien on animals.—After a judgment of the court a lien upon such animal shall enure for the benefit of the owner or tenant of such enclosed ground, and execution shall thereupon issue from the court or trial justice rendering the judgment, and the animal or animals so trespassing shall be levied upon by the officer to whom the execution was issued, who shall sell the same, as provided for by statute.

Impounding animals.—Whenever any such animal is found trespassing upon any such enclosed ground, the owner or tenant of such enclosed grounds shall have the right to take up such animal and impound the same until the damages provided for by the preceding sections shall have been paid, or until the same are taken under execution by the officer as hereinbefore provided, and the costs of taking up and impounding such animal shall be estimated as a part of the actual damage.

Duty to issue warrant when animal impounded.—It shall be the duty of such owner or tenant of such lands so trespassed upon, within three days after the taking up and impounding such animal unless the damages be otherwise settled, to apply to a justice of the peace of the district in which such land is situated for a warrant for the amount of damages so claimed by him, and such justice shall issue the same, to be made returnable at as early a date, not less than three days thereafter, as shall be deemed best by him; and upon the hearing of the case the trial justice shall give such judgment as is deemed just and right.

Lien of keeper of livery stable, garage, marina, etc.—Every keeper of a livery stable, marina or garage, and every person pasturing or keeping any horses or other animals, vehicles, boats, or harness, shall have a lien upon such horses and other animals, vehicles, boats, and harness, for the amount which may be due him for the keeping, supporting and care thereof, until such amount is paid.

Lien on offspring of stallion or jackass.—When the owner of a mare or jennet breeds the same to any stallion or jackass whereby such mare or jennet shall become in foal and is delivered of a live colt, the owner of any such stallion or jackass shall have a lien upon the colt for a period of twelve months, or until the price agreed upon for the season or service by the owner of the stallion or jackass and the owner of the mare or jennet be paid. Such lien shall not extend for a longer period than twelve months, and after judgment has been taken for the amount of such fee, then, unless the same is paid, the officer in whose hands the fieri facias is placed for collection may proceed to levy on and sell such colt for the aforesaid fieri facias and costs, and he shall be entitled to the same fees for his services as is provided for by the existing law.

Recordation of lien given by preceding section.—The lien given by the preceding section, if reduced to writing, shall be recorded in the miscellaneous lien book and shall be operative from the recordation thereof and if the lien is not reduced to writing, it shall, upon application of the owner of the stallion or jackass, be recorded by the clerk of the circuit court of the county in which the foal is foaled in such book in the following form:

_____ (giving the name of the owner of the stallion or jackass) versus _____ (giving the name of the owner of the colt). The owner of the stallion or jackass claims a lien on a colt less than twelve months old for $_____, for the get thereof.

The clerk shall be entitled to a fee of thirty cents for the recordation of each of such liens.

False pretense in obtaining registration of cattle and other animals and giving false pedigree.—Every person who by any false pretense shall obtain from any club, association, society or company for improving the breed of cattle, horses, sheep, swine or other domestic animals the registration of any animal in the herd register or other register of any such club, association, society or company, or a transfer of any such registration, and every person who shall knowingly give a false pedigree of any animal shall be guilty of a misdemeanor.

Washington

Liability for damages—Restraint—Any person making and maintaining in good repair around his or her enclosure or enclosures, any fence such as is described in RCW, may recover in a suit for trespass before the nearest court having competent jurisdiction, from the owner or owners of any animal or animals which shall break through such fence, in full for all damages sustained on account of such trespass, together with the costs of suits; and the animal or animals, so trespassing, may be taken and held as security for the payment of such damages and costs: *Provided,* That such person shall have such fences examined and the damages assessed by three reliable, disinterested parties and practical farmers, within five days next after the trespass has been committed: *And, provided further,* That if, before trial, the owner of such trespassing animal or animals, shall have tendered the person injured any costs which may have accrued, and also the amount in lieu of damages which shall equal or exceed the amount of damages afterwards awarded by the court or jury, and the person injured shall refuse the same and cause the trial to proceed, such person shall pay all costs and receive only the damages awarded.

Liability for damages—Restraint—Any person suffering damage done by any horses, mares, mules, asses, cattle, goats, sheep, swine, or any such animals, which shall trespass upon any cultivated land, inclosed by lawful fence or situated within any district created pursuant to RCW, may retain and keep in custody such offending animals until the owner of such animals shall pay such damage and costs, or until good and sufficient security be given for the same.

Liability for damages. If any stud horse, stud mule, jackass, ridgling or stag, while running at large out of the enclosed grounds of the owner or keeper, shall damage any other animal by biting or kicking him, or shall do any damage to person or property of any kind whatever, the owner of said stud horse, stud mule, jackass, ridgling or stag, shall be liable for all damages done by him.

Gelding animals at large. It shall be lawful for any person to take up and geld, at the risk of the owner, within the months of April, May, June, July, August, and September, in any year, any stud horse, jackass, or stud mule, of the age of eighteen months and upwards, that may be found running at large out of the enclosed grounds of the owner or keeper, and if the said animal shall die the owner shall have no recourse against the person or persons who may have taken up and gelded, or caused to be gelded, the said animal, if the same has been done by a person in the habit of gelding, and the owner shall pay one dollar and a half therefor.

Animal marks and brands

Definitions. For the purpose of this chapter:

(1) "Department" means the department of agriculture of the state of Washington.

(2) "Director" means the director of the department or his duly appointed representative.

(3) "Person" means a natural person, individual, firm, partnership, corporation, company, society, and association, and every officer, agent or employee thereof. This term shall import either the singular or the plural as the case may be.

(4) "Livestock" includes, but is not limited to, horses, mules, cattle, sheep, swine, goats, poultry and rabbits.

(5) "Brand" means a permanent fire brand or any artificial mark approved by the director to be used in conjunction with a brand or by itself.

(6) "Production record brand" means a number brand which shall be used for production identification purposes only.

Recording brands—Fee. The director shall be the recorder of livestock brands and such brands shall not be recorded elsewhere in this state. Any person desiring to register a livestock brand shall apply on a form prescribed by the director. Such application shall be accompanied by a facsimile of the brand applied for and a three dollar recording fee. The director shall, upon his satisfaction that the application meets the requirements of this chapter and/or rules and regulations adopted hereunder, record such brand.

Agister and trainer liens

Liens created. Any farmer, ranchman, herder of cattle, tavern keeper, livery and boarding stable keeper or any other person, to whom any horses, mules, cattle or sheep shall be entrusted for the purpose of feeding, herding, pasturing, and training, caring for or ranching, shall have a lien upon said horses, mules, cattle or sheep for such amount that may be due for said feeding, herding, pasturing, training, caring for, and ranching, and shall be authorized to retain possession of said horses, mules or cattle or sheep, until said amount is paid.

West Virginia

Stock trespassing on inclosed grounds; damages.

If any horse, mule, ass, jennet, cattle, sheep, swine, or goat shall enter into any grounds inclosed by a lawful fence, the owner or manager of any such stock shall be liable to the owner or tenant of such grounds for any damage he may sustain thereby, and the party so injured may, if he find such stock on his premises, impound them, or a sufficient number thereof, subject to the provisions of sections eight, nine and ten of this article, until such damages and costs of keeping have been paid.

Unlawful running at large of stock on road or railroad right of way.

It shall be unlawful for the owner or manager of any horse, mule, ass, jennet, cattle, sheep, goat or hog, to negligently permit it to run at large on any public road or highway or railroad right of way, and should any such stock, while so negligently allowed to run at large, injure or destroy the property of another while so running at large, the owner or manager thereof shall be guilty of a misdemeanor, and, upon conviction thereof, shall be fined not less than five dollars nor more than ten dollars.

Unlawful running at large of certain male animals and swine.

It shall be unlawful for any stallion, jack or bull over one year old, buck sheep over four months old, buck goat over six months old, or swine, to run at large, and the owner or manager of any such stock running at large shall be guilty of a misdemeanor, and, upon conviction thereof, shall be fined not less than five nor more than ten dollars.

Unlawful running at large of stock of nonresidents.

It shall be unlawful for any horse, mule, ass, jennet, cattle, sheep, swine, or goat owned by any person not a citizen of this State to run at large in this State.

Liability of owner for damage by stock unlawfully running at large.

Should any stock, while running at large contrary to the provisions of sections two, three or four of this article, injure or destroy the property of another, the owner or manager of any such stock shall, notwithstanding any penalty imposed by said sections, be liable to the party whose property shall have been injured or destroyed for the amount of damage sustained by him by reason of such injury or destruction. And the party so injured may, if he find such stock on his premises, impound them, or a sufficient number thereof, subject to the provisions of sections eight, nine and ten of this article, until such damages and costs of keeping be paid.

Impounding stock unlawfully running at large.

It shall be lawful for any person finding any stock running at large contrary to the provisions of sections two, three or four of this article, to impound such stock, subject to the provisions of sections eight, nine and ten of this article, until the costs of keeping such stock be paid.

Forcible retaking of impounded stock; penalty.

Any person who shall forcibly take possession of any stock impounded under the provisions of sections one, five or six of this article, or section one of article nineteen of this chapter, without paying the amount therein allowed the person so impounding such stock, shall be guilty of a misdemeanor, and, upon conviction thereof, shall be fined not more than fifty dollars.

Impounding stock when owner is known resident of State; arbitration of damages; right to sell impounded stock.

If the owner of any stock impounded under the provisions of this article, or article nineteen of this chapter, be a resident of this State and known to the person impounding the stock, such person shall, within three days from the date thereof, serve written notice on such owner stating therein, (a) the stock impounded, setting forth the number of each kind and the natural or artificial marks of each one of every kind, (b) the date such stock was taken up, (c) the place where impounded, (d) the cause for impounding the stock, and (e) the amount claimed as damages, if any, by reason of the injury or destruction of property by such stock and the costs for keeping the same, for which such person shall be entitled to an amount not to exceed that allowed a sheriff for keeping similar stock. If the owner considers the amount claimed excessive, he shall forthwith serve written notice on the person impounding the stock that he has appointed one freeholder, naming him, to ascertain the injury and damages sustained and the costs for keeping the stock. The person impounding the stock shall forthwith appoint one freeholder, and the two thus appointed shall appoint a third. Should either party fail or refuse to make such appointment within twenty-four hours after being notified so to do, any justice of the county may do so on application of either party. The freeholders appointed shall act as arbitrators and, after being duly sworn, shall ascertain the injury and damages sustained, if any, and the costs for keeping such stock. The decision of any two of the arbitrators shall be final and shall be reduced to writing and a copy thereof furnished to each of the parties. Each arbitrator shall be allowed a fee of two dollars for his services, which shall be paid by the party against whom the decision is made.

Lien of bailee of animals or vehicles.

A person keeping a livery stable, or boarding stable for animals, or a garage or storage place for automobiles or other vehicles, or who boards, pastures, feeds or trains animals for hire, has a lien upon such animals or vehicles for the sum due him for the care, boarding, pasturage, feeding, or training of such animals, or the care, keeping or storage of such vehicles, even though such animals or vehicles are permitted to be taken out of the possession of the one claiming such lien, if the contract between the owner and the person claiming such lien for keeping, boarding, pasturage, feeding, training or storage, has not been terminated at the time such animal or vehicle is taken out of such possession: Provided, however, that any purchaser of such animal or vehicle, while out of the possession of the person claiming such lien, shall take such property free of such lien, unless he had actual notice at the time of such purchase that such animal or vehicle was being kept, stored, boarded, pastured, fed or trained by some person other than the owner thereof: Provided further, that the lien hereinbefore provided for in this section shall not be valid as against any person other than the owner of such animal or vehicle, whether such other person have notice of the claim of lien or not, for any charges incurred more than three months prior to the time when such person other than the owner acquired his interest in the animal or chattel, unless the animal or chattel was, at the time of the acquisition of such interest, actually in the possession of the person claiming such lien.

Lien for service of male animals.

The owner of any stallion, jack or bull, that is duly registered under the laws of the State of West Virginia, shall have a lien upon the foal or calf thereof, whenever the service of such stallion, jack or bull was had by contract with the owner, or agent of the owner, of the dam or cow of such foal or calf, at the time of such service. Such lien shall cease unless the person desiring to avail himself thereof shall, within six months from the birth of such foal or calf, file before some justice, in the county in which such foal or calf may be, his own affidavit, or that of some credible person, stating the amount of his lien against such foal or calf, and that such amount is due by contract, also a description of the foal or calf upon which such lien is claimed. Such affidavit shall be filed and preserved by such justice, for which service he shall receive the fee provided by law. Upon the filing of such affidavit, such proceedings shall be had for the enforcement of such lien as are provided in section seventeen of this article.

Registration and enrollment of certain male breeding animals.

It shall be unlawful for any person to use or offer for use for public service, sell or offer for sale, exchange or transfer in this State, under the representation of being purebred, any stallion, jack, bull, ram or boar, unless such animal be purebred and registered in some stud, herd, flock or swine record book, as the case may be, recognized by the United States department of agriculture for the registration of pedigrees, and unless the owner thereof shall have procured a certificate of such registration. In addition to such registration the owner of a stallion or jack shall, and the owner of a bull, ram or boar may, cause the name, description and pedigree of such animal to be enrolled by the department of agriculture and procure a certificate of such enrollment from the department.

Enrollment certificate for stallion or jack; certificate of soundness.

In order to secure such enrollment certificate for a stallion or jack, the owner thereof shall obtain a certificate of its condition of soundness, signed by a practicing veterinarian approved by the commissioner of agriculture, who shall make oath to such certificate before some officer duly authorized to administer oaths, and shall forward the certificate, together with the original studbook certificate of registry of pedigree of the stallion or jack, and all other necessary papers relating to his breeding and ownership, to the commissioner. A certificate of the condition of soundness shall be made upon the application for the first certificate of enrollment, and every two years thereafter until the stallion or jack is ten years old, and if the stallion or jack is ten years old or over on the date of the issuance of the first certificate of enrollment, no subsequent certificate of the condition of soundness shall be required.

Acceptance and enrollment of stallion or jack as purebred: form of enrollment certificate.

STATE OF WEST VIRGINIA
Department of Agriculture

Certificate of Purebred Stallion (or Jack) No. ....
The pedigree of the (breed) .... Stallion (or Jack)
(name and number) .... owned by
.... P. O. ....
County .... color and marks .... foaled

in .... has been examined by the commissioner of agriculture or one of his duly authorized agents, and it is hereby certified that the said stallion (or jack) is of pure breeding, and is registered in a studbook recognized by the commissioner of agriculture.

The above-named stallion (or jack) has been examined by ...., a legally qualified veterinarian duly authorized by the commissioner of agriculture to make such examination and by him found to be sound.

....
Commissioner of Agriculture.

Dated at Charleston, West Virginia, this ....
day of ....

Wisconsin

Animals not to run at large

No stallion over one year old, nor bull over six months old, nor boar, nor ram, nor billy goat over four months old shall run at large; and if the owner or keeper shall, for any reason, suffer any such animal so to do he shall forfeit five dollars to the person taking it up and be liable in addition for all damages done by such animal while so at large, although he escapes without the fault of such owner or keeper; and the construction of any fence shall not relieve such owner or keeper from liability for any damage committed by an animal of the enumerated class upon the inclosed premises of an adjoining owner.

Liens of keepers of hotels, livery stables, garages and pastures

As used in this section:

Every keeper of a garage, livery or boarding stable, and every person pasturing or keeping any carriages, automobiles, harness or animals, and every person or corporation, municipal or private, owning any airport, hangar or aircraft service station and leasing hangar space for aircraft, shall have a lien thereon and may retain the possession thereof for the amount due him for the keep, support, storage or repair and care thereof until paid. But no garage keeper shall exercise the lien upon any automobile unless there shall be posted in some conspicuous place in his garage a card, stating the charges for storing automobiles, easily readable at a distance of 15 feet.

Lien of owner of breeding animal or methods

(1) Every owner of a stallion or jackass, or bull, or semen therefrom, kept and used for breeding purposes shall have a lien upon any dam served and upon any offspring gotten by such animal, or by means of such artificial insemination for the sum stipulated to be paid for the service thereof, and may seize and take possession of such dam and offspring or either without process at any time before the offspring is one year old, in case the price agreed upon for such service remains unpaid, and sell the same at public auction upon 10 days' notice, to be posted in at least 3 public places in the town where the service was rendered, and apply the proceeds of such sale to the payment of the amount due for such service and the expenses of such seizure and sale, returning the residue, if any, to the party entitled thereto; provided, no such lien shall be effectual for any purpose as against an innocent purchaser or mortgagee of such offspring or the dam thereof for value unless such owner having a claim for the service shall file with the register of deeds of the county where the owner of the dam served resides a statement showing that such service has been rendered and the amount due therefor.

(2) Any person who sells, disposes of or gives a mortgage upon any dam which to his knowledge has been so served, the fee for which service has not been paid, without giving written information to the purchaser or mortgagee of the fact of such service, shall be guilty of a misdemeanor and upon conviction shall be fined not more than $10 or by confinement in the county jail not to exceed 60 days.

Livestock brands, recording, misuse

Every town clerk shall, on the application of any person residing in his town, record a description of the marks or brands with which such person may be desirous of marking his horses, cattle, sheep or hogs; but the same description shall not be recorded or used by more than one resident of the same town. If any person shall mark any of his horses, cattle, sheep or hogs with the same mark or brand previously recorded by any resident of the same town and while the same mark or brand shall be used by such resident, he shall forfeit for every such offense $5; if any person shall wilfully mark or brand any of the horses, cattle, sheep or hogs of any other person with his own mark or brand he shall forfeit for every such offense $10; and if any person shall wilfully destroy or alter any mark or brand upon any of the horses, cattle, sheep or hogs of another he shall forfeit $10 and pay to the party injured double damages.

False pedigree

No person with intent to defraud shall obtain from any corporation, association, society or company organized for the purpose of improving breeds of domestic animals, a false certificate of registration of any such animal in the herd or other register of any such corporation, association, society or company, or the transfer of any such certificate, or shall, with intent to defraud, give a false pedigree of any such animal.

Misrepresenting breed of domestic animal

No person shall sell or barter or cause to be sold or bartered any domestic animal and represent, or cause to be represented that such animal is a pure bred animal, when in fact such animal is not registered, or entitled to registry, in any pure breed registry maintained for such animals; nor shall any person knowingly utter, pass or deliver to any person as true, any false, or altered pedigree; nor shall any person refuse to deliver proper certificate of registry for any animal sold or transferred by him, having represented at the time of sale or transfer, and as an inducement thereto, that such animal was registered and that he possessed and would deliver a certificate of registry as evidence thereof, or that such animal was entitled to registry and that he would secure such certificate and deliver the same.

Animals doing damage

The owner or occupant of any lands may distrain any beast doing damage on his premises, either while upon the premises or upon immediate pursuit of such beasts escaping therefrom and before returning to the enclosure of or to the immediate care of the owner or keeper, and may keep such beasts upon his premises or in some public pound in his town, city or village until his damages * * * *are* appraised as hereinafter provided. If the owner of such beasts * * * *is* known to the person distraining and resides within the same town, city or village the person distraining shall give a written notice to such owner within 24 hours, but if he * * * *resides* in the same county, but not in the same town, city or village, within 48 hours, Sundays excepted, specifying therein the time when and the place where distrained, the number of such beasts and the place of their detention, and that at a time and place, which shall not be less than 12 hours after the serving of such notice nor more than 3 days after such distress, he will apply to some *municipal* justice * * * of the county (naming him) *or to the town chairman, village president or city mayor of the municipality where found* for the appointment of 3 disinterested freeholders of such town, city or village to appraise the damages; but if such owner * * * *is* unknown or does not reside in the county he shall apply for the appointment of such appraisers without notice and within 24 hours after such distress; and upon such application such justice * * * , *chairman, president or mayor* shall appoint in writing disinterested Freeholders of such town, city or village to appraise the damages and shall receive Fifty cents therefor.

Wyoming

Leaving gates open; destruction of bars, gates or fence.— Any person who shall wilfully or negligently leave open, break down or destroy any bars or gate made and provided for the use and convenience of the public, or shall wilfully tear down, throw down or destroy in any manner any lawful fence, shall be deemed guilty of a misdemeanor, and shall, upon conviction, be punished by a fine of not more than one hundred dollars, or by confinement in the county jail not more than three months, or by both fine and imprisonment in the discretion of the court.

Damage by breachy animals generally; arbitration; duties of arbitrators; civil action.—Any person or persons owning or having in his or her or their possession or charge any horses, mules, cattle or any one of such animals which shall breach over or under or breach into any lawful enclosure belonging to any person or persons other than the owners of such animal or animals, shall be liable to the party or parties sustaining such injury for all damages he, she or they may have sustained by reason of such breaching as aforesaid, to be recovered in a civil action before any court having jurisdiction thereof, or by arbitration, each party to select a property holder and the two arbitrators to select a third, and said arbitrators, before entering upon their duties, shall be first sworn before a justice of the peace, and it shall be the duty of the arbitrators to carefully examine the fence, its condition, and assess the damage done; the arbitrators shall examine witnesses under oath, one of them to administer said oath to the witnesses; they shall make a written report signed by at least two of the arbitrators, to any justice of the peace in the county in which such damage is sustained. The finding of the arbitration, as provided for in this section, shall within three days after the same shall have been rendered, be filed with any justice of the peace in the county where said trespass shall have been committed, who shall enter the cost upon his docket and proceed to issue execution therein as in other cases originally commenced before him.

Notice to owner of animals of damage done.—The party sustaining the damage shall notify the owner or person having in charge such offending animals, of such damage, and the probable amount thereof; provided, he knows to whom such animal or animals belong, and that such owner or keeper resides within the county where the damage was committed.

Retention of animals to secure damages.—The person suffering such damage done by animals as mentioned in section four, may restrain and keep in custody as many of such offending animals as are equal in value to the damage done, until the finding of the court or arbitration be ascertained, unless, before such suit, the amount of his claim and expense of keeping such animals be tendered him.

Trial for damage done by breachy animals; proof of damages; judgment.—If, upon the trial of any action under the provisions of section three of this act, it shall appear by competent testimony, that the plaintiff's enclosure is a lawful fence under the provisions of this chapter, he shall be allowed to prove the amount of damage sustained; and (if he has retained in custody the animals committing such damage) the amount of the expense incurred for keeping such animals, and any judgment rendered for damages, costs and expenses against the defendant, shall be a lien upon the animals committing the damage. But if it shall appear upon the trial that the plaintiff's inclosure is not a lawful fence, or that no damage was sustained, judgment shall be rendered against the plaintiff, for costs of suit and damages sustained by defendant.

Proceedings when defendant is unknown.—If, upon the trial, it appears that the defendant is not the owner, or the person in charge of such offending animals, he shall be discharged from the action with his costs, and the suit may proceed against a defendant whose name is unknown; and if, at the commencement of the action, the plaintiff does not know the name of the owner, or keeper of such offending animals, he may bring suit against a defendant unknown, in which case service shall be made by posting copies of the summons in three of the most public places within the county, not less than ten days previous to the day of trial, which posting may be done by the proper officer, or by any voter of the county.

Stallions and jacks generally.—If any horse or ass not gelded, two years old or upwards, shall be found running at large, it shall be lawful for any person to take up such horse or ass, and forthwith give notice to the owner or keeper, if he be known to the taker up, and if the owner or keeper do not appear within six days thereafter and pay to the said taker up, five dollars, as compensation for his trouble, the taker up shall proceed to advertise said horse or ass, and the same proceedings shall be had in every respect as hereinbefore provided in the case of estray horses and mules; provided, that the taker up may, after the expiration of thirty days from the time of advertising, geld, or procure to be gelded, the said horse or ass, which shall be done at the risk and expense of the owner, except when such horse or ass is in the owner's herd, or in care of the owner's herder.

Unclaimed horses—Permit for rounding up.—Any person, persons, organization or corporation desiring to gather or round up unclaimed horses from the ranges within the State of Wyoming must, before commencing to engage in such activity, obtain written permission to do so. Such person may be entitled to a permit which must be obtained from the person, persons, organization or corporation who has ownership or control of the surface rights of the range whereon the unclaimed horses are to be gathered or rounded up. Such permit shall definitely contain the following:

(a) The name of the person, persons, organization or corporation desiring to gather or round up the unclaimed horses.

(b) The name and signature of the person, persons, organization or corporation who has ownership or control of the range whereon the unclaimed horses are to be gathered or rounded up.

(c) That the owner or controller of the range concerned gives his or its permission allowing the unclaimed horses to be gathered or rounded up.

(d) Said permit shall be presented to the county livestock inspector to be used for the basis for the issuance of any brand inspection permit for removal of such unclaimed horses from the county whereon such unclaimed horses are gathered or rounded up.

Same—Disposition.—Such unclaimed horses shall be deemed to be estrays and after gathering shall be disposed of under the laws pertaining to estrays.

Penalty for violation.—Any person, firm, or corporation violating any of the provisions of this act shall be deemed guilty of a misdemeanor and upon conviction shall be fined in an amount not exceeding one hundred dollars ($100.00) and imprisoned for not more than 30 days.

Liability for death.—Should any animal taken up as an estray, die while in the possession of the person taking it up, he shall not be liable for the loss, unless its death was the result of mistreatment or wilful neglect.

Stock at large in roads or lanes.—It shall be unlawful for any person, persons, company or corporation being the owner of livestock of any kind or having custody or charge thereof to permit said livestock to run at large in any fenced public lanes or fenced roads in the State of Wyoming. Any person, persons, company or corporation violating the provisions of this section shall be deemed guilty of a misdemeanor and upon conviction thereof shall be fined not less than ten dollars ($10.00) nor more than one hundred dollars ($100.00) and in addition shall pay all damage done by such stock unlawfully permitted to run at large in such lanes or roads; provided that the provisions of this act [section] shall not apply to range cattle drifting into lanes or fenced roads in going to, or returning from their accustomed ranges.

Any sheriff, deputy sheriff, county livestock inspector, deputy livestock inspector, or officer or patrolman of the Wyoming highway patrol, after notification to the owner of such livestock, if known, shall have authority to remove said livestock from said public lane or fenced road, impound the same in the nearest convenient place where feed and water are available and immediately notify the owner, if known, of such action.

Standard Bred Horses.

Cooperative agreement for propagation; location of breeding establishment.—The governor of the State of Wyoming is hereby empowered to enter into a cooperative agreement with the bureau of animal industry of the United States for the purpose of the propagation of standard bred horses within the State of Wyoming. The said breeding establishment shall be located at such place as may be agreed upon between the governor of the State of Wyoming and the representatives of the bureau of animal industry.

Horse Breeder's Lien.

Owner of stallion to have lien on mare and colt.—The owner of a stallion shall have a lien upon any mare bred to such stallion, and also upon any colt begotten by such stallion, for the sum stipulated to be paid for such service.

Certificate of registration—Required for owners, etc., of animals used for public service; posting copy, etc.—Every owner or keeper of any stallion or jack in this state, who uses such animal for public service, or who represents such animal as being fit for public service, shall procure a certificate as hereinafter provided, and keep same or an exact copy thereof posted in a conspicuous place within every barn, shed, or building where such stallion or jack is kept for service, and shall mention the same in all advertisements as hereinafter provided.

Stallions, mustangs, etc., running at large generally; castration permitted.—No mustang or other inferior stallion over the age of twenty-four months shall be permitted to run at large, nor shall any stallion over the age of twenty-four months be permitted to run at large within three miles of any town, city or village. It shall be lawful for any person to castrate or cause to be castrated, any such animal or animals found running at large contrary to the provisions of this section.

Designation of mustangs, etc.; finder may enclose and care for; notice to owner; contents of notice; unclaimed animals to be castrated; expense of care, etc., a lien on animal.—Stallions possessing one-fourth mustang or bronco blood shall be deemed mustangs or inferior stallions. Any person who shall find any stallion running at large, as described in the next preceding section, may take up such animal and keep the same in some secure enclosure, and take good care of such animal; and it shall be the duty of such person to immediately notify the owner of such animal, if such owner is known, and if said owner is unknown to said person, to immediately give notice by publication in some newspaper in the county in which such animal shall have been taken up, for a period of four successive weeks, and which notice shall contain a full description of all marks and brands, if any there be on such animals, and that unless the owner of such animal makes claim for the same within six weeks from the date of its first publication, said animal will be castrated. The notice shall be signed by the person or persons having taken up the same. Said notice, keeping and caring for such animal shall be paid for by the owner of such animal, and until paid the person taking up the same shall have a lien upon such animal for his or their claims; and in case of said owner refusing or failing to pay for such notice, keeping and caring for, within a reasonable time, the person having such claim shall be entitled to recover the same in the same manner as an agistor's lien.

Unlawful castration of stallions.—If any person shall castrate any stallion and it shall, on proper evidence before a competent court, be proven to the satisfaction of said court that such animal was not of a class of stock prohibited from running at large by the next two preceding sections, said persons shall be liable for damages to the amount of treble the value of said animal so castrated, and cost of suit.

Brands—Recording generally.— (A) *Application, contents, fees, procedure upon receipt.*—Any person, company, firm, association or corporation desiring to adopt any brand or marks to be used for the branding or marking of horses, cattle and sheep or other livestock in this state, shall before using the same make application therefor to the Wyoming live stock and sanitary board. Said application shall

(1) Contain a facsimile of such brand or mark;

(2) State the species of livestock for which the desired brand is to be used, that is, whether it is to be used on horses, cattle, sheep or other livestock;

(3) State the place on animal upon which the brand is to be applied, and the means to be used for application, that is, whether it is to be with hot iron, paint, tattoo or other means;

(4) State the range and counties on, and in which, the stock are to be grazed;

(5) Be accompanied by a fee of ten dollars ($10) for the first species of livestock, and five dollars ($5) for the second species of livestock, and five dollars ($5) for each additional

species of livestock for which the brand or mark is to be used. Said fee shall be used to pay for the recording of such brand or mark and for a certified copy of such brand or mark which the executive officer of the Wyoming live stock and sanitary board shall provide for the owner, which sum shall be paid into the state treasury for the credit of the brand recording and permit fund. Upon receipt of such application and fee, the executive officer of the Wyoming live stock and sanitary board shall immediately record the same in the state brand record, unless said brand or mark, has already been recorded in the said record on behalf of some other person, company, firm, association or corporation, for the same species of livestock, in which latter case the executive officer of the Wyoming live stock and sanitary board may suggest a brand or mark that can be recorded: provided, that the executive officer of the Wyoming live stock and sanitary board shall not record any brand or mark which in his discretion would conflict with any brand or mark of record in the same locality.

INDEX

335

Missouri, statutory regulations, 241
Montana, statutory regulations, 243
Mosiac Code, 12
Motorist's Liability for injuring or
killing horse on highway, 83
Care required, 84 .

Near-Dispersal Sale, 34
Nebraska, statutory regulations, 249
Nevada, statutory regulations, 253
New Hampshire, statutory regulations, 256
New Jersey, statutory regulations, 257
New Mexico, statutory regulations, 260
New York, statutory regulations, 265
North Carolina, statutory regulations, 267
North Dakota, statutory regulations, 269
Notice of breeder's lien, form, 166

Ohio, statutory regulations, 273
Oklahoma, statutory regulations, 275
Open range law, 67
Liability of owner, 68
Oregon, statutory regulations, 280
Ownership, 21

Pennsylvania, statutory regulations, 285
Personal property, horse as, 12
Plaintiff, definition, 17
Preface, 7
Production Sale, 34
Puffing, 44

Renting horse, liability, 46
Rhode Island, statutory regulations, 287
Riding stable, liability, 46

Sale of horses, 21
Actual transfer, 21
Implied transfer, 21

School, riding, 46
South Carolina, statutory regulations, 290
South Dakota, statutory regulations, 293
Span of horses, definition, 17
Stallion service agreement, 153
Stallion service contract, 152
Statutory regulations, 170
Stock Law, 170
Strays, definition, 18

Tax Reform Act of 1969, 116
Disposing of farm land, 128
Farm losses, 116
Livestock, depreciation, 125
Tennessee, statutory regulations, 299
Terms and conditions of auction sales, 35
Texas, statutory regulations, 303
Tort, definition, 17
Traffic laws governing animals, 87
Training and showing horses, contract, 148
Transportation of Animals Act, 90
Trespassing animal, definition, 18
Trespassing horse, liability of owner, 67
Twenty-Eight Hour Law, 90

Utah, statutory regulations, 305

Vaccine, liability of manufacturer, 95
Vermont, statutory regulations, 310
Veterinarian, 101
Action for services rendered, 108
Employment Contract, 105
Incorrect diagnosis, 102
Liability for acts of agents, 104
Malpractice, 101
Vicious animal, definition, 18
Virginia, statutory regulations, 314

Warranty, 23
Expressed warranty, 23
Implied warranty, 23

MELVIN POWERS SELF-IMPROVEMENT LIBRARY

COOKERY & HERBS

____ CULPEPER'S HERBAL REMEDIES *Dr. Nicholas Culpeper*	3.00
____ FAST GOURMET COOKBOOK *Poppy Cannon*	2.50
____ GINSENG The Myth & The Truth *Joseph P. Hou*	3.00
____ HEALING POWER OF HERBS *May Bethel*	4.00
____ HEALING POWER OF NATURAL FOODS *May Bethel*	3.00
____ HERB HANDBOOK *Dawn MacLeod*	3.00
____ HERBS FOR COOKING AND HEALING *Dr. Donald Law*	2.00
____ HERBS FOR HEALTH—How to Grow & Use Them *Louise Evans Doole*	4.00
____ HOME GARDEN COOKBOOK—Delicious Natural Food Recipes *Ken Kraft*	3.00
____ MEDICAL HERBALIST *edited by Dr. J. R. Yemm*	3.00
____ NATURE'S MEDICINES *Richard Lucas*	3.00
____ VEGETABLE GARDENING FOR BEGINNERS *Hugh Wiberg*	2.00
____ VEGETABLES FOR TODAY'S GARDENS *R. Milton Carleton*	2.00
____ VEGETARIAN COOKERY *Janet Walker*	4.00
____ VEGETARIAN COOKING MADE EASY & DELECTABLE *Veronica Vezza*	3.00
____ VEGETARIAN DELIGHTS—A Happy Cookbook for Health *K. R. Mehta*	2.00
____ VEGETARIAN GOURMET COOKBOOK *Joyce McKinnel*	3.00

GAMBLING & POKER

____ ADVANCED POKER STRATEGY & WINNING PLAY *A. D. Livingston*	5.00
____ HOW NOT TO LOSE AT POKER *Jeffrey Lloyd Castle*	3.00
____ HOW TO WIN AT DICE GAMES *Skip Frey*	3.00
____ HOW TO WIN AT POKER *Terence Reese & Anthony T. Watkins*	5.00
____ WINNING AT CRAPS *Dr. Lloyd T. Commins*	4.00
____ WINNING AT GIN *Chester Wander & Cy Rice*	3.00
____ WINNING AT POKER—An Expert's Guide *John Archer*	5.00
____ WINNING AT 21—An Expert's Guide *John Archer*	5.00
____ WINNING POKER SYSTEMS *Norman Zadeh*	3.00

HEALTH

____ BEE POLLEN *Lynda Lyngheim & Jack Scagnetti*	3.00
____ DR. LINDNER'S SPECIAL WEIGHT CONTROL METHOD *P. G. Lindner, M.D.*	2.00
____ HELP YOURSELF TO BETTER SIGHT *Margaret Darst Corbett*	3.00
____ HOW TO IMPROVE YOUR VISION *Dr. Robert A. Kraskin*	3.00
____ HOW YOU CAN STOP SMOKING PERMANENTLY *Ernest Caldwell*	3.00
____ MIND OVER PLATTER *Peter G. Lindner, M.D.*	3.00
____ NATURE'S WAY TO NUTRITION & VIBRANT HEALTH *Robert J. Scrutton*	3.00
____ NEW CARBOHYDRATE DIET COUNTER *Patti Lopez-Pereira*	2.00
____ QUICK & EASY EXERCISES FOR FACIAL BEAUTY *Judy Smith-deal*	2.00
____ QUICK & EASY EXERCISES FOR FIGURE BEAUTY *Judy Smith-deal*	2.00
____ REFLEXOLOGY *Dr. Maybelle Segal*	3.00
____ REFLEXOLOGY FOR GOOD HEALTH *Anna Kaye & Don C. Matchan*	4.00
____ 30 DAYS TO BEAUTIFUL LEGS *Dr. Marc Selner*	3.00
____ YOU CAN LEARN TO RELAX *Dr. Samuel Gutwirth*	3.00
____ YOUR ALLERGY—What To Do About It *Allan Knight, M.D.*	3.00

HOBBIES

____ BEACHCOMBING FOR BEGINNERS *Norman Hickin*	2.00
____ BLACKSTONE'S MODERN CARD TRICKS *Harry Blackstone*	3.00
____ BLACKSTONE'S SECRETS OF MAGIC *Harry Blackstone*	3.00
____ COIN COLLECTING FOR BEGINNERS *Burton Hobson & Fred Reinfeld*	3.00
____ ENTERTAINING WITH ESP *Tony 'Doc' Shiels*	2.00
____ 400 FASCINATING MAGIC TRICKS YOU CAN DO *Howard Thurston*	4.00
____ HOW I TURN JUNK INTO FUN AND PROFIT *Sari*	3.00
____ HOW TO WRITE A HIT SONG & SELL IT *Tommy Boyce*	7.00
____ JUGGLING MADE EASY *Rudolf Dittrich*	3.00
____ MAGIC FOR ALL AGES *Walter Gibson*	4.00
____ MAGIC MADE EASY *Byron Wels*	2.00
____ STAMP COLLECTING FOR BEGINNERS *Burton Hobson*	3.00

HORSE PLAYERS' WINNING GUIDES

___ BETTING HORSES TO WIN *Les Conklin*	3.00
___ ELIMINATE THE LOSERS *Bob McKnight*	3.00
___ HOW TO PICK WINNING HORSES *Bob McKnight*	5.00
___ HOW TO WIN AT THE RACES *Sam (The Genius) Lewin*	5.00
___ HOW YOU CAN BEAT THE RACES *Jack Kavanagh*	5.00
___ MAKING MONEY AT THE RACES *David Barr*	3.00
___ PAYDAY AT THE RACES *Les Conklin*	3.00
___ SMART HANDICAPPING MADE EASY *William Bauman*	5.00
___ SUCCESS AT THE HARNESS RACES *Barry Meadow*	5.00
___ WINNING AT THE HARNESS RACES—An Expert's Guide *Nick Cammarano*	5.00

HUMOR

___ HOW TO BE A COMEDIAN FOR FUN & PROFIT *King & Laufer*	2.00
___ HOW TO FLATTEN YOUR TUSH *Coach Marge Reardon*	2.00
___ HOW TO MAKE LOVE TO YOURSELF *Ron Stevens & Joy Grdnic*	3.00
___ JOKE TELLER'S HANDBOOK *Bob Orben*	4.00
___ JOKES FOR ALL OCCASIONS *Al Schock*	4.00
___ 2000 NEW LAUGHS FOR SPEAKERS *Bob Orben*	5.00
___ 2,500 JOKES TO START 'EM LAUGHING *Bob Orben*	5.00

HYPNOTISM

___ ADVANCED TECHNIQUES OF HYPNOSIS *Melvin Powers*	3.00
___ BRAINWASHING AND THE CULTS *Paul A. Verdier, Ph.D.*	3.00
___ CHILDBIRTH WITH HYPNOSIS *William S. Kroger, M.D.*	5.00
___ HOW TO SOLVE Your Sex Problems with Self-Hypnosis *Frank S. Caprio, M.D.*	5.00
___ HOW TO STOP SMOKING THRU SELF-HYPNOSIS *Leslie M. LeCron*	3.00
___ HOW TO USE AUTO-SUGGESTION EFFECTIVELY *John Duckworth*	3.00
___ HOW YOU CAN BOWL BETTER USING SELF-HYPNOSIS *Jack Heise*	3.00
___ HOW YOU CAN PLAY BETTER GOLF USING SELF-HYPNOSIS *Jack Heise*	3.00
___ HYPNOSIS AND SELF-HYPNOSIS *Bernard Hollander, M.D.*	3.00
___ HYPNOTISM *(Originally published in 1893) Carl Sextus*	5.00
___ HYPNOTISM & PSYCHIC PHENOMENA *Simeon Edmunds*	4.00
___ HYPNOTISM MADE EASY *Dr. Ralph Winn*	5.00
___ HYPNOTISM MADE PRACTICAL *Louis Orton*	5.00
___ HYPNOTISM REVEALED *Melvin Powers*	2.00
___ HYPNOTISM TODAY *Leslie LeCron and Jean Bordeaux, Ph.D.*	5.00
___ MODERN HYPNOSIS *Lesley Kuhn & Salvatore Russo, Ph.D.*	5.00
___ NEW CONCEPTS OF HYPNOSIS *Bernard C. Gindes, M.D.*	5.00
___ NEW SELF-HYPNOSIS *Paul Adams*	5.00
___ POST-HYPNOTIC INSTRUCTIONS—Suggestions for Therapy *Arnold Furst*	5.00
___ PRACTICAL GUIDE TO SELF-HYPNOSIS *Melvin Powers*	3.00
___ PRACTICAL HYPNOTISM *Philip Magonet, M.D.*	3.00
___ SECRETS OF HYPNOTISM *S. J. Van Pelt, M.D.*	5.00
___ SELF-HYPNOSIS A Conditioned-Response Technique *Laurence Sparks*	5.00
___ SELF-HYPNOSIS Its Theory, Technique & Application *Melvin Powers*	3.00
___ THERAPY THROUGH HYPNOSIS *edited by Raphael H. Rhodes*	4.00

JUST FOR WOMEN

___ COSMOPOLITAN'S GUIDE TO MARVELOUS MEN Fwd. by *Helen Gurley Brown*	3.00
___ COSMOPOLITAN'S HANG-UP HANDBOOK Foreword by *Helen Gurley Brown*	4.00
___ COSMOPOLITAN'S LOVE BOOK—A Guide to Ecstasy in Bed	5.00
___ COSMOPOLITAN'S NEW ETIQUETTE GUIDE Fwd. by *Helen Gurley Brown*	4.00
___ I AM A COMPLEAT WOMAN *Doris Hagopian & Karen O'Connor Sweeney*	3.00
___ JUST FOR WOMEN—A Guide to the Female Body *Richard E. Sand, M.D.*	5.00
___ NEW APPROACHES TO SEX IN MARRIAGE *John E. Eichenlaub, M.D.*	3.00
___ SEXUALLY ADEQUATE FEMALE *Frank S. Caprio, M.D.*	3.00
___ SEXUALLY FULFILLED WOMAN *Dr. Rachel Copelan*	5.00
___ YOUR FIRST YEAR OF MARRIAGE *Dr. Tom McGinnis*	3.00

MARRIAGE, SEX & PARENTHOOD

___ ABILITY TO LOVE *Dr. Allan Fromme*	6.00
___ GUIDE TO SUCCESSFUL MARRIAGE *Drs. Albert Ellis & Robert Harper*	5.00
___ HOW TO RAISE AN EMOTIONALLY HEALTHY, HAPPY CHILD *A. Ellis*	4.00

___ SEX WITHOUT GUILT *Albert Ellis, Ph.D.*	5.00
___ SEXUALLY ADEQUATE MALE *Frank S. Caprio, M.D.*	3.00
___ SEXUALLY FULFILLED MAN *Dr. Rachel Copelan*	5.00

MELVIN POWERS' MAIL ORDER LIBRARY

___ HOW TO GET RICH IN MAIL ORDER *Melvin Powers*	15.00
___ HOW TO WRITE A GOOD ADVERTISEMENT *Victor O. Schwab*	15.00
___ MAIL ORDER MADE EASY *J. Frank Brumbaugh*	10.00
___ U.S. MAIL ORDER SHOPPER'S GUIDE *Susan Spitzer*	10.00

METAPHYSICS & OCCULT

___ BOOK OF TALISMANS, AMULETS & ZODIACAL GEMS *William Pavitt*	5.00
___ CONCENTRATION—A Guide to Mental Mastery *Mouni Sadhu*	4.00
___ CRITIQUES OF GOD *Edited by Peter Angeles*	7.00
___ EXTRA-TERRESTRIAL INTELLIGENCE—The First Encounter	6.00
___ FORTUNE TELLING WITH CARDS *P. Foli*	4.00
___ HANDWRITING ANALYSIS MADE EASY *John Marley*	4.00
___ HANDWRITING TELLS *Nadya Olyanova*	5.00
___ HOW TO INTERPRET DREAMS, OMENS & FORTUNE TELLING SIGNS *Gettings*	3.00
___ HOW TO UNDERSTAND YOUR DREAMS *Geoffrey A. Dudley*	3.00
___ ILLUSTRATED YOGA *William Zorn*	3.00
___ IN DAYS OF GREAT PEACE *Mouni Sadhu*	3.00
___ LSD—THE AGE OF MIND *Bernard Roseman*	2.00
___ MAGICIAN—His Training and Work *W. E. Butler*	3.00
___ MEDITATION *Mouni Sadhu*	7.00
___ MODERN NUMEROLOGY *Morris C. Goodman*	3.00
___ NUMEROLOGY—ITS FACTS AND SECRETS *Ariel Yvon Taylor*	3.00
___ NUMEROLOGY MADE EASY *W. Mykian*	4.00
___ PALMISTRY MADE EASY *Fred Gettings*	5.00
___ PALMISTRY MADE PRACTICAL *Elizabeth Daniels Squire*	4.00
___ PALMISTRY SECRETS REVEALED *Henry Frith*	3.00
___ PROPHECY IN OUR TIME *Martin Ebon*	2.50
___ PSYCHOLOGY OF HANDWRITING *Nadya Olyanova*	5.00
___ SUPERSTITION—Are You Superstitious? *Eric Maple*	2.00
___ TAROT *Mouni Sadhu*	8.00
___ TAROT OF THE BOHEMIANS *Papus*	5.00
___ WAYS TO SELF-REALIZATION *Mouni Sadhu*	3.00
___ WHAT YOUR HANDWRITING REVEALS *Albert E. Hughes*	3.00
___ WITCHCRAFT, MAGIC & OCCULTISM—A Fascinating History *W. B. Crow*	5.00
___ WITCHCRAFT—THE SIXTH SENSE *Justine Glass*	5.00
___ WORLD OF PSYCHIC RESEARCH *Hereward Carrington*	2.00

SELF-HELP & INSPIRATIONAL

___ DAILY POWER FOR JOYFUL LIVING *Dr. Donald Curtis*	5.00
___ DYNAMIC THINKING *Melvin Powers*	2.00
___ GREATEST POWER IN THE UNIVERSE *U. S. Andersen*	5.00
___ GROW RICH WHILE YOU SLEEP *Ben Sweetland*	3.00
___ GROWTH THROUGH REASON *Albert Ellis, Ph.D.*	4.00
___ GUIDE TO PERSONAL HAPPINESS *Albert Ellis, Ph.D. & Irving Becker, Ed. D.*	5.00
___ HELPING YOURSELF WITH APPLIED PSYCHOLOGY *R. Henderson*	2.00
___ HOW TO ATTRACT GOOD LUCK *A. H. Z. Carr*	5.00
___ HOW TO DEVELOP A WINNING PERSONALITY *Martin Panzer*	5.00
___ HOW TO DEVELOP AN EXCEPTIONAL MEMORY *Young & Gibson*	5.00
___ HOW TO LIVE WITH A NEUROTIC *Albert Ellis, Ph. D.*	5.00
___ HOW TO OVERCOME YOUR FEARS *M. P. Leahy, M.D.*	3.00
___ HOW YOU CAN HAVE CONFIDENCE AND POWER *Les Giblin*	5.00
___ HUMAN PROBLEMS & HOW TO SOLVE THEM *Dr. Donald Curtis*	5.00
___ I CAN *Ben Sweetland*	5.00
___ I WILL *Ben Sweetland*	3.00
___ LEFT-HANDED PEOPLE *Michael Barsley*	5.00
___ MAGIC IN YOUR MIND *U. S. Andersen*	6.00
___ MAGIC OF THINKING BIG *Dr. David J. Schwartz*	3.00
___ MAGIC POWER OF YOUR MIND *Walter M. Germain*	5.00

_____ MENTAL POWER THROUGH SLEEP SUGGESTION *Melvin Powers*   3.0
_____ NEW GUIDE TO RATIONAL LIVING *Albert Ellis, Ph.D. & R. Harper, Ph.D.*   3.0
_____ PROJECT YOU *A Manual of Rational Assertiveness Training Paris & Casey*   6.0
_____ PSYCHO-CYBERNETICS *Maxwell Maltz, M.D.*   5.0
_____ SCIENCE OF MIND IN DAILY LIVING *Dr. Donald Curtis*   5.0
_____ SECRET OF SECRETS *U. S. Andersen*   6.0
_____ SECRET POWER OF THE PYRAMIDS *U. S. Andersen*   5.0
_____ STUTTERING AND WHAT YOU CAN DO ABOUT IT *W. Johnson, Ph.D.*   2.5
_____ SUCCESS-CYBERNETICS *U. S. Andersen*   5.0
_____ 10 DAYS TO A GREAT NEW LIFE *William E. Edwards*   3.0
_____ THINK AND GROW RICH *Napoleon Hill*   5.0
_____ THINK YOUR WAY TO SUCCESS *Dr. Lew Losoncy*   5.0
_____ THREE MAGIC WORDS *U. S. Andersen*   5.0
_____ TREASURY OF COMFORT *edited by Rabbi Sidney Greenberg*   5.0
_____ TREASURY OF THE ART OF LIVING *Sidney S. Greenberg*   5.0
_____ YOU ARE NOT THE TARGET *Laura Huxley*   5.0
_____ YOUR SUBCONSCIOUS POWER *Charles M. Simmons*   5.0
_____ YOUR THOUGHTS CAN CHANGE YOUR LIFE *Dr. Donald Curtis*   5.0

SPORTS

_____ BICYCLING FOR FUN AND GOOD HEALTH *Kenneth E. Luther*   2.0
_____ BILLIARDS—Pocket • Carom • Three Cushion *Clive Cottingham, Jr.*   3.0
_____ CAMPING-OUT 101 Ideas & Activities *Bruno Knobel*   2.0
_____ COMPLETE GUIDE TO FISHING *Vlad Evanoff*   2.0
_____ HOW TO IMPROVE YOUR RACQUETBALL *Lubarsky Kaufman & Scagnetti*   3.0
_____ HOW TO WIN AT POCKET BILLIARDS *Edward D. Knuchell*   5.0
_____ JOY OF WALKING *Jack Scagnetti*   3.0
_____ LEARNING & TEACHING SOCCER SKILLS *Eric Worthington*   3.0
_____ MOTORCYCLING FOR BEGINNERS *I. G. Edmonds*   3.0
_____ RACQUETBALL FOR WOMEN *Toni Hudson, Jack Scagnetti & Vince Rondone*   3.0
_____ RACQUETBALL MADE EASY *Steve Lubarsky, Rod Delson & Jack Scagnetti*   4.0
_____ SECRET OF BOWLING STRIKES *Dawson Taylor*   3.0
_____ SECRET OF PERFECT PUTTING *Horton Smith & Dawson Taylor*   3.0
_____ SOCCER—The Game & How to Play It *Gary Rosenthal*   3.0
_____ STARTING SOCCER *Edward F. Dolan, Jr.*   3.

TENNIS LOVERS' LIBRARY

_____ BEGINNER'S GUIDE TO WINNING TENNIS *Helen Hull Jacobs*   2.
_____ HOW TO BEAT BETTER TENNIS PLAYERS *Loring Fiske*   4
_____ HOW TO IMPROVE YOUR TENNIS—Style, Strategy & Analysis *C. Wilson*   2.
_____ INSIDE TENNIS—Techniques of Winning *Jim Leighton*   3
_____ PLAY TENNIS WITH ROSEWALL *Ken Rosewall*   2
_____ PSYCH YOURSELF TO BETTER TENNIS *Dr. Walter A. Luszki*   2
_____ TENNIS FOR BEGINNERS, *Dr. H. A. Murray*   2.
_____ TENNIS MADE EASY *Joel Brecheen*   4
_____ WEEKEND TENNIS—How to Have Fun & Win at the Same Time *Bill Talbert*   3
_____ WINNING WITH PERCENTAGE TENNIS—Smart Strategy *Jack Lowe*   2

WILSHIRE PET LIBRARY

_____ DOG OBEDIENCE TRAINING *Gust Kessopulos*   5
_____ DOG TRAINING MADE EASY & FUN *John W. Kellogg*   4
_____ HOW TO BRING UP YOUR PET DOG *Kurt Unkelbach*   2
_____ HOW TO RAISE & TRAIN YOUR PUPPY *Jeff Griffen*   3
_____ PIGEONS: HOW TO RAISE & TRAIN THEM *William H. Allen, Jr.*   2

The books listed above can be obtained from your book dealer or directly from
Melvin Powers. When ordering, please remit 50¢ per book postage & handling.
Send for our free illustrated catalog of self-improvement books.

Melvin Powers

12015 Sherman Road, No. Hollywood, California 91605